Can Business Management Save the Cities?

Can
Business Management
Save the Cities?

The Case of New York

DAVID ROGERS

THE FREE PRESS
A Division of Macmillan Publishing Co., Inc.
NEW YORK

Collier Macmillan Publishers
LONDON

The Free Press
A Division of Macmillan Publishing Co., Inc.
866 Third Avenue, New York, N.Y. 10022

Collier Macmillan Canada, Ltd.

Library of Congress Catalog Card Number: 77-18594

Printed in the United States of America

printing number

1 2 3 4 5 6 7 8 9 10

Library of Congress Cataloging in Publication Data

Rogers, David
    Can business management save the cities?

    Includes bibliographical references and index.
    1. New York (City)--Executive departments--
Management. 2. New York (City)--Politics and
government--1951-   3. Government consultants--
New York (City). 4. Economic Development Council
of New York City. I. Title.
JS1234.A1R63   352.0747'1   77-18594
ISBN 0-02-926730-7

Contents

Acknowledgments

Many people helped in the preparation of this book. First, I would like to thank Tony Cline of the Russell Sage Foundation, which provided the main grant for the study. Cline, who was president of the foundation at the time, was supportive throughout and took a strong personal interest in the study's being done and completed. George Vickers, the main staff person working on the study in its early stages, was also most helpful. Barbara Newsom of the Rockefeller Brothers Fund had enough confidence in my work and in the importance of the study to provide a supplemental grant that enabled me to complete it. I am most grateful for her strong support through some difficult times between the study's completion and its publication. She endorsed my work on several critical occasions when the politics surrounding its findings and publication became fairly heated. Jerry Davenport, also of the Fund, was helpful in this regard as well.

The many officials and staff members of the Economic Development Council, the subject of this book, also deserve thanks. They spent literally hundreds of hours going over their experiences with me, and they opened their files for my continued use in this study. George Champion, Joe Grazier, Paul Busse, Roland Delfausse, Ed O'Rorke, Floyd Flom, Dick Coyne, and Harold Finley were all helpful. As one might expect, some were much more open, balanced, and nondefensive than others, and they deserve special thanks. Some of the others, unfortunately, felt that my book might well destroy their program (would that social scientists had such power), despite the assessment of several social science reviewers that the book was not biased either for or against EDC. People whose programs get evaluated often don't take well to parts of the evaluation, but I hope that those findings and conclusions that some EDC people objected to will seem more acceptable to them in the future. Despite my differences with some of them, EDC officials' reactions to an early draft did help me in making the final revisions.

Many on-loan business people also spent time with me reporting on their experiences with EDC. Bill Korwan and Richie Herrink, both from IBM, reviewed with me at considerable length their experiences and their interpretations of EDC's programs. Herrink later read a near-final draft and offered comments. Of all the EDC staff, I want to particularly acknowledge Ed O'Rorke, for providing me with extensive background information for the study.

Staff members in the target agencies of EDC's management consulting programs also cooperated, including those in the Board of Education and in various criminal justice agencies. The confidentiality of their comments and the potential damage to many involved in reporting who they were preclude my mentioning them by name here. Their cooperation, however, was indispensable to completing the study.

The study was conducted under the auspices of the Institute of Public Administration, and I could not have asked for a more supportive setting in which to work. Lyle Fitch, its director, offered penetrating insights about New York City and, more generally, about urban problems. And the support staff—Xenia Duisen, director of IPA's excellent library, and Bob Kirkwood, its business manager—were always available for assistance. The extensive typing services of Elinor Wentworth and her constant good humor and editorial suggestions are also acknowledged.

It would not have been possible for me to be at the Institute of Public Administration were it not for the generous support of Dean William Dill and my area chairman, Dale Zand, at New York University. I want to thank them for their permission to do the study at the Institute and to benefit from its resources, while retaining my academic appointment at the University.

The study was done, as were previous ones I have conducted, with a very small staff. Steve Banks did interviews and field reports in the early stages. Art Springer did field work and writing on EDC's work in the courts and also provided editorial assistance on early drafts of a few chapters. John Lubey helped summarize and draft material for one chapter.

A major person in the successful completion of the book was my close friend and colleague Ken Lenihan, who read many drafts and provided comments and editorial assistance that went far beyond what I had any right to expect. Providing usable editorial assistance is a rare talent, and he has it in great abundance. Many of the main connecting themes in the book, particularly those relating to the conflict between management efficiency and political constraints in the public sector, emerged as a direct result of his critical reading of early drafts.

Finally, I want to acknowledge the strong support of my wife Terry, who combines the skills of editor, researcher, and social analyst in ways that continue to amaze me. Her critical reading of several chapters helped immeasurably. Our three sons, Edward, Alex, and Paul, must also be given credit for their continued patience, along with that of their mother, while I was completing the book.

Introduction

This is a book about an important social experiment in New York City. It involved a non-profit consortium of large corporations engaged in an intensive effort to transfer to local government management technologies and practices that are in common use in business. The consortium was the Economic Development Council (EDC). Founded in 1965 and composed of more than 200 of the largest corporations in the world, it has gone through many stages of experimentation and development, each of which contains lessons for business and civic groups in other cities that may want to undertake similar programs. The purpose of this book is to assess EDC's programs from that perspective, indicating the problems it faced and how they were handled.

It is always difficult to generalize from a single case study, particularly one conducted in New York City, and as this book will show, New York is probably one of the most difficult places in which to undertake such a program. Its size, diversity, and turbulent politics constitute tremendous obstacles to the effectiveness of municipal reforms, regardless of the skills, resources, or good will of the participating groups. Despite that, an analysis of what happened to EDC and to New York City as a result of EDC's activities has national relevance. New York's recent problems may simply represent an exaggeration of those faced by many large inner cities and a preview of what may well happen in still others, if they don't act to prevent what happened there. In casting about for a preventive-action strategy, cities may well be helped by tapping the expertise of business and other groups helping cities with administrative reform (e.g., management consultants, public administration institutes, university-based policy analysts and specialists in administration). EDC has begun that process in New York, and the story of how it proceeded there and what lessons emerged therefore merits national attention.

The EDC program has several key components. (1) It is a *good-government, non-profit consortium* of corporations; (2) It attempts to reverse New York City's economic decline through the use of *on-loan executives who provide free management consulting services;* (3) The executives are organized in a series of *task forces,* one for each agency in which EDC works; and (4) It *is part of a larger program of activating business resources* for the city's economic and social development. It has been one of the main mechanisms in New York City for getting business involved in civic problems, by providing a program through which on-loan executives could work and offering informal advice on how corporations might help the city in other ways as well. Many cities have business associations to promote civic projects, but the combination of elements just listed and the degree of business involvement that EDC reflects don't appear elsewhere.

Unlike other management consultants, EDC provides these services at no fee to city agencies, both through retired executives and through people on loan from its member companies. The latter do this on "public service sabbaticals," with their salaries paid by their corporate employers. Moreover, EDC does not just do management studies and then leave, but actively presses for their implementation. EDC is in both these respects a unique species of management consulting work in cities.

EDC's work has national significance from another perspective as well, in that it represents a potential new direction in the exercise of corporate "social responsibility." With the deepening urban crisis and the ghetto riots of the 1960's, business spokesmen emphasized their obligation to help improve economic opportunities for minorities. The National Urban Coalition, the National Alliance of Business, and other, similar programs in cities all reflected this outlook, providing jobs, money, and other services to enable minorities to move more readily into the mainstream of American society.

EDC's approach is quite different: it deals with the urban crisis through the transfer of management techniques from business to the public sector. The program is based on the following assumptions: (1) There is, in fact, a transferability of management skills, because all large organizations, whether business or government, face similar problems, notwithstanding their differences; (2) A successful transfer may significantly improve the delivery of services in public-sector agencies, even within existing budget constraints; (3) Such improved service delivery may improve the quality of life in the city and help stem the exodus of business and the middle class; and (4) These developments, in turn, will strengthen the city's economic base and provide jobs for minorities and the poor.

The point of this case study, then, is not just to gain some understanding of a business program in one city, but rather to appreciate what that program represents: a unique social experiment in the management transfer strategy that may well be taken up elsewhere. The fact that the program has operated in the nation's largest city, with some of the most intractable urban problems, (with those problems emerging in their most dramatic form in recent years), and that it involved in this instance some of the largest and most powerful corporations in the world is what gives it significance. EDC is important, then, largely as a way of exploring management transfer as an approach for dealing with the urban crisis.

Actually, the EDC program bears on several policy issues: (1) *the management of cities* and how it can be improved; (2) *strategies for changing organizations generally*, not just public-sector ones; (3) *the extent to which the public and private sectors are becoming more alike*, as this bears on the potential effectiveness of the management transfer approach; and (4) *the political and civic role of economic elites in cities*, to the extent that their collective actions may affect both the emergence of and resolutions of the urban crisis.

An awareness of these issues runs through the entire study. One theme that emerges throughout is *the tension between management efficiency and political constraints* in the public sector. While that tension exists in business and other organizational settings, as well, it is particularly pronounced in government. The EDC management transfer strategy in New York is essentially a technocratic one, emphasizing the redesign of local government and the introduction of new management procedures to improve efficiency. It has run into all kinds of predictable vested interests—unions, the civil service, agencies and civic groups comfortable with the status quo—which have made the implementation of management reform proposals extremely problematic.

The very politics that have contributed to the city's decline, then, also constitute a constraint on improvement. This is not to argue that management reforms in local government are not possible—even in New York, where the political obstacles are so formidable. Rather it is to indicate that bringing about such reforms in a highly political setting like city government is a very complex process. If other cities are to learn from this experiment and if EDC is to develop and improve its own programs, that complexity must be understood. And it is only after an analysis of programs like that of EDC in New York that one can begin to assess the efficacy of the management transfer strategy. Rather than arguing that issue in the abstract, then, we take it up through an analysis of this important case.

As for the intended audience, my primary interest was to write a book that would be useful to people actively concerned with doing something about the socioeconomic problems of big cities: public officials, business, labor, civic group leaders. They should know how the management transfer strategy worked out in this case, so that they can apply some of the lessons learned to their own situation. My other audience is policy-oriented social scientists. Since there are so few case studies analyzing the problems involved in implementing planned social changes, I felt that the book would make a contribution to social science as well.

In this regard, one of the central themes of the book, equal in importance to that mentioned above, relates to *what strategies are most effective in changing organizations*. Two broad strategies come immediately to mind. One is what has been called the *collaborative strategy*, wherein the outside change agent works cooperatively with staff members in the target agency, playing a technical assistance and consulting role. The other is an *advocacy or adversarial strategy*, a la Ralph Nader, wherein one publicly attacks the agency for its mismanagement, corruption, lack of accountability, and the like. It is based on the assumption that organizations have an enormous amount of inertia and change only in response to strong outside pressure. In contrast, the collaborative strategy assumes that change can take place only through enlisting the cooperation of agency staff, many of whom are quite competent to be effective change agents in their own right, if only given the support that a consultant can sometimes bring.

Each of these strategies has strengths and weaknesses, and one of the keys to being effective is to know when and how to orchestrate them. EDC consciously pursued the collaborative one, and this book constitutes an assessment of how a strong and single-minded dedication to that strategy works out.

1. The Mismanagement of Big Cities: Proposed Solutions

This is a book about the prospects of transferring or adapting to local government management practices that seem to work well in the private sector. Rather than pursue this issue in the abstract, I have chosen to explore, as a case study, a business organization that has been engaged in such an activity for several years. That organization is the Economic Development Council (EDC) of New York City, an association of over 200 of that city's largest employers that has worked intensively to improve the management of city government.

The central questions of this study are: (a) whether one can in fact transfer the management practices and expertise of business to local government; (b) what types of management expertise can be transferred, with what adaptations, to what types of agencies by means of what types of political and organizational strategies, and with what effects on agency structure, procedures, and performance; (c) what problems accompany such an effort; and (d) what lessons have been learned from EDC's experiences. An important policy issue in this regard is whether similar programs (with appropriate adaptations) should be attempted elsewhere and, if so, whether one can develop some preliminary recommendations as to tactics and strategy for business associations and other private-sector groups elsewhere that are interested in making the effort.

Big cities in America are, by most standards, very badly managed—if, indeed, they are managed at all.* Some historical and

---

*By "management" in this context, I mean a concern with both "goals" and "means" in complex organizations—with both "effectiveness" and "efficiency," as those terms are commonly used.

analytical perspective on the issue of the mismanagement of cities is essential if we are to place our case study in its appropriate context.

Many municipal agencies, having been designed in the nineteenth century, when simple housekeeping and the dispensing of patronage were their main functions, have failed to adapt to an increasingly changing and complex urban environment that requires sophisticated political and administrative skills.[1] If this well-documented institutional lag were a simple problem, it might have been dealt with more adequately than it has. The forces producing it, however, are incredibly complex, embedded as they are in the political/legal and social history of urban America and, more generally, in the entire federal system.

STRUCTURAL CONSTRAINTS ON CITIES

Unlike corporations in the private sector, with their relatively stable by-laws and their considerable autonomy, American cities have been burdened by legal anachronisms, piecemeal reforms, a long tradition of growth by accretion, and state and federal policies that limit their capacity for effective management. As creatures of their states, cities have not been free in many instances to develop new sources of revenue, new structures, or new programs. Furthermore, local government has historically developed in a dialectical fashion, with each organizational or political form that was set up to solve old problems creating, in turn, many new ones. A particularly critical manifestation of this historical process has been the steady increase in fragmentation in the evolution from the political machine to the centralized downtown bureaucracies to the recent push for decentralization. Each of these new forms overlapped on older ones that were themselves not completely eliminated.[2] Certainly the proliferation by the federal government of multiple programs for cities, often leading to considerable duplication in delivery systems and numerous turf struggles, has been a problem, especially since cities don't control many of these systems.

The structure and workings of the federal system and of federal-state–city relations place further constraints on local government. Political scientist Morton Grodzins characterized American federalism as "an inseparable mingling of differently colored ingredients, the colors appearing in vertical and diagonal strands and unexpected whorls."[3] Drawing on an industrial analogy, Grodzins has drawn attention to the fact that the nation's intergovernmental production system has critical functions (e.g., financing, budgeting, planning, purchasing, service delivery) so randomly and chaotically distributed across various levels that it is difficult for cities to consolidate and gain control over them—making effective management, let alone reform, quite problematic. The resultant fragmentation, both within any given level of government and across levels, with its attendant duplication, overlapping, conflict, and lack of coordination, makes it very difficult to develop integrated, simplified structures in which more rational management might take place.

There are other major constraints on effective management in cities. The criteria by which voters elect top officials—even including "experience in government"—are not necessarily those that characterize effective managers. Furthermore, government and business may well attract entirely different kinds of people. Those with strong managerial talents may have more incentive to move into business rather than government, since the opportunity to exercise management skills may be perceived as limited in government, given its vulnerability to political pressures.

Although none of the forces just discussed that limit effective management in cities are easily reversed, pressures keep building to do so. Indeed, one item on the agenda of urban management specialists, city planners, and policy makers which is becoming more widely endorsed by citizen groups as well is to modernize and rationalize local government.[4] This is undoubtedly a response to the fact that America continues to face an "urban crisis," the dimensions of which were extensively documented in such major publications as the U.S. Riot Commission Report and have not changed significantly since then—except, perhaps, insofar as they have gotten worse.[5] They include: segregation; a concentration of poverty in inner cities; runaway cost inflation of public services, with salary increases generally not tied to productivity; public employee union strikes and breakdowns; a substantial exodus of industry, jobs, and taxpaying populations; decaying housing, schools, and other physical plant and equipment; increasing crime, delinquency, and drug addiction; intensified conflicts among citizen groups and between minority communities and city agencies for scarce services, housing, and neighborhood control, often along racial, ethnic, and religious lines; and an accompanying lack of hope or expectation on the part of many citizens and city officials that they can do anything about these problems. It is simply not possible for city government to be run in the same old ways when such multiple and escalating problems confront it.

The traditional way in which cities have tried to resolve these problems has been to pass on urban costs to state and federal tax systems, a policy that may now be obsolescent. The taxpaying public is a saturated group, and the public's willingness to have more taxes and federal funds directed to cities may increasingly depend on governmental productivity reforms. Interest groups and associations representing big cities that have lobbied extensively for more federal funds—for example, the U.S. Conference of Mayors/National League of Cities—will have to face up to the productivity issue in the future much more than they have in the past, as will municipal employee unions and civil service groups.

The need for changes in local government has been increasingly documented in numerous policy and commission reports over the past several years. They point to a combination of defective delivery systems and inadequate or nonexisting management procedures as the main weaknesses of local government.[6] Underlying both failures has been the absence of any strong governmental commitment to do anything about them, reflecting the limited political constituencies for management reform in the public sector. Evidence of increasing taxpayer revolts and of resistance to municipal bond issues suggests a gradual change in this regard, but it could not be characterized as a groundswell movement. Politicians haven't particularly helped it, either. Most elected officials like to point out to their constituents how successful they have been in securing more money from Washington for local programs, without any reference to how the money was used and what impact, if any, it had on agency performance.[7] In fact, they habitually neglect the latter and usually do little to dramatize the shortcomings of local government itself, shortcomings that may contribute quite substantially to diluting the potential impact of such new resources. The management structure and operations of local government has not been an attractive political issue— at least not until recently, as citizen concern about accountability and productivity in all large institutions, including government, has begun to grow.[8] Its neglect in the past has severely hampered efforts to improve the delivery of services in cities.

It would be a mistake to attribute the nation's contemporary urban crisis mainly to shortcomings of local government. The crisis is a result of numerous forces, including urbanization, industrialization, technological change, and massive population shifts—forces largely outside the control of cities. Nevertheless, the shortcomings of local government certainly impair the limited capacity of cities to deal with their many socioeconomic problems. As economist Lyle Fitch has noted, "Urban governments in the United States are performing inadequately at best in meeting the demands laid upon them, and at worst they are failing miserably as measured by general discontent with public services."[9]

What to do, given this seemingly dismal state of affairs, is, therefore, a critical question of social policy. Most of the social science and social policy writings of the 1960s were of limited value in this regard. They documented pathologies, but they gave little indication of what social change strategies might improve the delivery of services and the quality of life in cities.[10] One contribution social scientists can now make is to do historical studies on the dynamics of implementation of those strategies that have some promise of reversing the cities' decline. Such studies should indicate why implementation proceeds as it does and what lessons can be learned and applied to similar efforts elsewhere. This book seeks to make such a contribution.

DIAGNOSES AND PROPOSED SOLUTIONS

No single solution for the many problems of the cities just described has been proposed. There is an increasing consensus, however, that providing additional resources without at the same time markedly improving the management and delivery systems of cities and of the wider federal system may not help at all. Indeed, it may simply spread inefficiency and lead to more shattered expectations, both among reformers and among the disadvantaged populations whom the programs were designed to serve. Such disappointment regularly followed in the wake of many of the Great Society programs of the 1960s, leading to disenchantment with much of the social legislation for the poor, both among political conservatives and among moderates and liberals as well.[11]

Some reformers advocate centralization strategies involving consolidation of authority and power at the top, as in superagencies, metropolitan authorities, Councils of Government, and interagency coordinating councils, and sometimes expansion of the geographical scope of agency jurisdictions as well. City charter revisions to create strong mayoral systems, often taking place in cities with effective reform coalitions, are another example of this principle. Such approaches often include complementary efforts to make top agency officials more effective managers by introducing them to new management techniques, such as program planning budget systems (PPBS), project management, and management information systems. The diagnosis on which they are based is that agency fragmentation, a diffusion of authority at the top, and limited management capability are the main obstacles to effective service delivery, and that the basic need is to strengthen the authority of top city officials, both elected and appointed.

A second approach, seemingly antithetical to the first, emerged from the community action programs and community control movement of the 1960s. It calls for a political decentralization of authority and power from city agency officials to elected boards of citizens. It is based on the view that professional and civil service power have prevented city agencies from adapting to change by permitting them to become insulated from citizen demands for accountability and for new programs.

Still another strategy calls for creating alternative agencies parallel to existing ones, eroding their monopolistic position through a more competitive market system. The argument for this strategy is that monopolistic public agencies, like their counterparts in the private sector, almost never make major changes in established patterns of behavior unless strongly pressured to do so by outside agencies competing for clients. Anthony Downs, one of the advocates of this strategy, suggests that even a small dose of competition might conceivably produce important, perhaps even radical, changes in the nature and quality of services.[12]

The many public authorities set up by Robert Moses and later by Governor Rockefeller in New York State are examples of this parallel-systems strategy. These authorities have a degree of flexibility and independence in financing (through raising their own bonds), staffing, and other critical functions that would not have been possible if their programs had been run through established government agencies.

Considerable interest has recently developed in one version of this competition strategy—namely subcontracting out to private-sector organizations, such as, business firms or nonprofit private corporations, for the delivery of services.[13] This approach is based on the diagnosis that the public sector has several unchangeable characteristics that prevent it from ever becoming an effective manager. They include the separation of policy from execution, the splintering of subunits within government agencies that zealously guard their own turf, fail to coordinate, and act as veto groups when innovations are proposed; the power of the civil service to effectively prevent anybody from holding them accountable for their performance; and the politicization of programs, making it difficult to change them based on "objective" evaluations.

Finally, decentralizing the entire federal system, in conjunction with block grants and revenue sharing, has been urged. The diagnosis behind this strategy is that too much centralization of the federal system in Washington has led to a proliferation of programs with rigid national guidelines, imposed, in turn, without regard for variations in local need and institutional capability and hampering local planning and political accountability. Originally proposed by President Johnson as "creative federalism" and then relabeled as the "new federalism," this strategy gained some impetus in the Nixon administration's revenue-sharing push of the early 1970s. Localism does not guarantee administrative competence or equity for minorities any more than privatization does, as critics of both strategies have pointed out, but both approaches continue to generate support in and out of government, as things worth trying.

Many of these proposals (with the possible exception of the first two, centralization and community control) may not necessarily be contradictory. They have not yet been tried out on any significant scale, however, either singly or in combination, owing to both the the marked divergence of opinion on what to do and the absence of the strong political coalitions necessary for implementation. The proposals have, however, been a focus of increasing public discussion, especially in the form of policy reports; and some, at least, have been selectively implemented in particular states, counties, and localities. [14] It seems likely that considerable experimentation and debate regarding all of these alternatives will take place in the coming years. Whatever new forms are developed and implemented ought to be carefully assessed, so that policy makers and citizen groups will begin to know what works, what doesn't, and why. This book attempts a careful evaluation of one effort.

REPRIVATIZATION: THE BUSINESS-IN-GOVERNMENT VERSION

One strategy that seems to have gained support in recent years is reprivatization. Besides divesting government of direct management and service delivery responsibilities through subcontracting, reprivatization attempts to transfuse government with more rational management techniques—usually based on classical management writings and business practice. The incorporation of PPBS and "systems analysis" in the 1960s, followed by the recent productivity movement in the seventies, are examples.

This business-in-government approach is a fairly old one in American society and has usually had all the earmarks of a movement, since its proponents have generally propounded it with some degree of missionary zeal, and for some it has had many elements of a fundamentalist faith or theology. It first appeared in an organized fashion in the Progressive Era, at the turn of the century, when business leaders were attempting to make government more efficient and "businesslike" and to eliminate patronage and spoils.15 These business leaders had several operating codes that guided their activities. They advocated classical management principles: standardized rules and procedures, hierarchy, unity of command, formal job descriptions, specialization, and centralization of authority.* By and large, they used the corporation model in trying to reform the public sector and were convinced that centralization of authority under a single appointive manager was the most effective way to organize local government. Both the city manager and the commissioner forms were developed and tried in many cities as a result.

A second and related assumption was that the public sector should be depoliticized as much as possible, not only to eliminate patronage and spoils but also to improve performance. The reformers pushed for nonpartisan government, in which agencies would employ only people with administrative expertise.† Another guiding principle was the emphasis on strong executive rule, to override parochial, ward-politician interests and to plan on an area-wide (county, city) basis. And still another was the importance of separating politics from administration, a view very much in vogue among those business and civic reformers in the early part of the century who were attacking municipal corruption. The emphasis, then, was on efficiency, standardized procedures, centralization and strong executive rule, technical expertise, and the elimination of partisan and political considerations from government.

These views reflected deeply held American values regarding business and government that did not die at the end of the Progressive Era. Indeed, they have been advanced since then by many good-government groups. They coincide with the traditional American view that business is inherently rational and efficient, while government is just the opposite—mired in corruption, red tape, and bureaucratic procedures and generally mismanaged. Americans from many strata, especially those in the upper middle and upper classes, who have much to do with setting national values, have long regarded careers in business and the professions much more highly than those

---

*Raymond Callahan points out in his *Business and the Cult of Efficiency* how enamored many businessmen in this period were with the work of Frederick W. Taylor and with applying Taylor's principles of scientific management to government.

†Ironically, the chief result of these efforts was the very civil service structure that today's reformers criticize so vigorously.

in politics, which was often seen as a corrupt calling.[16] The spectre of Boss Tweed and Tammany Hall was often conjured up as representing standards of conduct typical of municipal government. The popular notion among those who wanted to improve the public sector was that government was simply an inefficient business, compounded by corruption, and that if government could be transfused with business management techniques, it would become much more efficient and corruption would be eliminated.

The more zealous and missionary of the business leaders who pursued this strategy were fairly elitist in their views and in their patronizing treatment of government officials, evoking considerable resistance from the latter when they engaged in efforts at reform.[17] They regarded business as far superior to government in virtually every respect: the quality of people it attracted, their leadership abilities, their moral codes of conduct, and the general management procedures they followed. Business success was seen as a direct consequence of these institutional and personal characteristics, while government officials, especially at the local level, were looked down on as inferior managers and, in some instances, inferior people. Consequently, business's attempts to rationalize and modernize government almost took on the tone of "bringing Christianity to the natives," an enterprise in which poorly trained government officials were patronizingly instructed in the art and "science" of management.

Underlying this view of business and government was a basic conflict in life styles, backgrounds, and political interests between these outsider reformers and those ethnic, religious, and economic groups who had moved into local government in great numbers since the late nineteenth century. It was in large part a conflict between the Yankees and the immigrants, one that has pervaded urban politics over the past century and contributed to cycles of reform and reaction.[18] The reformers generally comprised an upper-middle- and upper-class, college-educated, and predominantly Protestant group that had a good-government, "public-regarding" ethos about urban politics. The insiders, by contrast, were a working- or lower-middle-class, predominantly Irish, Italian, and East European Catholic group who had a more machine-oriented, "private-regarding" immigrant ethos about local government.[19] Government was seen by the reformers as appropriately serving only a "public interest." Generalized, universalistic standards of efficiency, effectiveness, equity, and the like were to be applied to make government work better for all the people. By contrast, followers of machine politics saw government in particularistic terms, in terms of what it could do for particular ethnic, religious, and neighborhood groups in a very concrete way, such as by providing jobs and better local services.* They were less interested in abstract principles, which their leadership regarded as the luxury of the upper classes, than in concrete services. What the reformers negatively defined as spoils and patronage was seen by these white ethnic groups as governmental responsiveness to the needs of the people.†

While both conceptions have merit, with city government probably requiring some combination of both to function well, the reformers, especially intellectuals, businessmen, and the managerial class, tended to be intolerant of machine-style politics. As already discussed, they resisted any kind of politics in government, regarding it as immoral and detrimental to efficiency and naively assuming that they themselves were free of political interests. They had their own organizations and patronage—for example, management consultant firms—and concomitant stakes in city jobs and contracts. The work they did might in many cases have contributed to improved urban management, but it makes little sense to overlook their economic and political interests.

This is not at all meant to debunk the attempt to bring business management techniques to local government. By all indications, they are desperately needed now, as they were in earlier periods of history. Serious doubt exists, however, as to whether practices and techniques that seem to work in the private sector can automatically be "transferred" to government without taking into account what may be marked differences between the public and private sectors. On that score, the more enthusiastic of the business-in-government advocates may have been too simplistic and missionary in their efforts, thereby increasing governmental resistance and discrediting the important reform strategy they were pressing.

Businessmen were not alone, however, in espousing this strategy, and the experience of the sixties and seventies indicates its widespread support from a broad spectrum of groups. Peter Drucker, for example, one of its foremost advocates, has noted that liberals and even radicals, who have become increasingly disenchanted with what

*Merton's quote from Boston ward leader Martin Lomasny to Lincoln Steffens on what local government should do for the poor is particularly apt: "I think," said Lomasny, "that there's got to be in every ward somebody that any bloke can come to—no matter what he's done—and get help. Help, you understand; none of your law and justice, but help." Robert K. Marton, *Social Theory and Social Structure*, rev. ed., New York: The Free Press, 1957, p. 75.

†This decline of the old political machine obviously affects the immediate needs of the two most recent immigrant groups, blacks and Puerto Ricans, who have enjoyed much less structured and powerful local political machinery than the white ethnics.

they see as the paralysis of government, have urged that the private sector be contracted with to manage many social programs. Liberal business associations like the Committee for Economic Development (CED) have been involved for over a decade in policy studies seeking to rationalize local and state government; they urged much more private-sector involvement in local government, both through subcontracting and through management assistance, in their recent publication, *The Social Responsibilities of Business* (1971). Among conservatives, the U.S. Chamber of Commerce, the National Association of Manufacturers, and Chicago economist Milton Friedman, to cite three prominent examples, have all urged greater involvement by business in local government—through vouchers, performance contracting, and business management of social programs.

The question is how to get beyond such normative statements for or against the privatization strategy. It is particularly important to question the many assumptions on which it is based and to bring social science perspectives to bear on the matter. It is to these questions that we now turn.

2. Theoretical Perspective

PUBLIC AND PRIVATE SECTORS:
THE NEED FOR A COMPARATIVE THEORY

Few systematic studies or analyses exist of the strengths and limitations of the business-in-government strategy. Most of the literature consists of ideological assertions by "true believers" that privatization is a good thing, usually including a statement about how well the private sector works relative to government. Drucker asserts, for example, that business is much more efficient than government, without mentioning the many industries and sectors of the economy of which this is not true at all. The railroads, aerospace firms, and the construction and transit industries are just a few instances in which the private sector is not well managed, and they are not isolated cases.[1] Indeed, Richard Cyert and James March state in their scholarly text on management science, *The Behavioral Theory of the Firm*, that what they call "fire department" administration, a style of non-planning and crisis management, is characteristic of all large organizations, including business. Recent work by the National Commission on Productivity, established in 1970 to improve productivity in the private and public sectors, pointed to serious problems in the private sector. As its first annual report indicated: "In the four years ending in 1970, output per manhour rose at an annual rate of only 1.7 percent, as compared with a 3.1 percent rate for the preceding 16 years. This rate was far slower than the rate of increase in wage rates over the same 4-year period and fell considerably short of the rates of productivity growth among our major foreign competitors."[2] It is not easy to compare productivity in many industries with that in government, since governmental services are still largely labor-intensive, but there certainly are productivity problems in the private

12

sector. Such popular critics of American corporations as Whyte, Townsend, and Parkinson further underscore this point.

If proponents of the business-in-government strategy, including many business executives themselves, make unrealistic comparisons between the private and public sectors, defensive counterreactions from government officials and anti-business liberals are also prevalent, and are equally invalid. Many local government officials in New York City and elsewhere, for example, have some of the same negative feelings about businessmen as the latter have about them. They often tend rigidly stereotype business as predatory, as well as self-interested in a narrow economic sense, and therefore as working against the public welfare. Recent generations of corporate managers, however, may be more likely to take into consideration in making decisions the broader social consequences of those decisions. At the very least, their background, education, and experience make them much more sophisticated about the relationship of business to society than were their entrepreneurial predecessors of the late nineteenth century.*

One way to place the business-in-government strategy in some analytical perspective would be to look in a comparative way at the main characteristics of the private and public sectors; to ascertain what their similarities and differences are with respect to structure, procedures, management styles, technologies, constraints, and environmental pressures. This may begin to suggest the extent to which similar or different types of management are required in the public sector.

Unfortunately, the literature of public administration theory, from which one would expect to gain some perspective on the business-in-government strategy, is limited. Indeed, that field is now acknowledged to be in a state of considerable disarray,† a state of

---

*Francis X. Sutton et al., *The American Business Creed*, Harvard University Press, 1956, contains one of the early analyses of the shift from a "classical, free enterprise" to a "managerial" ideology among American business leaders and their spokesmen. This ideology emphasizes business's perceptions of its obligations or social responsibility to serve outside constituencies. At the same time, however, many observers note the continued negative societal impacts of business decisions. See, for example, Jack Newfield and Paul Dubrul, *The Abuse of Power*, Viking Press, New York, 1977, for a discussion of business and New York City.

†One of the main reasons for this is that public administration theory derives largely from classical management theory and has never freed itself from the many limitations of that tradition. Frederick W. Taylor, Max Weber, and Henri Fayol were among the many classical writers who influenced early theory in public administration. See Vincent Ostron, *The Intellectual Crisis in American Public Administration*, University of Alabama Press, 1973.

affairs which is directly relevant to our task. Challenged first for its failure to take into account the negative consequences for productivity of following classical principles (e.g., rules, hierarchy, specialization), it later came under attack for overlooking political forces—for example, political party, interest group, civil service, and municipal employee union politics—as they affected public sector management.[3] Certainly any theory that does not take such forces into account will be of limited relevance in trying to assess the business-in-government strategy.

With this in mind, what does the broader social science literature on complex organizations have to say about similarities and differences between the public and private sectors? One view, reinforcing the business-in-government strategy, is that the similarities far outweigh the differences, thereby justifying any attempt to introduce or transfer business techniques to government.[4] Proponents of this view argue that all large organizations engage in planning, goal setting, design, control, staffing, performance appraisal, and the like, and that they all face both "economic" and "political" problems.[5] By "economic" problems is meant a concern with the rational allocation of resources—with cost effectiveness, as measured by the relation of inputs to outputs. "Political" considerations relate to securing legitimacy for the organization and its leadership from inside and outside groups, mobilizing support for implementation of programs, and handling problems of succession. In brief, any differences between the public and private sectors, say these advocates, are ones of degree more than of kind. If one accepts this view, and it has some validity, then there is much logic in trying to incorporate business management techniques into government.

A second view, however, points to differences between the public and private sectors which make the application of business management techniques to government problematic, to say the least. These differences are conceived of in terms of a variety of constraints that exist in the public but not nearly to the same degree in the private sector, and that limit both the adoption and the implementation of business management techniques in their original form.*

These constraints on efficiency in the public sector are seen not as peripheral characteristics, but rather as quite basic.[6] They include:

*It is important to note in this context that the line between the public and private sectors has become increasingly blurred. Each sector is becoming more like the other, owing largely to the fact that corporations have come under increasing pressures to become more socially accountable for their decisions. The development of social audits to assess the wider societal impact of corporate decisions reflects this phenomenon. Also, as corporations become more diversified, they develop large, bureaucratic structures that more closely resemble government agencies.

(1) *the lack of measurability of the public sector's service or "product"*, especially in human resources (health, education, welfare, manpower training) agencies; (2) the consequent *absence of any clear pricing or market test* as an outside control on performance and accountability; (3) the *monopolistic market* situation of many local agencies, which limits their incentive to innovate or adapt; (4) the existence of a complex and often turbulent public sector "politics," which makes decision makers, especially elected officials, highly vulnerable to pressures from outside publics; (5) *the unique role of the civil service* in limiting administrative flexibility, employee motivation and performance, efficiency, innovation, and accountability; (6) the existence of a fragmented intergovernmental production system that limits local autonomy and flexibility; (7) *financing arrangements* that reflect such an intergovernmental system and have the same constraining effects; (8) a reversal of the pattern of staff (expert)- line (manager) relationships that prevails in business which reinforces a pattern of "insider rule" by professional practitioners and downgrades management to a secondary or means activity; (9) the short term of office and high turnover of top agency officials, reflecting the vulnerability of public agencies to the forces of electoral politics and further reinforcing the pattern of insider rule and professional power that civil service and staff- line relationships support; and (10) the consequent time horizons of government officials, which tend to be generally more short-term than those of top management in the private sector. These differences are summarized in the table on p. 16.

It must be understood that not all business is more efficient and more rationally managed than government, and the structural distinctions made in this context between "business" and "government" are obviously very gross. Indeed, there is great diversity within each sector. Some government agencies, for example, have very sophisticated management procedures, and there are many corporations quite deficient in this regard.[7] Just within the private sector, the range of management structures and practices is so great that there is no definable body of principles applicable to the diversity that exists. At a minimum, corporations differ in terms of sector of the economy, extent of diversity in product line, extent of vertical and horizontal integration, age, size, scope of markets, and the like. These differences require comparative data not now available to indicate the range of management practices in the private sector.

Furthermore, comparing business and government is not that simple. Since government is obviously quite different from the typical corporation, a different conceptualization may be required as to the most appropriate type of management. Government agencies usually confront a larger range of needs and demands than a corpora-

T A B L E 1. Characteristics and Environment of Business and Government

SERVICE OR PRODUCT	BUSINESS	GOVERNMENT
Measurability	High	Low
Market Situation a) Quantitative, "bottom-line" standards, market test of performance	High	Low or nonexistent.
b) Competitive situation, alternative client or consumer	Existent, though variable by industry and economic sector	Nonexistent in most public service agencies
Client Relations Vulnerability to outside political pressures from clients and other political interests	Increasing, but still limited	Very high, turbulent, fluid, and functions in uncertain political environment
Employee Relations a) Extent of constraints on management decisions resulting from personnel (civil service) and collective bargaining policies	Increasing, but still limited	Very high and perhaps even increasing
b) Limits on establishing and enforcing incentives, rewards related to performance	Some, but competence and high performance likely to be rewarded through salaries, promotions	Strong limits. Promotion largely based on seniority and conformity. Competence and performance not as likely to be rewarded
Inter-Organizational Relations a) Extent of autonomy and control over production or service delivery-related activities.	Very high. Tendency toward much vertical horizontal, and conglomerate integration; much control over production and distribution	Very low. Part of a complex interdependent intergovernmental system that includes many state and federal agencies
b) Extent of fragmentation of the production or service delivery system	Very low, because of corporate integration patterns noted above	Very high
c) Financing arrangements	Internal financing for existing or new programs, out of profits.	Completely dependent on external bodies or agencies

TABLE 1 (Con't)

SERVICE OR PRODUCT	BUSINESS	GOVERNMENT
Internal Structure and Operations		
a) Line manager authority	High	Low. Rule by expert practitioners
b) Status of "management" relative to "expert-staff" functions	High	Low. Management downgraded to secondary or means activity
c) Promotion from within vs. recruitment of outsiders	Much variability, but many outsiders	High recruitment from within. Few outsiders, except at very top
d) Term of office of top management	Long. Much continuity, allowing for longrange planning, R&D, innovations, etc.	Short. Extreme turnover and discontinuity
e) Prospects for decentralization	High. With greater measurability of performance and market test, use of "profit center" concept	Low, from management point of view. Few existing criteria for evaluation, monitoring, and control
Outlook and Culture of Management		
a) Time horizons	Longer term	Very short-term
b) Extent to which a management tradition exists	High	Very low

tion and respond with a larger array of "services," including jobs for their constituencies. Government is not a "service," then, in any simplistic sense. The essence of its operations, which are so heavily political, is to reconcile conflicting interests—an open-ended and continuous process. It is subject to a "political rationality," related to party and interest-group politics, that is different from the more economic rationality of the corporation. There is nothing inherently moral or virtuous about incorporating the latter into government, except insofar as it might contribute to a better delivery of services, but that involves normative considerations, which takes us back to politics. The political rationality of government is thus different from the economic rationality and marketplace constraints of business.

For all its constraints, however, even government must maintain some minimal levels of productivity. Given the present situation of rising costs, inflationary collective bargaining agreements, and increasing citizen demands for better services delivered more efficiently, this goal is all the more imperative. Yet, it cannot be achieved by most local agencies, with their presently archaic administration, owing largely to all of the characteristics of government listed above. Considered together, they constitute a formidable array of obstacles to the modernization of local government that is so needed. Some may constitute nonmanipulable variables, given the political power of entrenched groups and the difficulties of putting together the coalitions needed for legislative changes; but that condition may well be changing, as local government fails to meet the demands of citizens. A business-in-government program that attempts to affect such a modernization thus has an increasing probability of success.

To understand better what obstacles such a program faces—obstacles that must be at least partially neutralized if the program is to have a chance of success—it is important to review briefly how the various public sector characteristics listed in Table 1 affect governmental management. The first three, relating to the service or product and to the market situation, are particularly difficult to overcome. As numerous observers of the public sector have noted, developing clear and measurable "bottom line" indicators of agency performance constitutes a formidable task. Many governmental services are so diffuse that they are simply not amenable to quantitative or clear-cut measurement and control systems.[8] This is a source, incidentally, of considerable frustration on the part of business executives trying to help improve the management of local government. Furthermore, there are so many diverse interest groups and outside organizations seeking to influence agency administrators in making policy and establishing program priorities that it is almost impossible to establish any consensus, let alone clarity, on agency objectives. These constituencies have different expectations and standards of evaluation with regard to agency performance. They also have different ways of rewarding and punishing agency officials, depending on how they meet such standards. The sanctions they use include reducing or increasing budgets (as exercised by a budget bureau in a city or OMB at the federal level); pressing for the promotion or firing of particular public managers (which is ultimately done by a mayor, a governor, or the President); or developing coalitions to support or sabotage agency programs as they get reviewed by legislative bodies. It is difficult to develop clear, consistent, and qualitative standards of performance and to have a policy of management by objectives in such a politically turbulent context.

One other condition further accentuates this problem of having few, if any, performance standards that are measurable and that control agency management. That is the monopolistic position of most public sector agencies, which shields them from the effects of the market. There simply is no market test. Even nonprofit, government agencies, with all the political pressures they face that prevent the development of usable performance standards, might well be forced to develop such standards and improve their productivity if they operated in a competitive market situation. Recent attempts in this regard to develop and publicize performance data—comparing productivity in similar units across several agencies in the same city; comparing the same units over time; comparing the same agencies or units in different cities; and comparing similar agencies and units in the public and private sectors—show some promise of reversing this situation.[9] The problem remains a severe one, however, involving as it does major structural constraints limiting the clarity of measurement and feedback.

The functional equivalent in the public sector of the market pressures that operate in the private sector is the pluralistic, interest-group politics that continually impinges on government administrators. A critical difference between business and government in this regard is the much greater exposure, openness, and vulnerability of managers in government to the pressures of a much larger number of interested constituencies. Government simply has many more constituencies to satisfy than has business, and these constituencies' support is vitally needed to give legitimacy to its agencies and their programs. Whenever program and policy decisions are made in the public sector, the question of their political feasibility—i.e., their acceptability—is always raised. Furthermore, there are often short-term political visibility considerations to be faced that relate to the immediate electoral needs of the mayor and his party. The result of these forces is that programs inevitably get modified as government administrators recognize and respond to them.

Defenders of the public sector and its management argue that it has a "political rationality" that naive business executives refuse to accept, but that leads to effective decisions—that is, to decisions that best meet the needs of various constituencies. That view is now under considerable question, however, as reflected in the writings of such political scientists as Theodore Lowi, who maintains that the outcome of pluralist interest-group politics impinging on government is often not that beneficial, either to particular interest groups and individuals or to the broader social welfare, however defined.[10] In brief, there may not even be a political rationality to the workings of government anymore, making efforts to improve public sector management even more imperative.

The public sector manager thus operates within a much more fluid, uncertain, turbulent, and fragmented power system than does his counterpart in business. This limits his capacity for planning, for long-term approaches to problems, and for administrative efficiency. As we will discuss below, however, even these constraints may be overcome or partially neutralized by some management reform strategies. Individual corporations, by contrast, have much more power in relation to clients and the market and are more able to manipulate and control both, notwithstanding all the business rhetoric and ideology about consumer sovereignty.

EMPLOYEE RELATIONS

Another seemingly compelling difference between business and government is in the area of employee relations. The public sector faces the severe constraint of civil service, even though some government administrators develop ingenious ad hoc ways of getting around it. Originally introduced to free municipal government from outside political party influences and from the patronage and corruption that were assumed to follow, civil service has created an independent, insider-dominated, countervailing power group of long-term career officials who often defy top administrators, the latter being political appointees who only serve for short terms. The career civil servants can always wait them out and are in that sense often a major stumbling block to management efficiency, to innovation, and to agency flexibility in adapting to changing conditions. Examinations often have no relationship to skills required on the job; the requirement of rigid adherence to civil service lists and seniority prevents top agency officials from bringing in competent outsiders, engendering instead a tradition of "promotion from within"; the use of seniority as an automatic basis for promotion breeds much mediocrity, limiting employee motivation to innovate or excel; and with no standards for defining competence, there can be no quality control and no incentive to improved performance. Finally, civil service, often masquerading under the guise of professionalism, actually promotes highly nonprofessional practices, by protecting government personnel from demands for accountability and protecting the upward-mobility opportunities of those who already have access to agency jobs and control over examination procedures as well. Without some system that—unlike civil service—recognizes and rewards good performance, it is difficult to have efficient or effective management.

INTERORGANIZATIONAL RELATIONS

A particularly critical characteristic of public agencies in cities relates to the fact that they exist in a complex, interorganizational network of other agencies that limits their autonomy and control. Key program and policy decisions in local government are often strongly circumscribed if not completely determined by such outside government agencies. Social service agencies in inner cities, for example, are subject to rules on welfare eligibility and programs that are set by their state and by the federal government. Local boards of education are often subject to controls from City Hall and from state education departments. And all line agencies in cities are reviewed by a variety of city overhead agencies. In New York City, the Department of Personnel maintains civil service standards through an elaborate examination system and passes on agency staffing decisions, often distorting and delaying them; the Bureau of the Budget shapes critical budget and program priority decisions; the Department of Purchase affects many procurement decisions; and the Comptroller helps make most agency payroll decisions, in addition to issuing checks and expense vouchers. One result of all of these reviews is that several different sets of standards are often used in shaping line agency decisions, and the line agencies are thereby subject to numerous and frustrating delays, with respect to both routine administrative decisions and innovative programing. Furthermore, poor management in the overhead agencies compounds similar problems in the line agencies, making it very difficult to modernize the latter without also taking on the whole network of overhead agencies that control them.

Municipal agencies are involved in other networks as well. The criminal courts in New York City, for example, are part of a wider criminal justice system that includes the Police Department, the District Attorneys, the departments of Corrections and Probation, and the Legal Aid Society. The policies and practices of all these other agencies vitally affect the performance of the courts, especially as related to reducing their case backlog, cutting detention time, and generally speeding the movement of defendants through the criminal justice system.

Being enmeshed in such networks severely hampers the management of municipal agencies. They function in a situation characterized by what public administration theorists commonly refer to as "elongated decision chains," involving so many checkpoints and outside controls that it takes much longer to reach decisions than in the private sector and affords public agencies much less flexibility, control, and autonomy. Unless these problems are dealt with—either by simplifying such fragmented structures or by speeding up the decision process within them—efforts at modernization and rationalization will not be very effective. Yet, there are possibilities for such corrective actions, as we will indicate below in this study.

Financing arrangements, a reflection of this intergovernmental system, further compound the problems of municipal agency management. Other, outside agencies—city, county, state, and federal—are often the primary revenue-producing sources for city line agencies and have considerable control over them as a result. Frequently, long delays in providing these line agencies with budget commitments for the next fiscal year prevent them from engaging in even short-term planning. They also hamper them from maintaining staff morale and in some instances from retaining competent staff. Moreover, the revenue system has generally been one in which government agencies are not required to reduce costs, improve services, or develop a better delivery system so as to use their resources more productively. The situation is, in fact, quite the opposite, with agencies rewarded more for lower than for higher levels of efficiency. As Richard Cyert notes: "The amount of revenue raised was frequently related to the level of deficit incurred rather than the surplus. Thus, instead of high quality of performance, the size of the deficit became a basis for increasing revenue. . . . In the case of non profits, however, since the revenue was in many respects adjusted to the level of costs or to the deficit there was no incentive for increasing revenue nor decreasing costs. As a result, non-profit organizations lacked the pressure that leads to problem-oriented research and to innovation."[11]

INTERNAL STRUCTURE AND OPERATIONS

Municipal agencies have a set of structural characteristics in addition to those mentioned above that are particularly critical in affecting the likely success of any management reform strategy. They differ from business structurally in ways that may then limit the applicability of the corporate model and make the transfer or even the adaptation of business management techniques highly problematic. Most of the differences relate to patterns of line-staff relations and to some political and organizational consequences that flow from those patterns. There is basically a reversal in many municipal agencies of the pattern of line–staff relationships that prevails in industry. Line managers who are not insider practitioners have low status and authority; the professional practitioners or "experts" run the agency; management is systematically downgraded to a secondary or means activity; and there is a consistent pattern of recruitment from within, except at the very top, where appointments are generally made through electoral rather than civil service politics. [12]

The "professionals" (staff) in many municipal agencies—e.g., teachers, social workers, police, physicians—have generally moved up the ranks into top administrative positions for which they are often singularly ill fitted. As we discussed above, civil service procedures encourage this kind of promotion of agency practitioners from within, rather than recruitment of managers from outside. The notion of a "generalist executive" has been rejected by professionals in these agencies as obsolete or irrelevant. People trained in administration and other "outsiders," then, are not given much status, as a professional and civil service politics prevails, protecting the upward-mobility opportunities of insiders. Instead of the professional experts standing in something of an advisory capacity to line administrators, as in the business model, it is the administrators who are given little status, income, or power by the professionals, unless such administrators have come up through the ranks and are professionals themselves.

These are bureaucracies of "insiders," then, who define outsiders very broadly to include anybody who has not come up through the ranks in the agency. In the encrusted, status-quo politics that develops, insiders not only control entry into the agency at lower-level positions, but control access to top administrative positions as well. The insiders assume that only people like themselves who are thoroughly experienced in the work of the agency are qualified to run it. This perpetuates inefficiency and incompetence at high managerial levels, since many of the insiders who eventually make it to the top have limited administrative training or expertise. An examination of the quality and level of sophistication of management training in graduate schools of education, social work, public health, and hospital administration indicates how limited that training is.*

In conclusion, the professional service agencies of city government are structured along line and staff lines in a way precisely the opposite from that which obtains in business. Related to this are

---

*The author has informally evaluated the course programs of several New York City universities in this regard. In recognition of this problem, top graduate school administrators at New York University have begun to discuss the possibility of developing university-wide courses in management to upgrade the training in several of its professional schools, especially social work and education.

sharply defined notions of insiders vs. outsiders and a protectionist professional and bureaucratic politics which operates to keep control in the hands of insiders. Since the outsiders are frequently a "cosmopolitan," upper-middle-class, college-educated, and predominantly WASP group, while the insiders are much more lower-middle-class, white-ethnic "locals," with markedly different values and lifestyles, the conflict is all the more intense. The insiders define the outsiders as an unfeeling, arrogant, elitist group who think they can throw their power around any way they like at the expense of the common people; the outsiders see the insiders as enmeshed in machine, agency, and neighborhood politics of a petty and parochial nature. These sharp differences and negative stereotypes only make it all the more difficult to achieve collaboration, which results, in turn, in poor management, limited innovation, and strong resistance to attempts by outside reformers to change these conditions.

In contrast to the permanence of insider practitioners and professionals who run city agencies from middle- and upper-middle management positions is the short tenure of the political appointees at the top—superagency administrators, deputy administrators, and some commissioners and their deputies who are generally appointed by the mayor and his party leaders. Their limited tenure gives them little time to develop their own power base from which to deal effectively with the insider practitioners and engage in the long-term planning necessary to get significant innovations underway. As Horwitch notes: "The new political appointee frequently faces the difficult situation of entering an agency populated with long-term career bureaucrats who have seen his like come and go. These bureaucrats frequently have a different background than does the appointee and may hold different conceptions of what services or functions the agency is supposed to perform."[13] In the private sector, though there is always turnover at the top and an active "succession politics," there is much more continuity of top management, enabling it to develop a much stronger political base inside from which to ensure greater compliance from middle managers than exists in government. There may be large cadres of middle managers who have been in the corporation for a long time and constitute formidable power centers, but they usually don't compare to their counterparts in local government in permanence, in protection from company evaluations, or in political power.

A final aspect of the internal structure and operations of local government that may distinguish it from many corporations is its limited capability for effective decentralization. Large corporations that develop diversified products and markets often benefit considerably from some form of decentralization—along geographical, divisional, or product lines.[14] They are able to do so through the profit-center concept, which involves the systematic use of quantitative indices of performance, by means of which each decentralized unit is evaluated and controlled. With no such measures available in the pusblic sector and with inadequate central monitoring and control, it is difficult to decentralize in a way that improves the delivery of services, notwithstanding all the recent political pressures to do so or even the administrative rationale for it (for example, central downtown bureaucracies in city government are correctly seen as too remote from local neighborhood and service-district needs and as obstructing rather than facilitating the delivery of services locally). Furthermore, the public sector usually has a scarcity of management talent, such talent being essential to monitor and service the decentralized units from some central headquarters as well as to run those units.

OUTLOOK AND CULTURE OF MANAGEMENT

In order to accommodate to all these pressures and constraints, government administrators generally develop much shorter time horizons than their counterparts in business, which poses even further obstacles to improving agency management. This is not to say that they necessarily prefer to be constantly involved in meeting crises or that they are inherently less competent as executives than those in business. Rather, they are forced into such a posture, and into a perennially crisis-management style, by the very nature of their situation (including their short tenure). The fact that their agencies face little competition, but exist instead in a quasi-monopoly position with no market test, only reinforces this style.

As a result of these forces, the public sector was characterized until quite recently by the relative absence of any management tradition. There has been little effort made to develop any significant management training programs, though they are sorely needed; little use has been made of sophisticated or in some cases even primitive management control techniques, such as accounting, auditing, program evaluation, and information systems; and performance appraisal and other personnel techniques are at an equally primitive level. In short, the wide variety of methods, both quantitative and qualitative, now available to improve the "rationality" of management decision making have yet to be incorporated on any scale in local government.

Moreover, the underlying values of many government administrators militate against the widespread use of such techniques. These administrators are much more concerned with effectiveness—with the delivery of more (and hopefully better) services to clients—than with efficiency. They tend to be, as I indicated, practitioner professionals who see in any undue emphasis on economic efficiency an assault on their ideals and mores.[15] Those in human resources or other people-serving agencies often find efficiency approaches particularly irritating, seeing them as dehumanizing their clients and as basically trivial by comparison with their broader concerns with improving programs, responding to the needs of all of their constituents, and redressing inequities that the wider society has imposed on minority populations. The goal of administrators in the public sector, then, is not to cut costs, but rather to keep expanding services. Such administrators rarely consider whether they might be more effective in serving clients if they managed their agencies in a more efficient way.

In sum, a wide range of characteristics of the public sector contributes to the absence of any management tradition and to consequently archaic management structures and procedures. This is not to suggest that such a state of affairs is either desirable or irreversible. Instead, it is to indicate that unless a program to transfer management practices from business to local government takes such considerations into account, it will probably not be very successful. With all these considerations in mind, we turn to an analysis of the Economic Development Council and its urban management programs.

3. The Economic Development Council

The Economic Development Council of New York (EDC) was founded in late 1965 at the initiative of George Champion, then chairman of the board of Chase Manhattan Bank, and several of his business associates. Champion had been president of the New York City Chamber of Commerce in the early sixties and had tried unsuccessfully at that time to merge the Chamber with another business association, Commerce and Industry, so that business might act as a single force to help stem the city's economic decline. As analyses of the city's economy had predicted, the business exodus had become quite severe over the previous decade, seriously weakening the city's employment and fiscal base just when demands for city services were increasing. Though there had been an expansion of jobs in some sectors (government, real estate, insurance, finance, and health), reflecting a change to a service-oriented economy, this had not made up for the loss of manufacturing and white-collar (clerical and executive) jobs resulting from the industrial and corporate headquarters exodus. Thus, manufacturing employment had declined from an estimated 946,800 jobs in 1960 to 865,000 in 1964, and, most importantly, the aggregate number of jobs in the city had also declined in this period.[1]

Champion and his associates did not see the Chamber and other existing business associations as providing leadership on this problem. They decided to try to reverse the business exodus by forming an entirely new organization with a very broad corporate membership.*

*The Chamber's charter limited its activities to lobbying and performing related functions for business. EDC, as a nonprofit corporation, got into broader, public-interest activities. Many early EDC members, incidentally, were also members of the Chamber.

27

To that end, they raised $250,000 from several corporations for start-up costs and approached Clarence Francis, retired board chairman of General Foods and then in his late seventies, to become its first president. Francis, having spent a lifetime in civic affairs, and being as distressed as Champion and his associates about New York City's decline, agreed to serve, with the understanding that EDC would be a nonpartisan organization whose programs would be oriented toward a broader public welfare than that comprehended by its business members. Francis even contacted both Beame and Lindsay, the two mayoral candidates at the time, to make sure that whoever was elected mayor would work with the organization.

To understand how and why EDC got established, it is important to know what was going on in New York City at the time. By the mid-1960s, the urban crisis had hit hard. Other cities had also suffered, but New York's size, its massive demographic changes, its decreasing resources relative to need, and the limited initiatives taken by City Hall, business, and civic leaders to deal with its many problems made its situation particularly acute. Many citizen groups were increasingly dissatisfied with what they saw as the absence of leadership from Mayor Robert F. Wagner, Jr., just when city problems were getting worse. Indeed, no matter where one looked—schools, housing, the economy, welfare, crime, or the city's fiscal situation—the decay was marked and accelerating.[2] The exodus in the past decade of over a million whites, most of them middle-class, and of many private-sector jobs—two critical indicators of urban decay—was particularly pronounced.

That same year, 1965, John Lindsay ran a spirited campaign for mayor whose success reflected the dissatisfaction with the Wagner style as well as the hopes and reformist dreams of the sixties. Lindsay's victory over his Democratic opponent, city comptroller Abraham Beame, was that of a Republican "outsider," who had never served in New York City government and knew little about its complexities, over an "insider" who had been a New York City civil servant for almost thirty years. There was some hope, however, at least among Lindsay's supporters, that as an outsider with fewer obligations than Beame or Wagner to groups with a stake in the status quo (such as civil service and municipal employee unions), he might be much more effective than they.

Indeed, Lindsay's victory, despite his inexperience and outsider status, seemed for a while to offer the promise of providing the leadership and optimism about the city's future that had declined so much in the fifties and sixties. This hope was given added impetus by the establishment of EDC. It marked the first time in several decades that New York City had the kind of potential leadership, both in

City Hall and in business, that was needed to improve its economy. Still, serious questions existed as to how effective either Lindsay or EDC might be, given the poor performance of their predecessors.

It was not going to be easy for EDC to overcome the limited civic involvement of business in New York. That situation reflected many deep-rooted characteristics of the city—most notably its size, its diversity, the institutional competition that exists, and the fact that it is part of an international economy and that its business leaders are often not "homegrown" but have migrated from other areas.*

New York's business community, like its other institutions, is characterized by extreme fragmentation. Unlike big cities such as Boston, Philadelphia, Pittsburgh, Detroit, Chicago, Atlanta, Dallas, and St. Louis, where one can locate a business "power structure," often in the form of a peak association of large corporations, New York has no such coalition of business interests.[3] There had never been any single downtown renewal program (such as has existed elsewhere) that might have helped in the development of a business coalition. Rather, there have been several such projects—for example, Chase Plaza, the World Trade Center, Battery Park, the Bedford-Stuyvesant Restoration Corporation, the 125th Street office buildings—but the size and scale of the city are such that none of the large corporations responsible for these projects could develop into a citywide coalition. The city's many local economies, spread over five boroughs, helped to prevent even a loosely joined business power structure from coming together. Numerous citywide, borough, and local business associations existed, including (among the citywide groups) the Chamber of Commerce, Commerce and Industry, the Board of Trade, the Real Estate Board, and a civic watchdog group with many business members, the Citizens Budget Commission.† All these groups represented business interests in a narrow sense, having been concerned with lowering taxes, cutting municipal budgets, and improving governmental efficiency.

Given the characteristics of New York just mentioned, it may not be possible to form enduring and broad-based business coalitions. Even if they could be formed and linked closely with City Hall, they might have only minimal impact on the local economy. Some urban economists contend, for example, that outside, "macro" forces—for

*Many New York City businesses, especially the large ones, are multinational. Moreover, the city is merely their headquarters location, not the place from which they derive much of their income. Furthermore, not only do business leaders live out of the city, but many live in other states (Connecticut, New Jersey) as well.

†The first two of these business associations merged in the late 1960s, and the new organization is called the Chamber of Commerce and Industry.

example, national monetary and fiscal policies, domestic programs like welfare and manpower training, tax incentives for business to locate in inner cities, general business conditions, and even international economic trends and foreign policy commitments—are more important than local actions in affecting the city's economy.

THE CIVIC FUNCTIONS OF EDC AND OTHER BUSINESS REFORM GROUPS IN CITIES

In order to assess the role of EDC in relation to other organizations and to New York City's problems, it is useful to consider the range of contributions that business can make to any city's economic development.[4] They include (1) *performing a symbolic or "boosterism" function*—attempting to publicize the city's amenities and other benefits as a basis for attracting more business; (2) *doing special-interest lobbying* to promote business interests; (3) *providing technical assistance in the form of management consulting to local government*, to improve its efficiency; and (4) *playing a role as active, outside critic of local government*, which involves an alternative to the management consulting strategy.

Trying to orchestrate these activities, either within the same organization (or set) or through different ones, raises a number of dilemmas. New York reflects to a large degree the specialization approach. Thus, there is an organization called the Association for a Better New York that is particularly oriented toward promoting the city. Some New Yorkers have a cynical view of the association's programs, since it represents many large realtors who may gain economically from them, but boosterism is a critical civic function that can increase the number of private-sector jobs in the city. Another business organization, the Chamber, has concentrated on the second function, doing lobbying and providing services to business that might encourage some corporations to stay and others to want to locate in the city. EDC, in turn, has been the organization most involved in providing management assistance to local government that, if successful, might improve services and the quality of life in the city, thereby inducing more companies and more of the middle class to stay. Finally, good-government groups such as the Citizens Budget Commission and the City Club have pursued the research and citizen advocacy strategy, hoping that this might improve government efficiency and perhaps keep corporations from leaving.[5]

Such specialization—though it does have survival value, in the sense that it allows an organization to retain its separate identity and autonomy—limits the power of any individual organization. The problem is in large part that of leverage. Given the size of city agencies and the power of civil servants and unions to resist change, no single outside organization doing critical studies and issuing "white papers" on agency mismanagement can have much impact. If the civic organizations in New York concerned with governmental efficiency were to pool their resources, however, and to concentrate at any given time on a narrower target—such as evaluating a single agency or program—they would have much greater impact than they do now.

Consolidation, however, can pose other problems. It may make little sense, for example, for the same organization to have one unit collaborating with city agencies as a consultant and another engaging in partisan lobbying or in writing reports as an outside critic. Its consulting relationship may be hurt by the lobbying or outsider roles. Conversely, spreading limited resources over three areas may hamper an organization's effective performance in any one of them. Perhaps what is needed are coalitions of organizations that orchestrate separate strategies while individual organizations specialize in particular ones.

With his scheme in mind, we turn now to a description of EDC.

EDC: ITS MEMBERSHIP, STRUCTURE, AND ACTIVITIES

Membership

One of the most striking features of EDC, in contrast to the city's other business associations, is the elite nature of its board and general membership. Essentially, EDC is George Champion and the network of business and personal relationships that he and his colleagues have established over their many years in the corporate world. EDC's membership list includes some of the largest banks, public utilities, oil companies, insurance companies, and New York City-based corporate headquarters in the world.[6] The wealth and potential power that such EDC member companies represent are enormous, though they had never before been directed toward programs to improve the economy and quality of life in New York. Chase Manhattan, Citibank, Manufacturers Hanover, Chemical, Morgan Guaranty Trust, and Bankers Trust are all members, with Chase and Citibank playing particularly active roles in EDC programs. There are, in addition, large insurance companies such as New York Life,

Metropolitan Life, and Equitable and, among corporate headquarters firms, Exxon, Mobil, Union Carbide, Continental Can, General Motors, Western Electric, RCA, Pfizer, and Sperry Rand, among others. IBM and General Electric are also active members, even though their headquarters are no longer in the city. The more locally oriented corporations include New York Telephone, Brooklyn Union Gas, and Con Edison, among public utilities; Bloomingdale's, Macy's, and Federated Department Stores, among retailers; and one of the city's largest realtors, Helmsley-Spear. EDC members also include prestigious law firms, some in the Wall Street area with ties to key banks, along with securities firms, management consulting corporations, and national retailers. This is undoubtedly the largest single organization of corporations ever assembled to deal with urban problems.

Structure

EDC was established in November 1965 as a nonprofit corporation chartered in the state of New York. Like most nonprofit corporations and even many major businesses, it is run mainly by its staff. Its board members, with few important exceptions, are not highly sophisticated about the complex problems of New York City or about the nationwide urban crisis. Many are board members of numerous other organizations as well and thus cannot be informed about the problems of all of them. In general, these are business leaders who have a keen interest in New York City and hence in EDC programs. They ask intelligent questions about how EDC programs are going, but take their cues from Champion and the EDC staff. Though there are now various committees of board members working on particular projects, the staff still runs the organization and takes the initiative in setting policy.[7]

EDC is like most nonprofit corporations in another sense, in that it reflects a combination of concern about the public interest and some initial confusion about its goals and how best to pursue them. It has gone through a long and often painful evolutionary process in the course of developing and refining its various programs; the lessons learned from that experience are highlighted throughout this book. Its many activities designed to improve the economic climate of New York have reflected much effort, goodwill, and intelligence, along with limited experience at the start in the complexities of New York City politics and a moralistic, crusading spirit that made it overlook those complexities when they were hampering EDC programs.[8] Over time, through self-examination and outside review, EDC has learned from past mistakes and improved on some of its programs. It has also failed to overcome some problems, indicating the uneven developmental experience that any organization moving into such unchartered territory must invariably have. To cite examples of operational improvements, EDC is now more systematic than before in trying to recruit competent business people on loan and in selling its programs to its member corporations. It is also more aware than before of political obstacles to implementing its reform recommendations and has begun to work more on trying to increase its political leverage. At the same time, it still faces severe problems of recruitment and of corporate support for many of its management consulting activities; and it faces equally severe problems in getting agencies to act on management reform recommendations.

The organizational structure of EDC is very simple. It has a board of roughly fifty corporate leaders, almost all of them either board chairmen in their corporations, presidents, or senior partners. Half of them attend monthly meetings to review EDC programs. Beyond that, EDC has evolved the concept of a three-tiered staff composed respectively of retired executives in pro bono positions, some of them heads of particular task forces; a small, full-time professional staff; and on-loan personnel who do much of the actual work.

EDC's board chairman, George Champion, has always taken a very active leadership role, helping to set policy, run the organization, maintain relations with business, government, and civic officials, and recruit people on loan. EDC policy is mainly made, however, by a few full-time staff members and the directors of its task forces, each of which provides management assistance to a particular city agency. The task forces are, with two exceptions, headed by retired senior executives.*

A key staff person has been Paul Busse, now president of EDC, who has worked extensively on its economic development activity and who is responsible for internal administration as well. As soon as EDC was established, Clarence Francis recruited Busse from Newark, where he had worked on municipal affairs for many years with a business group and for a much briefer time at City Hall. He also had worked in federal and state agencies. Busse arrived along with a colleague from Newark, Roland Delfausse. A student of public finance and administration, and an urban economist, Delfausse is also an important figure in EDC: he has served as its one-man research

---

*One was the director of EDC's high school program, Dr. Floyd Flom, who had been a college professor before working as a public relations executive in industry and then joining EDC. The other is Richard Coyne, a lawyer, who has been with EDC since 1969.

office (that office now has two people) and has written voluminous policy papers and research reports that have become the basis for many EDC programs. Busse, Delfausse, and Charles Coates, whom Francis had recruited from General Foods and who had also served on the Hoover Commission,* were EDC's main staff members at its inception.†

By and large, EDC has been structured and run much more like a professional management consulting firm than like a corporation, with its task forces functioning fairly autonomously. Each task force director has developed his own strategies—subject, of course, to review by Champion and, in the high school program, by an outside group of policy advisors. Some task forces have been managed more loosely and others less so, reflecting the particular style of the director. Most of the present directors have served in that capacity for several years, such continuity probably contributing to whatever success these task forces have had.††

This small, informal cadre of people, with its strong leader, senior staff, task force directors, and people on loan, has maintained the three-tiered structure described above since the early 1970s. New positions have been established—for example, a full-time on-loan staff person working just on recruitment—and EDC now shares a joint board with the Chamber; but neither these developments nor other, similar ones have basically changed the three-tiered structure.

The one group that does keep changing, however, is the people on loan. Many are loaned for a year and others for shorter periods, and the turnover makes it difficult to manage the projects to which they are assigned. This has led to serious problems in maintaining continuity with the public agencies, as well as in developing momentum and having a cumulative impact. It usually takes a few months for a person on loan to even begin to have a working knowledge of the agency. Then, after several months of more productive work, the person becomes understandably preoccupied with reentry into his or her firm or with relocating elsewhere. The problems of doing effective management consulting in municipal agencies are so complex that even several months' time is hardly adequate to more than begin

*The Hoover Commission was an investigative agency, originally headed by former president Hoover, to help streamline and rationalize the management of the federal government.

†Coates retired from EDC in 1976.

††The heads of EDC's high schools program and courts task force have served since 1969 and 1970, respectively, while those in the school headquarters and Human Resources Agency (HRA) task forces have been in those positions since early 1972. A new school headquarters director was appointed in late 1976, but his predecessor also continued to work part-time on education.

the effort. Bringing in new people every year means almost starting from scratch, unless they are given a substantial orientation to the work, both by EDC and by the agency; and they are often not given an adequate orientation.

It is particularly important for EDC to be able both to specify in advance the nature of the assignment for which it is recruiting and to match people and their skills to it. That is often not possible in city agencies that function under such turbulent conditions, making it difficult for EDC to rationalize its recruitment procedures.

Given all these conditions, recruitment is certainly enormously complex. Moreover, the programs can succeed only if EDC sells them to its member companies. This requires securing qualified people, not corporate castoffs; getting them in enough numbers and at the times needed; and protecting them on reentry so that they will be willing to come in the first place and will not have their performance on the assignment adversely affected by concern about what awaits them on their return. These matters required much more attention than Champion and his task force directors could give them. The absence until June 1974 of any single staff person working on recruitment meant that this important function had been neglected until then.

Goals and Membership

EDC's main goal throughout its existence has been to reverse the business exodus from New York City and to help stimulate private investment there. It differs from all other business associations both in its broad emphasis on economic development and in its nonpartisan style. Champion and his associates who helped found EDC immediately dissociated their organization from any identification with narrow lobbying efforts of such traditional business groups as the Chamber. They publicized instead EDC's concern with serving a "broad public interest." Notwithstanding these statements of purpose, EDC did, in fact, serve business interests as well. Its research office, for example, did many studies that dramatized inefficiencies in government and inflationary collective bargaining agreements which EDC maintained contributed to increased taxes on business. The ultimate concern, however, was with the corporate exodus and the city's economic base. Furthermore, the studies were presented simply as fact-finding reports; there was no lobbying to encourage implementation of their recommendations.

EDC should also be distinguished from the city's many civic reform groups. It has an almost exclusively business membership—in contrast to, say, the Citizens Union, the City Club, and the Citizens

Budget Commission, all of which include New York's political and civic elites, in the person of, for example, distinguished lawyers, public officials, and representatives of universities and nonprofit agencies. Moreover, EDC concentrated much more than did other reform organizations on the city's economic climate and on jobs.

Nevertheless, there is some overlap in membership and in program priorities with these organizations, though the latter pertains more to stated goals than to actual practice. The Citizens Budget Commission, for example, had twelve members of its board from EDC-member corporations, and it has done many studies of governmental efficiency.

Such a proliferation of organizations with overlapping membership and programs could exist on this scale only in New York. Elsewhere, business and civic leaders with an interest in governmental reform, economic development, and the quality of life locally might well have come together in a Chamber, a Rotary or a Kiwanis Club. Instead, New York has many specialized civic organizations, each involved in a particular aspect of the city's problems but none having enough resources to exert any significant political impact. Were these organizations to pool their resources and form broader-based coalitions on such issues as productivity in government, on which they have common positions, they would be much more effective politically than they have been.

PROGRAM HISTORY

All this discussion of EDC's structure, membership, and civic functions makes sense only in the context of its main activities. In line with the modern architect's dictum that form follows function, we turn now to a discussion of EDC's program history and of how and why it came to have the particular task force structure and to be involved in the kinds of management consulting activities that have been briefly described.

EDC was formed to help Mayor John Lindsay deal with the city's economic decline and, in particular, with the conditions leading to the exodus of corporate headquarters and industry.[9] New York was faced with increasing numbers of poor minority residents who were placing tremendous demands on services, including the welfare system. While the city was struggling to marshall the resources necessary to provide jobs and services to this population without taking them away from others, the state and federal governments appeared uninterested. Also, at just this time, municipal employee unions were becoming better organized and more militant. As a result, they were demanding higher wages and salaries without offering increased productivity, and they were demanding retirement benefits generally beyond the city's capacity to pay. By the late 1960s, the costs of running city government were increasing about 15 percent a year, as opposed to about a 3 percent increase in revenues.

Most of this revenue gap had to be closed by taxes, and business was a main target. Top EDC officials maintained that an increased tax burden, along with deteriorating city services, was contributing directly to the exodus of business. They then became involved in exploring a series of interrelated problems that they saw as underlying causes of the city's economic decline. These included the increased service and welfare demands of the new minority poor; the decline in the quality of the public schools; the increasing crime rate; the city's labor relations practices; and, in later years, rent control, deteriorating housing, the high costs of the City University of New York under the Open Admissions program, and the mismanagement of the city hospital system.

Several central themes kept recurring in EDC's early discussions of these matters. One was the costs of local government, which the city was unable to meet without substantially increasing taxes on business. Another was the decreasing efficiency and productivity of city government; and a third was the city's lack of any consistent or long-range policy on these matters, particularly with respect to its labor relations. All these issues formed the agenda for a series of programs that EDC was to evolve over time and that it is still evolving.

One of EDC's first programs related to the city's use of land, as this affected the local economy. It helped form a nonprofit agency, the Public Development Corporation, that became a vehicle to rezone land for industrial use. It later helped establish several industrial parks and development projects—one in downtown Jamaica, another in the South Bronx. Still another was the convention center in Manhattan.

At the same time, EDC did not abandon its broad interest in the many facets of the urban crisis. In late 1967 and 1968 it conducted a series of surveys on city problems, leading to the establishment of its Committee on Public Policy, which helped coordinate the studies. One of that committee's key members was Roland Delfausse, EDC's research director, who produced an important policy paper in this period, known internally as the "Delfausse memo." It developed in quite explicit form his and EDC's diagnosis of how the city's lack of leadership was contributing to its economic decline. His argument was that the city's deteriorating services, its increasing taxes, its poor economic climate, and its decline in private investment, with more corporations leaving, were the inevitable results of its failure to take any clear and effective initiatives on such issues as governmental efficiency, labor relations, crime, public education, health, housing, and taxes.

In early 1969, as a result of this committee's studies and other explorations of what EDC might do to improve the schools and to ease the crime problem, it decided to assume the role of management consultant to city government, with its services to be offered without cost to city agencies. It evolved the strategy of forming a task force to deal with each separate agency. A retired corporate executive would be the director of each task force, with on-loan people from EDC's member corporations functioning as staff people, conducting management studies of key agency problems. EDC would play a low-key role in each instance, not entering with preconceived solutions and not taking a strong policy position, but rather acting as a management analyst, making recommendations for change and then seeking to develop support inside the agency for their implementation. EDC also adopted the strategy of getting the agency itself to implement the recommended changes, rather than have EDC do it. It didn't always work out this way, as agencies tried to retain EDC staff to do much of the staff and administrative work, but that was the goal.

EDC's task force concept was first developed for use in its consulting work in the city's criminal courts, with the many elements just described only evolving over time. It was later applied to projects involving the Board of Education; several individual high schools; the Human Resources Administration, the city's superagency for social service and antipoverty programs; the Housing and Development Administration; and other parts of the criminal justice system. All these task forces got underway as a result of favorable early publicity EDC received in the courts, which stimulated top officials from other agencies to invite EDC in. As will be shown in the ensuing chapters, however, the value of the work that EDC did for these agencies was extremely problematic. Many of the changes it helped institute were not easily discernible and were reversible unless there was continuing support for them within the agencies. Getting municipal agencies to accept new management techniques and then institutionalize them is quite difficult, as EDC was to learn.

Having given this brief history of EDC's program development, we now seek to provide a more analytical perspective on what EDC has done. Such a perspective will indicate more clearly some of the main assumptions behind EDC's programs and the key turning points in their development.

Phase One: The Jobs Strategy

EDC has gone through two phases in its economic development efforts and is perhaps moving into a third as of this writing. The first involved working intensively to try to create more private-sector jobs. The two major figures in this work were Clarence Francis, EDC's president, and Kenneth Patton, a new staff person who later went to work for the city. Francis was active in trying to attract and retain corporate headquarters and industry, and he felt that this should always be EDC's main mission. During his three years as president of EDC, he made certain that it was the organization's primary activity. "I got in touch with Mayor Lindsay," he reported, "and we spent a lot of time together, persuading companies not to leave. The mayor actually went out with me to see the corporations. When he was not at meetings, one of his top assistants was. This was a very high-priority item for him, and we worked closely together on it."

EDC hired Kenneth Patton in June 1967 from a company whose main service, ironically, was finding suburban sites for New York City-based companies. Patton was only with EDC for a year and a half, but during that time he became involved in many projects related to how the city might use land for the creation of private-sector jobs. They included an industrial park at the Brooklyn Navy Yard; working with the Regional Planning Association, a nonprofit civic group, on a study for developing a business and industrial center in downtown Jamaica, Queens; getting the City Planning Commission to provide capital-budget money for urban renewal; and laying out an industrial parks and economic development strategy for the entire city. Patton continued this work when Mayor Lindsay recruited him from EDC in November 1968 to serve as commissioner of the Department of Commerce and later as administrator of the Economic Development Administration, the superagency responsible for economic development in the city.

Working through the Public Development Corporation while at EDC and then with the city, Patton was largely responsible for the establishment of industrial parks throughout the outer boroughs. There were three in Queens, one in Staten Island, and two in Brooklyn.* EDC has also helped set up a new development corporation in the South Bronx to bring in more industry there. Roughly 12,000 to 15,000 jobs were created by all of these parks, according to city agency estimates, but this has done little to limit the continuing and massive loss of manufacturing jobs from the city, which

*The Queens parks included one at College Point, a Springfield Boulevard Air Services Park in southeastern Queens, and a JFK Air Service Park. The two in Brooklyn were at the Brooklyn Navy Yard and in the Canarsie area of southeast Brooklyn.

amounted to an estimated 194,500 from 1969 through 1974, the peak years of the industrial parks program.[10] The parks, then, seem to have been at best a "holding action" while New York was going through an inevitable change so characteristic of most old cities in the Northeast—from a blue-collar industrial to a white-collar service economy.

Some of the forces that affect the city's employment picture appear to be well beyond its power to control, almost regardless of local programs. As we have just indicated, the overall shift in the city's economy seems inevitable. No systematic data are available on why industry and corporate headquarters move out, but one factor that many urban economists and business leaders agree is important is business's perception that the quality of the inner-city labor force has deteriorated with the influx of poor blacks and Spanish-speaking people from rural areas. Even for lower-level white-collar jobs (clerical, some sales), business may see the quality of that labor force as so poor that it would prefer to move out to recruit the seemingly large supply of suburban women. Corporate executives also speak of the problems of crime, deteriorating schools, inadequate and expensive housing, and a general decline in city services. When Union Carbide, for example, publicly announced in 1976 its decision to move out, its spokesmen stated that the city's poor schools were an important factor in limiting the company's ability to persuade promising executives to move to its headquarters in New York.[11] Finally, business may also fear racial confrontations within the workplace and in the wider community and may prefer to have a more tractable and culturally compatible labor force. Though these interpretations are all largely speculative, the business exodus from New York City is very real. Indeed, the city has lost over 600,000 jobs since 1969, most of them in the private sector; and with the city's budget crisis, the public sector is now diminishing as well.*

One may thus question how productive it was for EDC and later for the city to keep pressing for industrial parks in the face of business decisions that negated that strategy. "The city will never be a center for manufacturing," suggested a top Lindsay administrator, "and we must support those sectors that had until very recently shown growth—offices, government, health, the services, entertainment, and universities."†

*The speculations above are from personal interviews with urban economists studying corporate move-outs from cities and from corporation executives.

†Actually, EDC had developed a proposal in 1967 to have Welfare Island turned into an urban research and policy center where urban specialists from many city universities would work on a comprehensive economic development strategy for the city. The proposal went to a foundation but was never funded.

The main emphasis in this early period, then, was on jobs. Paul Busse, EDC's top staff person, referred to it as his organization's "materialistic" phase, where the emphasis was more on "retooling land" than on "developing its human resources," which was to be part of the next stage. In retrospect, what is clear about EDC's job strategy is that EDC did not have the leverage necessary to effect a turnabout in the city's economic decline. No other organizations have been able to do that either.

Phase Two: The Management Consulting Strategy

After Patton left for his city post in November 1968 (which, incidentally, coincided with Francis's retirement), EDC shifted to a totally different set of activities, and acquired many new staff. Francis, having passed 80 by this time, prevailed on George Champion to become president. With Champion's ascendancy, EDC took on a new set of priorities. Its policy studies and the "Delfausse memo" referred to previously suggested that the corporate exodus could be stopped and possibly reversed only if the entire infrastructure of city services that business complained so much about—schools, housing, transportation, crime prevention, manpower training, welfare—were substantially improved. It was all right to try to persuade business to stay, but unless the deteriorating conditions that led it to leave were corrected, no job creation or economic development strategy would work.

Furthermore, one part of the infrastructure—namely, those agencies responsible for the education and training of the city's human resources—needed special attention, since business was particularly concerned about the inadequate local labor force on which it had to draw. (Whether it was a reflection of the racism of employers or of the limited training and skills of many blacks and Puerto Ricans, or some combination of the two, this concern was present.) EDC officials argued that if the city could produce a larger employable population, perhaps some corporations who would otherwise leave might be induced to stay.

These concerns led to two related program developments after Champion became president in late 1968. One was a concentration on management consulting, intended to improve the delivery of city services. The other was a direction of much of the consulting effort initially toward the schools. Throughout 1968 and early 1969, EDC surveyed various industry-school partnerships that had been tried throughout the nation. It concluded that bad schools were a distinct threat to the city's economic development and that the EDC should try to establish partnerships with high schools in which innovative programs might be developed to upgrade those schools.

The main strategy, then, became one of providing management assistance to those agencies responsible for training and educating the local labor force—the schools in particular, but later welfare and manpower training agencies as well. Thus, a study that EDC had commissioned documenting the mismanagement of the Welfare Department led to the later development of a task force providing management assistance to that agency.[12]

The increasing incidence of crime, as related to the city's deteriorating economic climate, was still another concern of EDC at this time. Street crime, burglaries, and particularly a rash of bomb threats and some actual bombings swept mid-Manhattan in 1968. They became a focus of much internal discussion at EDC, and the council formed a Crime and Public Safety Committee to try to deal with the problem. After providing extensive management assistance to the Police Department and then trying to identify and support those organizations involved in court reform, EDC set up its own city court task force in 1970, through which it developed a program of management assistance to the criminal courts.

All these separate concerns coalesced in 1971 into a fairly coherent program of free management consulting to several city agencies—the courts, the schools, and welfare, manpower training, and related departments within the Human Resources Administration. Early programs helped pave the way for later ones, in the sense that favorable publicity on the criminal court project and the school partnerships led to subsequent invitations from the Board of Education and the Human Resources Administration. EDC's philosophy regarding these projects was indicated in its 1973 annual report: "Government costs are a crucial element in the urban economic 'climate.' Taxes enter heavily into the cost of goods and services to all the City's consumers. Excessive tax burdens put a blight on the ability of business to prove employment for the City's people. By helping to make government more efficient, therefore, EDC's task forces are serving an essential and primary purpose."[13]

Lessons from an Early Failure

Before analyzing some of the complexities of the EDC consulting program, it is important to describe a management assistance project that EDC undertook long before these others got underway. Even while EDC was concentrating on its jobs strategy (through 1968), it had one management consulting effort that turned out quite badly and that contained important lessons about what not to do in the future.

As soon as EDC was established, several of its top staff members recommended that it help the city revamp the entire structure of local government. They urged that it press for a "modified Hoover Commission approach" and make its management expertise available to the mayor. Top EDC staff then called on the Deputy Mayor–City Administrator, Dr. Timothy Costello, in early 1966, offering free management assistance to city government.

Reading the city charter fairly literally (too literally, as it turned out), EDC officials saw Costello as the key person at City Hall with whom to work. At the time this made a lot of sense, since Mayor Lindsay had announced publicly in early 1966 that he was increasing the authority of the city administrator's office to work on needed management improvements.[14] This office had rarely been strong in the past, but Lindsay's was seemingly a reform administration, and EDC took seriously his stated intention to increase its authority and powers. Moreover, the office's main competitor, the Bureau of the Budget, was particularly weak at that time, with Lindsay's first budget director having a lot of trouble establishing relationships in city government. EDC formed a Management Advisory Committee (MAC) to work with Costello, and by early July 1966 he had publicly endorsed a program of management assistance for the city that he and EDC had put together, to begin the following September.

The program called for as many as twelve management teams to work on different city agency problems. Each team was to have two EDC representatives and one each from the Bureau of the Budget, the city administrator's office, and the agency under study. There would be no publicity about the activities, except as indicated by the city administrator. EDC would do research, recommend management changes, and monitor their implementation.

Costello and the mayor warmly endorsed the project, issuing a press release to that effect. As Lindsay noted: "[EDC's] commitment to serve the city in this way means that, at long last, the city government is tapping the vast pool of management talent that exists in New York."[15]

EDC and the city agreed that the program would be conducted on a trial basis for about a year, with EDC working on the following projects: developing administrative reforms for the city's retirement system and Pension Bureau; instituting a cost accounting system for the voluntary Blue Cross and Blue Shield programs in the new Health Services Administration, providing its administrator with an executive assistant to advise on management matters; developing an information system for the Fire Department; introducing computer operations into the Finance Administration; streamlining the administration of the Mitchell-Lama program; and helping with management improvements in the Human Resources Administration.

All this was going on while Lindsay and Costello were attempting to consolidate city government into several superagencies. The superagency strategy actually complemented what EDC was doing, providing as it did a more receptive administrative environment in which such consulting could take place. Thus, the superagency itself could become the site of management improvement activity, whereas under the old, fragmented structure, it would not have been clear who the client was. EDC strongly supported the Lindsay administration's superagency efforts, and Clarence Francis testified at City Council hearings in favor of the strategy.

Some time in the late summer and early fall of 1967, a year after these projects got started, Birny Mason, the head of the EDC group and chairman of the board of Union Carbide, asked an associate to evaluate the entire program. The report was generally positive, indicating that many city agency officials liked having EDC-recruited executives as management consultants and that EDC should try to continue and expand the program. It documented what it claimed were many "positive results" of the projects, including the streamlining of procedures in several agencies, the development of new management systems, and the speeding up of administrative decisions on such matters as budget, personnel, and service delivery.

Mason and his associates then agreed to go ahead only on the condition that the mayor personally support the project and mandate that it be run through the city administrator's office. To their dismay, Mason and EDC were never able to get that support, and the program died shortly thereafter. What they hadn't realized until the very end was that their program had gotten caught up in some political infighting at City Hall and had been dropped along the way.

The main problem was that the program fell between the city administrator and the Bureau of the Budget. Both offices had always competed as to who would become the management arm of the mayor, regardless of the particular personalities involved, and the city administrator never had the political resources to prevail. There was a short time, in mid-1966, when Costello might conceivably have taken on more power, as Lindsay's budget director had resigned and no successor had yet been found. Costello's style was not one of empire building, however. In addition, he reportedly realized that as a Liberal Party patronage appointee, he could not get the mayor's support to increase the powers of his office.

More importantly, however, the office had no resources to establish its authority. The budget director had control over the money, and the other deputy mayor had by tradition been the mayor's political arm. Meanwhile, there was little left for the city administrator to do except some ceremonial functions and the running of high-visibility programs (Office of the Aging; contract compliance; student internships in city government) that no other agency wanted.

The main City Hall efforts at management reform, it turned out, were being initiated by the innovative and influential new budget director, Fred Hayes, who came to that position in late 1966 with an imposing agenda of strategies for improving city government. Hayes became a close advisor and confidant of Lindsay soon after he arrived, and Costello's limited influence then diminished even more. Having recruited a cadre of young "management activist" types from Washington, from the campuses, and from such organizations as Vista and the Peace Corps to become program planners and management analysts, Hayes also brought in RAND, McKinsey, and other management consultants to city government. A New York City RAND office was established in 1968, and Hayes initiated many consulting contracts through it and McKinsey, working assiduously to transform the Bureau of the Budget from a traditional cost accounting agency to a management development one. He had no particular interest in EDC at the time, professing little awareness of its activities; and Costello's office could not establish any management reform programs in the face of Hayes's influence.

In brief, this management consulting effort that EDC had developed with all good intentions dissolved after only a year, mainly because there was no central place in city government for it to link up with. Furthermore, the project did not reflect a casual involvement by EDC. Mason had on his council some of the most powerful and prestigious business leaders in America, including Fred Borch, president of General Electric; Gilbert Fitzhugh, chairman of Metropolitan Life; Philip Reed, director of American Express Company; A. L. Williams of IBM; and A. E. Perlman, president of New York Central. The executives they brought in as consultants were in most cases high-level management people, not castoffs. And their services were being offered free. Yet, the city was not organized to use them. The whole experience caused dismay at EDC and among some staff people in the city administrator's office, and EDC was forced to find another way of making its management expertise available to city government.

A final episode illustrates the problems of outsiders working in such a consulting relationship with city government. Costello and

Lindsay, in their last meeting with Mason, implored him not to go public with an EDC version of how and why the project fell through, but to just let it die away. In deference to their request, as well as for self-interested political reasons (e.g., they wanted to maintain close future ties to City Hall), EDC never did go to the press on this. Some of its members and staff wanted to do so, but those angry enough to want the public to know what had happened did not prevail.

For EDC, the lesson from this experience was never again to go through any single office at City Hall, but rather to approach particular agencies individually and to do so only by informing many top city officials of what it was doing. EDC concluded that effective management consulting would require letters of invitation from each agency where it might work, plus the approval of such city government officials as the mayor, various deputy mayors, the City Council president, and the comptroller. In addition, task forces would be needed to develop a carefully nurtured relationship with the agencies. Only when all of these things took place could EDC undertake projects that might not be buried like this first one.

AN OVERVIEW OF EDC MANAGEMENT CONSULTING

The projects that EDC later undertook, then, were not just one-shot efforts, but rather involved long-term commitments by EDC to this free management consulting strategy. There were, of course, many problems that EDC would have to face. First, how would it gain entree into agencies that already had many paid consultants? Could it secure the cooperation of agency officials to do studies, and then to implement its recommendations for change?

Beyond that, how would EDC organize for such an ambitious effort? Could it sell this program to its corporate members? Would they then be willing to provide needed executives on loan of sufficiently high quality, in sufficient numbers, and during the time periods required for such assignments? Would EDC be able to maintain such commitments over time, in agencies where it was very difficult to demonstrate conclusively the "bottom line" impact of the program, and as it became obvious that the program could not easily achieve dramatic results, no matter how competent the executives might be? Since this was such a new concept to most EDC members, could it, indeed, ever create the critical mass necessary to effect significant change, without EDC having to align itself with many other organizations?

Basic to the entire effort was the more general issue raised in the preceding chapter: namely, can one significantly improve the performance of municipal agencies by transferring management practices from business, given the constraints of the public sector? How much "transferability" is there? Or are there other, perhaps better, strategies for improving productivity in local government?

By working as a management consultant, EDC was of necessity assuming a posture of collaborating with the "insiders," and thereby perhaps running the risk of either being coopted or absorbed by them, or being frozen out. In concentrating solely on management issues, it also ran the risk of getting bogged down in the administrative details of the agencies, while critical policy questions relating to civil service, collective bargaining, decentralization, and citizen participation, all of which also affected the delivery of services, went unresolved. It was possible, for example, for the teachers union and the Board of Education to reach contractual agreements on salaries and working conditions that might wipe out several years of EDC efforts to effect cost savings and management improvements.

Since no business group had ever undertaken such a consulting program to improve local government in New York City, at least not on this scale, there were no precedents on which EDC could rely. It was moving in new directions and could evolve its strategy only from experience.

To raise all of these questions is only to indicate how problematic such a program is. Many of the problems of agency mismanagement were a result of years of neglect; and conditions that took fifty to seventy-five years to develop could not be rectified that quickly. New York City's long record of unimplemented management studies, some dating back to the 1920s and 1930s, indicated that. And yet EDC had to show results if it were to keep its members committed to the effort.

On the more positive side, the city agencies EDC worked with were willing clients, and most wanted it to stay on. It made them look good to have a prestigious business group doing management consulting on their problems. Moreover, some agency administrators were keenly aware of how management deficiencies had severely hampered their ability to function. They saw EDC's management expertise as potentially valuable to them, and the fact that it was free and that EDC brought in other resources as well made it even more attractive.

EDC's strategy of approaching the agencies also contributed to a deepening of the relationship. It never came in with any preconceived solutions and rarely questioned the goals and program priorities of agency officials. Instead, it emphasized its desire to make management techniques available to better implement whatever programs were in effect. EDC was not another annoying constituency in this regard, and many agency officials with whom it worked appreciated that.

One fairly standard practice that EDC followed was to do a lot of preliminary interviewing of agency staff at all levels, to find out their definitions of key problems. It responded to some of those definitions in order to gain initial credibility, even though it realized that doing so might not necessarily increase the long-term ability of the agency to manage itself better. For example, the constant request by court and school officials for more resources (money, staff, space), as though that was their main obstacle to good management, was something that EDC responded to at first; though it soon refused to do so, telling agency officials that they had to decide on their priorities and manage better what resources they already had.

Most importantly, EDC agreed not to go "public" with critical reports (with the exception of its work in the courts), and as a result, it soon became a repository of voluminous information on agency inefficiency and mismanagement.* The reports it produced were often not given wide release. Moreover, many of them reflected the ideas of agency officials themselves, who wanted the innovations proposed but didn't have enough inside support for them and felt they would be undermined in the future if they spoke up. Like most consultants, EDC thus became a catalyst for change, giving legitimacy to the ideas of agency staff, taking the heat off of them, and often even becoming the scapegoats for agency personnel who had successfully blocked change in the past.

This is not to say that EDC's relations with these agencies were free of problems and conflict. There were many problems, some quite severe, and they will be discussed in the case studies to follow.

Given the marked difference in background, experience, and values between members of EDC and officials of local government that they worked with, it is not surprising that the two groups sometimes came into conflict. Some EDC people had very negative views about government officials, regarding many as "unbusinesslike," as too "political," and generally as not as capable as their counterparts in the private sector. On occasion they communicated such feelings (however indirectly), usually after they felt the agency had not responded to important recommendations for management

*The courts task force released all its studies and for a variety of reasons circumvented many of the problems discussed here. See chapter six for a further analysis.

changes. As EDC gained experience, however, its people became more realistic about the public sector's characteristics and softened some of their negative attitudes. (Impatience with agency delays, for example, became less associated over time with personal short-comings of particular officials and was seen more in institutional terms.) If they hadn't, these consulting relationships would have ended earlier than they did, and certainly the agencies would not have asked EDC to keep doing work for them.

On their side, government officials had many negative views about EDC, regarding some EDC staff as naive about the public sector. They felt that some EDC recommendations could not be implemented because of constraints (political or financial) that EDC had not adequately taken into account. Many grew impatient with what they regarded as the unreality of some of its consultant reports. "They tell us we need so many more people for our data processing unit and that it should be set up in a particular way," reported one top agency official, "and we knew that long before they came on the scene. If they can't provide us with the bodies or with enough clout to get such people, we don't need another consulting report from them."

Many of the agency administrators impatient with EDC were looking for short-term operational assistance on pressing problems in payroll, budget, accounting, data processing, information systems, and the like. Traditional management consulting reports were the last thing they thought they needed. EDC, by contrast, didn't want to get coopted into doing operational work, but preferred rather to diagnose problems and recommend structures and procedures to eventually get the city out of its crisis-management mode. It partic-ularly wanted to have the agencies take more initiative and become more self-sufficient in programming for their own improvement.

One agency criticism of EDC related to the mixed quality of its on-loan staff. Some were seen as quite competent, but others as much less so. EDC was aware of this, and the uneven quality of the people on loan was one of the program's biggest weaknesses. As we already reported, EDC has had a person working full-time on just this problem since 1974. We will take up in chapter seven the extent to which any improvements have resulted from this work.

Partly in the context of this criticism, and also reflecting an impatience with the short time that most on-loan people served, some local government officials were not that cooperative in ori-enting the consultants to conditions in their agency. They were annoyed at having to spend time dealing with each new EDC group that came in; yet these consultants had to be oriented if they were to be helpful.

As the case studies below will suggest, all of these problems were symptomatic of a more basic one that any group like EDC will have to deal with in order to be effective in such a program. Many of EDC's on-loan staff and task force directors were not trained as consultants either to the public sector or to business. If one accepts the premise that there are particular kinds of skills required for work of this nature, then EDC was at a disadvantage. At least one task force director had arranged for day-long training sessions for his people with McKinsey staff, but a few training sessions may well be a poor substitute for actual experience.

One top city official well acquainted with EDC's work suggested an entirely different role for EDC from the one it chose. "The city desperately needs lots of trained people to do the hard work of redesigning systems," he noted. "EDC may well be good at early diagnostic work and at advising city agencies how to proceed, but it has to recognize that it cannot do the big half-million dollar job that would be required, say, to put together a management information system in an agency like the Board of Education. That requires much more personnel and expertise than EDC has. EDC should indicate to the agencies the areas where they should spend money and give them the customer sophistication they need on these matters. It might also politic with the mayor, the City Council, the Board of Estimate, and other budget bodies to get the funds. But it should not and cannot get into actual on-line work, and we don't need any more City Club-type studies telling us what is wrong with these agencies. EDC did both, and that was wrong."

In conclusion, EDC's management consulting is an important program, an understanding of which has national implications in the sense that many cities face the fiscal and management problems that New York does, even if only in preliminary form and on a smaller scale. If only to avoid the worsening of such problems elsewhere, other cities and civic-minded groups should learn from EDC's attempts to improve the management of local government in New York. Even if the program turns out to have been unsuccessful, that in itself may contain important lessons on what *not* to do elsewhere.

The main policy issues that one must be sensitive to in analyzing the cases to follow include: (1) whether any program like this could ever attain the leverage required to effect significant changes in a city of the size and diversity of New York; (2) related to that, whether any business or civic group like EDC could ever overcome the many political obstacles to governmental reform in New York; (3) whether governmental reform is really that relevant a strategy for revitalizing the cities and resolving the urban crisis; (4) whether policy decisions on such issues as decentralization, civil service practices, or collective bargaining agreements may not affect efficiency much more than EDC's management consulting; and, finally, (5) whether EDC's diagnosis of what went wrong with New York, which constituted the rationale for its consulting work, was valid.

We will be addressing all of these issues in the course of the case studies and in the concluding chapter. The issue of EDC's diagnosis, however, does merit some comment here. EDC has a particular view of the city, not always spelled out in great detail, on which it based its management consulting programs. Presented as a "nonpartisan" position, it essentially argues that profligate spending both on social programs and on city employee salaries, fringe benefits, and pensions has contributed to creating a downward spiral in the city's economy and has put it in a precarious fiscal position from which it may not recover for many years, perhaps decades. This spending was largely a capitulation by politicians to pressure-group demands; it involved many questionable budgetary practices; and it had to be financed largely through increasing taxes on business and on city residents. Meanwhile, too little attention was given to improving productivity, efficiency, and accountability in government.

EDC felt strongly that "politics," by which it meant the capitulation of elected officials to pressure-group demands so that those officials could get reelected, had contributed to the downfall of New York. That "politics" had to be counteracted, EDC argued, by strong leadership, better "management," and more "businesslike" practices in government. This was not so much an antiminority and antipoor position as it was one that argued that government at all levels, particularly in this instance local government, was being run so inefficiently and had perpetuated such inflationary labor contracts that it was sapping the vitality of the nation. The main villains in this scenario were municipal employee unions, the civil services, and politicians who capitulated to their demands.

Though many of EDC's views are valid, they oversimplify the reasons for the urban crisis and for New York's decline. As indicated in chapter one, many national developments over which cities have no control—the automation of agriculture in the South, the mass migration of blacks to the North, and the development of communication and transportation networks that facilitated the exodus of the middle class and the dispersion of business and industry—contributed to the urban crisis in America. Furthermore, just looking at New York alone, there are many other possible villains besides the ones EDC indicates. While labor and politicians are partly responsible for New York's decline, business and other large institutions must share some of the blame as well. As Jack Newfield, journalist and social critic, has noted, much public money that might have been used to deal with the city's many social problems [16] has gone instead to construction firms, real estate interests that don't pay city taxes, and institutions like Con Edison. An analysis of the social and economic costs of projects such as Yankee Stadium, the World Trade Center, and the Albany Mall indicates that big business and monopolistic utilities have cost the city millions of dollars and also contributed to its bankruptcy. Until there are controls over their actions so as to make them act more in the public interest, New York City may continue to decline.

What follows is a detailed analysis of EDC's various management consulting programs to see how they have worked and with what impact.

4. The School Headquarters Task Force

Our first case, illustrating well the ways in which public-sector characteristics make the management transfer strategy so difficult of attainment, is the headquarters bureaucracy of the New York City schools. The New York City Board of Education, like all other public-sector agencies, is a supremely political organization. The central board and top agency administrators make decisions on such issues as staffing, budget, and curriculum mainly in response to interest-group pressures, including those from the "insiders"—e.g., the teachers union and supervisory associations. Furthermore, it is an "insider-dominated" monopolistic agency with little incentive to innovate, and it has no clear bottom line, no management traditions, and no consensus about agency goals except those that are defined by the political process.

These are among the major public-sector constraints discussed earlier in chapter two, which make the application of a rational efficiency model from the private sector so difficult. To anticipate, this case will not necessarily conclude that the management transfer strategy is without merit or that EDC was largely unsuccessful. Quite the contrary: it will indicate important benefits derived from EDC's work in this agency and suggest that such efforts should be increased in the future. They must be carried out, however, with full awareness of the political realities of the public sector that limit what can and cannot be accomplished.

This case is more than just another case study, testing the merits of the management transfer strategy. EDC's free consulting efforts in this agency were by far the largest of their kind anywhere in the country. Since 1971, EDC has provided over fifty person-years of executives on loan, involving over $1 million worth of talent. Relative to the size, complexity, and problems of the Board of Education this was not much; but it constitutes an important pilot test of the management transfer strategy in a large educational agency and has relevance for other cities and for states as well. Furthermore, the project has added national importance because it involved helping the New York City schools deal more effectively with the many new problems and relationships that decentralization brought about. New York's was the first big-city school system that began to decentralize citywide.

THE SETTING

Before assessing EDC's efforts, it is important to indicate what the New York City Board of Education was like at the time of EDC's arrival. Numerous studies and commission reports,[1] going back several decades, had indicated many deficiencies in the board's structure and management. The main ones when EDC began work there included: (1) *a pronounced absence of management procedures and systems* throughout the agency; (2) *much internal fragmentation* (organizational and political) across bureaus, divisions, and educational programs, as well as across different levels in the hierarchy; (3) *no clear lines of authority*; (4) *no adequate incentives for performance*; (5) *much ambiguity and conflict in relations between the central board and professional staff*, with the board becoming deeply involved in administrative detail, partly forsaking its policy role; (6) *a general pattern throughout the agency of not delegating authority or engaging in much planning*; (7) *a particularly dysfunctional relationship between headquarters and the districts*, with little adequate standard setting, monitoring, or technical assistance flowing from the center and a marked mutual distrust; and (8) *an insulation of the agency* from outside review and demands for accountability.*

Perhaps most basic of all, this was an "insider-dominated" agency, with highly particularistic loyalties having been built up over many years. The insiders, it should be noted, were largely pedagogues

*Though most of these deficiencies have been extensively documented in the many studies and reports mentioned above, including the author's own work, more concrete illustrations and examples would undoubtedly help here. Rather than parting from the story now, however, we have chosen to give such examples in the context of EDC's actual consulting work, which dealt with most of these deficiencies.

who got promoted to supervisory and administrative positions with very little management training or experience.*

Moreover, the agency had successfully resisted any infusion of competent managers from the outside. As the authors of the State Charter Revision Report correctly noted, "It was hoped that decentralization would hasten the 'opening up' of the system to bring 'new blood' into leadership positions. This does not seem to have happened."[2]

In addition, the agency's fiscal dependence on the city had led to a condition of divided authority with City Hall, which resulted in limited board control over key administrative decisions, tremendous delays in decisions on such matters as payroll, staff appointments, vendor payments, and construction, and limited accountability. Since the city provided so much of the Board of Education's budget, top city officials and agencies—in particular, the mayor, the comptroller, the Bureau of the Budget, the City Planning Commission, and the Board of Estimate—influenced school decisions; yet the board and the chancellor were held responsible for them.

EDC faced other constraints as well. The polarized educational politics of the city with respect to school decentralization made it difficult to innovate in the context of the stalemate among contending groups that had resulted. The educators and those citizen and parent groups advocating decentralization still regarded one another with distrust. There were in particular the recurring politics of ethnic succession that were associated with the decentralization controversy, and were given impetus by the schools' failure to educate many minority students. That politics got played out, for example, in the hiring of black and Puerto Rican paraprofessionals and educators in the districts and placed further demands on the school system's scarce resources.

Finally, there were the city's increasing budget problems, which made school reform difficult. Some of the reforms EDC was suggesting would invariably require more funds, at least initially. Many reforms required new staff, and not all of the old staff they would replace would be phased out right away.

Related to the budget problem was Mayor Abraham Beame's increasing reluctance to allow any city agency to hire non-civil service "provisional" people for high administrative positions. Any management reforms would require at least some outsiders, since the system itself was not producing many competent administrators.

*One top budget official in the Lindsay administration who had helped direct its attempts at management reform reported that in the late sixties the New York City Board of Education had one of the most poorly trained central administrative staffs of any in all of city government.

EDC was to run up against strong City Hall resistance when it tried to recruit from outside, even when the staffing requests grew out of joint Board of Education—EDC recommendations.

Students of organizations indicate that innovations are more likely to occur where there is considerable "organizational slack"— that is, where there are unused or potentially transferable resources available.[3] Given the severe budget crisis, EDC was moving into an agency almost bereft of such resources. Again, this is not to say that the odds were hopelessly against EDC's having much impact, but merely to indicate the political realities of the situation.

Any consulting effort like EDC's begins with a diagnosis as to what is wrong with the agency. A basic issue for the New York City Board of Education, given its archaic structure and management, is modernization, meaning by that developing a new organizational structure and procedures that permit headquarters and the districts to relate to each other in the context of decentralization. That involves rationalizing headquarters so that it can perform the necessary support and control function while at the same time rationalizing the decentralized districts so they can perform their new responsibilities effectively.

There were actually two management issues facing EDC. There was first a reorganization of headquarters and the districts specifically in response to the problem of decentralization. Beyond that, however, there was a reorganization that would have been necessary even without decentralization, as a result of the obsolete nature of the Board of Education's bureaucracy.

In brief, this was a large agency seriously deficient in the most basic and accepted management procedures. Furthermore, it was an agency whose central headquarters had by the late sixties become increasingly discredited, through a series of studies, commission reports, and exposés. And that was the situation that EDC confronted when it arrived.

A Model of Prerequisites for Effective Change

Given the fact that these conditions had been recognized for many years, and that past reform proposals, commissions, consultants, boards, and "outsider" superintendents had come and gone without having had much impact, it is reasonable to ask why EDC should have been expected to have any different fate. In trying to assess and interpret EDC's impact I developed a general model of what might be required to change an agency like the New York City Board of Education and that might help interpret the failures of these past reformers.

The model includes the following conditions: (1) Any change agent must have the *strong support of a client or sponsor within the agency*, having both a commitment to management reform and the power to get it implemented; (2) the agency should have some *management capability among its top administrators*, who might constitute a *core group* to help the change agent and the agency implement reform recommendations; (3) the change agent should have a body of *skilled management analysts and consultants* who, along with this insider core group, would provide the *critical mass* required for change; (4) the change agent and the agency should then *establish the coalition necessary* to overcome the inevitable resistance to change on the part of vested interests inside; and (5) *the agency should be in such a state of acute crisis as to force it to reform*.

By most of these standards, especially the first four, the New York City Board of Education was an agency fairly unreceptive to management reforms, and EDC was going to be hard put to generate the resources necessary to overcome that.

ESTABLISHING A RELATIONSHIP

EDC was invited into the New York City Board of Education in early 1971 by Chancellor Harvey Scribner, who was seeking outside assistance to reorganize headquarters in the context of decentralization, and by the central board as well.* Scribner arrived in the fall of 1970 and faced an immediate problem: how to restructure headquarters to maintain standards, monitor performance, and provide technical assistance for the decentralized districts.† While he may not have realized it at the time, Scribner also faced a strong board whose views on decentralization and many other matters differed from his.

EDC was not Scribner's only potential consultant. McKinsey, working with the board since early 1969, had also bid for this consulting job. It had already conducted a series of decentralization studies for the Board of Education and had submitted several reports outlining its views on how to make decentralization work. It advo-

---

*Scribner wrote a letter of invitation to George Champion, president of EDC, dated March 16, 1971, outlining the kinds of questions he wanted EDC to address in developing a headquarters reorganization plan. Before he did so, however, his board checked EDC out on its own.

†The 1969 Decentralization Law gave the community school districts new budgetary, staffing, and other powers over elementary and junior high (intermediate) schools.

cated a "bottom-up" strategy: first build a management capability in the community districts and boards, and then, based on such an analysis of local problems, work on headquarters.

McKinsey's last effort was a sixty-six-page document, dated December 30, 1970, briefing Scribner and the board on what it saw as the "management requirements for successful decentralization." There was considerable substance in this document, as there was in the many that preceded it, but Scribner and his associates rejected McKinsey to do the bigger headquarters reorganization study.*

Meanwhile, one of Scribner's assistants heard about EDC's work in the criminal courts. Though EDC had been in the courts for but a little over a year, its work had been favorably reported in the *New York Times* and other media. An EDC report on the criminal courts that contained an elaborate scheme for analyzing management functions in any organization particularly impressed Scribner's assistants. As Scribner wrote to Champion in his March 16, 1971, letter of invitation to EDC: "I was impressed by the several kinds of problems you look for in assessing the strengths and weaknesses of business organizations, and I think they apply at the Board of Education as well." Another of Scribner's assistants had met Floyd Flom, the director of EDC's high schools program, and was impressed. "We had heard that some good things were going on in those high schools," he said. "Also, they never pushed themselves on us, and we liked that."

Scribner and his board quickly concluded that EDC's courts work was quite good and that it should be asked to do similar work at school headquarters. That decision was reinforced by Commissioner Nyquist's refusal to provide state funds for McKinsey. EDC's work, of course, was free, and its involvement brought the board a lot of prestige as well. As one of Scribner's staff reported: "Even if EDC did not come free and had cost roughly the same as McKinsey, we would have taken EDC. Its work seemed so good that we wanted to have it."

Essentially, Scribner asked EDC to help him restructure headquarters so that it could "become an agency responsible mainly to service the districts, to maintain minimum city-wide educational standards, and to monitor the districts' programs." This also involved strengthening community school boards and district office staffs, "so that they can assume as broad a role as possible in the management

---

*McKinsey could not compete with EDC on fee, since EDC came free. In addition, Mayor Lindsay had come under particularly strong criticism for his use of management consultants, and McKinsey was singled out by some critics, including Comptroller Beame and the City Council, for consulting studies and fees that they found unacceptable.

of their schools and absorb as many of the present central services functions as possible."

The letter made very clear Scribner's strong advocacy of decentralization. Some powerful board members, however, were not nearly as enthusiastic about decentralization as was Scribner. Nor were they impressed with his running of the school system.

EDC thus had a client, the chancellor, who soon had little power within his own agency. The central board was also, by definition, EDC's client. But the fact that it and Scribner were divided on the decentralization issue and that some board members had little confidence in his administrative skills placed EDC in a very difficult position. The board and Scribner were too involved in their own internal differences to respond readily to EDC's management reform plans. More important, those plans might or might not be used to support decentralization, depending on who in the Board of Education had the final say in interpreting them.

HEADQUARTERS REORGANIZATION:
THE TOP-DOWN STRATEGY

EDC began its headquarters reorganization study in early 1971. It was conducted mainly by a management consultant on loan from one of EDC's member companies. "I interviewd a broad spectrum of people in vertical fashion throughout the system," he reported, "starting with Scribner and the central board members and going out to offices, bureaus, and some districts." Based on his interviews, his review of district and headquarters studies by EDC's people on loan, and other available documents, EDC presented a reorganization plan to Scribner in November 1971. He reviewed it and got EDC to make a presentation to the board that month. It then took fourteen months for the board to accept and adopt the plan, which went through several revisions in response to objections of particular board members and professional staff.* For EDC business people, accustomed to a much faster pace of decision making in the private sector, this seemed like an unconscionable delay. For school officials, facing constant crises and other priorities, it wasn't that long at all.

There seemed to be at least two reasons for the delay. One was the board's practice of moving on major policy matters only by consensus, something that often took a long time to reach. A second

*Irving Anker, in particular, who was Scribner's Deputy Chancellor at the time, raised many objections, reflecting largely an "insider" point of view.

was the conflicts between Scribner and his board and the board's increasing lack of confidence in him. It may not have been a coincidence that the board finally moved to accept the plan in March 1973, just after it had decided not to renew Scribner's contract. As one top EDC official reported: "We presented it and wrote it up in January 1972, and it took until Harvey left before we could get it through. I really think the bad relations between him and his board had a lot to do with the delay. I couldn't prove it, and you couldn't get the board to acknowledge it. If you interviewed them, they'd probably deny it. But in fact, they didn't want to pass on Harvey's reorganization plan. They simply weren't going to give him a reorganization. It was going to be theirs or nothing at all."

The reorganization plan was an attempt to improve the management of the agency by restructuring it at the very top, including the offices of the chancellor, the deputy chancellor, various executive directors reporting to each, and the central board. EDC officials concluded that much of the Board of Education's lack of responsiveness and inefficiency had resulted from poor leadership and faulty organization at the top.*

EDC then set out to simplify and streamline the structure, based on the view that if all of the Board of Education's main activities could be consolidated and divided up among a small number of divisions, this might conceivably minimize the agency's administrative deficiencies. If one chooses to extract from EDC's diagnosis and recommendations a "management theory" on which they are based, it is the conventional one of classical management writings, which emphasize an essentially "top-down" approach.[4]

The original EDC plan involved the creation of four deputy chancellor positions to replace the single deputy chancellor in the existing structure. One of the four was to be in business and administration and the other three in education.† The plan was designed to release the chancellor from having to tend to so many business and educational

---

*To illustrate: EDC kept emphasizing the tremendous amount of administrative detail flowing to the top; the central board's deep immersion in administrative matters, which was not its function; its tendency to set up committees that duplicated what the professional staff was supposed to be doing; its and the chancellor's unwillingness to delegate authority; blurred lines of authority; the tendency of many top administrators to work on an emergency basis on the same crisis; and constant turf struggles throughout the agency, all of which reflected its bad management.

†The education ones were for the remaining centralized programs in high schools and special education, for a central curriculum and instruction unit that would also promote innovations, and for a central office that would link headquarters to the community school districts.

matters, so that he could concentrate more on broader policy issues and on long-range planning. Much of the detail matters and unresolved controversies that used to flow up to him would, it was hoped, no longer do so, but would rather be handled by the deputy chancellors, each one of whom would be held accountable for matters in his or her bailiwick. A key theme in the plan was the proposed separation of business from pedagogical or educational program activities, and this was to be elaborated on more in later versions.

Not surprisingly, the central board and top professional staff did not initially endorse the entire plan. To review the criticisms briefly, there was strong objection to having four deputy chancellors, on the grounds that it would undercut the chancellor. As one top headquarters administrator said: "I thought having four deputy chancellors would dilute the chancellor's authority and create more rather than less confusion at the top." At least one board member thought it would add to succession problems for the chancellorship. Another common reaction was that the plan for four deputies was geared too much to personalities, being predicated on a recognition of Scribner's limited management ability. "All they were doing was compensating for his bad management by having four people do what he should have been doing all along," reported a school official.

EDC ended up keeping the functional divisions but having them headed by executive directors rather than deputy chancellors. Some headquarters staff remained cynical, having lived through many past reorganizations and being wary of still another, which several referred to as "old wine in new bottles." What they meant was that few of the divisions were that different from those of the past.*

Still another criticism related to the way that EDC had designed the functions of the Division of Community School District Affairs, a key headquarters unit under decentralization. Reflecting Scribner's views, EDC proposed that it be an ombudsman for the districts as well as interpret headquarters policies to them. The central board overruled Scribner on this and voted strongly against the office's serving an ombudsman role.

After EDC lost on the four deputy chancellors,† it pressed to have a single deputy chancellor for management, arguing the importance of

---

*The divisions were for business and administrative services, community school district relations (elementary and junior high schools), centralized school administration (high schools and special programs for the handicapped), and educational planning and support (a curriculum and instruction staff unit that would service all schools, centralized or decentralized).

†Actually, EDC just changed the titles from deputy chancellors to executive directors but retained all the functions of those positions. In that sense, then, it didn't lose out on that part of its original reorganization proposal.

consolidating all business functions and separating them from education. EDC even defined the office as having equal status with the chancellor, reporting directly to the central board rather than to him.* Again there was objection from some top school officials. "I told the board I thought it would be bad for that office to have an independent power base from the chancellor," one explained, "undercutting him and diluting his authority, and complicating the board's relations with him."

Events surrounding the board's final adoption of a revised EDC reorganization plan reveal something of how innovation takes place in the public sector. After over a year of board inaction, EDC finally threatened to pull out if the board didn't adopt and implement the plan. It was only after that threat that the board did move ahead. In effect, the board responded only when EDC acted like a demanding constituent, rather than as an amiable consultant who wanted to keep in its good graces. Also, EDC's timing was good. If it had made the threat before Scribner had left, the reorganization might not having been approved.

The main point of the reorganization, then, was to streamline the structure so that decisions could be made and implemented faster while the chancellor, freed from having to tend to administrative details, could concentrate more on broader program and policy questions. As one school official explained: "Before this reorganization, stuff piled up on Scribner's desk and he never got to it. A lot of the problem was Scribner, but the way the system was set up encouraged that. When Anker was deputy, he had all these business matters like payroll and the school lunch program to attend to that weren't his bag, and stuff was piling up with him, too. And we had one person in charge of curriculum and instruction, and he was absolutely inundated with problems."

Selecting Top Management in the New Structure

One strong concern of EDC that the board shared was that simply changing the structure was not enough. Competent administrators had to be recruited to the new top management positions— including the Chancellor, deputy Chancellor, and executive directors of key divisions. The central board not only agreed with EDC on this, but asked EDC to conduct a national search for the best-qualified people. At no time did the board indicate that EDC would

---

*When the central board designated Irving Anker in 1973 as chancellor, Anker being an educator and not oriented toward business and administrative matters, EDC felt it was particularly important to have a strong deputy chancellor.

actually select these top administrators, but it did communicate its high regard for EDC's experience in executive recruiting. "They told us they had no confidence in their Personnel Department," an EDC official related at the time, "and they also said several times that we were more experienced in such executive search activities than they and that they would appreciate it if we would help them out."

EDC, quite anxious that its reorganization plan be well implemented, immediately plunged into a vigorous executive search activity. This involved its contacting and interviewing scores of potential candidates from all over the country over a period of several months. One of the people on loan made elaborate ratings of candidates, indicating how seriously EDC took this assignment. EDC's main criteria related to administrative experience and competence and did not consider to any degree political or social considerations—for example, the ethnic backgrounds of the candidates, their "local" knowledge of the schools or of city government, or their relationships with key educational interest groups in the city. Indeed, some EDC officials were interested in eliminating the use of such "political" criteria, which they regarded as irrelevant.

At the final stage, the board invited in Ed O'Rorke, the EDC task force director, to help conduct the interviews, and he was even asked for his judgment on many candidates. From his and EDC's point of view, then, recruitment was something they had a big stake in, as a critical first step in making the new organization work. What they didn't completely realize was that, as "good government" reformers, they were trying to change the rules of the game by taking politics out of the selection process, and that was simply not going to be possible.

Though EDC was to lose out in recruiting, the board, on its side, benefited a lot from having EDC involved. EDC took the heat off the board, which could now direct individuals and groups with preferred candidates for those positions to EDC. It also gave the board more time for deliberating, since the board could legitimately say that it had an "expert" group helping it with the recruiting which hadn't completed their work yet. And the board might eventually abdicate responsibility for selections that some constituencies might not like. EDC could be used, then, as any consultant in such a situation would be.

What happened was that EDC presented the board with a list of its selections, assuming that the board would take the list seriously. Instead the board rejected many of EDC's candidates.* It was a

---

*Some top EDC officials report that all of its candidates were rejected. Others note that EDC agreed with some central board selections and that it had, in fact, also supported them.

classic case again of the "insiders" and "outsiders" problem, with the board's candidates almost exclusively insiders and EDC's outsiders. Not only were the board's selections made with political and ethnic criteria in mind, but in virtually every case, the board's final selection was either a career civil servant within the school system or part of the political network of board members. Thus, Irving Anker, the board's selection for chancellor, had been in the school system for thirty-nine years, in contrast to EDC's nationally recognized candidate, who had never been in it. Bernard Gifford, whom the board selected as deputy chancellor, had come highly recommended by Deputy Mayor Edward Hamilton and other top people in the Lindsay administration, was black, had lived in Bedford-Stuyvesant, and had gone through the New York City schools. EDC's candidates were a retired Chase Manhattan Bank executive and a federal civil servant from the comptroller general's office who was also near retirement. Dr. Edythe Gaines, the board's selection for executive director of the Division of Educational Planning and Support, was a black woman who had been a teacher, principal, district superintendent, and then director of the Learning Cooperative, a unit Scribner had set up to develop and disseminate innovative programs. EDC's candidate was a white male who had never worked in the New York City schools and was the director of innovative programs in the New York State Department of Education. Finally, the board selected as executive director of the Personnel Department an Italian with extensive experience in city government who had strong support from Democratic and Liberal Party leaders. EDC's candidate had most recently served as deputy superintendent of schools in a big city and had no experience in the New York City schools.

EDC was, from the board's point of view, both naive and presumptuous. "When they thought they could tell us who the top people should be," said one board member, "they overstepped their bounds." "They were really naive on the appointments," reported another, "and they tried to get into things and take over power when they shouldn't have. We had to make them back down." Still another indicated: "They had moved out of their traditional role as consultants and wanted some of their own people in, some of them old, retired executives, and most of them not at all fit for the jobs. Their people would have been killed if they came in. They were really naive about the politics of education, and you can't separate the management of education from its politics."

The board's final selection reflected a broad ethnic balance, responsive to the demands of all of its constituencies. Thus, the chancellor and one executive director were Jews, the deputy chancellor and a second director were blacks, and other appointees included a Puerto Rican, an Italian, a career educator of Irish background, and two women. These criteria were not made known in advance to EDC, which assumed or at least hoped that only "objective" and "technical" ones would be used. The board saw EDC at this time not just as a benign consultant but as another pressure group, recommending people from a homogeneous ethnic, age, and economic background (older or retired corporation executives, often WASPS) whose qualifications the board questioned.

Some EDC officials felt that the board's use of ethnic and related criteria was symptomatic of the public sector's main management problem—its unwillingness to recruit people of high competence who could provide needed leadership. When it became obvious to EDC that the board had taken such criteria so strongly into account, it felt betrayed and used. The board's definition of an "insider," which so informed all its selections, was a person of the right ethnic background who had spent all or most of his or her career in the school system or who was part of the political networks and constituencies that the board members saw as important. Though EDC had become deeply involved in the schools since the late 1960s through its high school programs, it was still very much an "outsider" in the context of the political networks most important for the board.

The fact is that public-sector agencies are essentially what political scientists have called "representational bureaucracies," serving the many interest groups that have a stake in their operations—as recipients both of their services and of jobs. The central board was in this instance simply mediating among conflicting interests like all its predecessors had done, and EDC was wrong in assuming that the board would suddenly abandon this approach.

As a result of conflicts between EDC and the board over appointments, EDC again threatened to pull out, but then did not act on that threat. Internal differences in EDC on appropriate future strategy were resolved in favor of staying on, as O'Rorke's more politically pragmatic position prevailed.

The broader issues that the appointment controversy raises relate back to our earlier discussion about prerequisites for effecting change in city government. The episode made clear the EDC was involved as an outsider in a political setting in which the rules of the game were made by insiders. Traditions of social criteria affecting such appointments had existed long before EDC arrived and are likely to endure long after it leaves. The key consideration in this episode, as in all others, was politics and where EDC was in relation to that. Despite the fact that EDC's membership included nearly 200 of the largest corporations in the world, it had very little power to affect such key Board of Education decisions.

A final element in this situation was the class and ethnic differences between EDC and the central board. The board included a Puerto Rican, a black, two Jews, and an Irish Catholic, all from working- or lower-middle-class origins, who were deeply involved in city affairs and were more sensitive to political forces that affected how the city functioned than were most EDC executives. These members were acutely conscious of the WASP nature of EDC and sometimes complained that EDC was "talking down" to them. As one top school administrator analyzed it: "I really think that our board came into conflict with EDC because of the board's lower-middle-class and ethnic character. It hadn't earned the respect of some EDC people, even though it was more sensitive to political undercurrents in education than EDC. EDC really knew little about the politics of education. And yet, because of its being a more high-status group than the board, it thought it could have its way on these appointments."

Implementation

After the appointments controversy died down, EDC remained on to assist the board in the reorganization plan's implementation.* It offered advice on such problems as clearly defining the responsibilities attaching to new headquarters positions and divisions; deciding which lower-level units belonged where and to whom they were accountable; securing as much coordination as possible among these new divisions and their executive directors; and resolving their many turf struggles.

Recent writings on organizations have increasingly emphasized that interdepartmental conflicts create some of the most intractable problems that organizations face and are not at all limited to the public sector.[5] Such conflicts have been particularly acute in the New York City Board of Education and have prevented the reorganization from being more effective than it has been. They reflect once more the play of educational politics in limiting management reform.

A main source of the difficulty is that most of the new appointees are ambitious "insiders," each with a strong political base and high career aspirations. Moreover, they represent different sets of constituencies. Also, they were appointed by the central board, not by the chancellor, and yet he is responsible for coordinating and

*EDC stayed on, despite the controversy, because of its strong commitment to change the Board of Education and to demonstrate the many benefits that could result from business involvement in city government.

supervising them, tasks for which the present chancellor is not well suited. His greater interest in educational policy as opposed to administration, his reluctance to exercise authority over "fellow insiders," many of them life-long professional colleagues and friends, and his highly developed political survival skills—all combined to limit his leadership on the implementation problems mentioned above. While one can seriously question the capacity of any top administrator to push through major administrative reforms in so crisis-ridden and politicized a public agency, the success of any reorganization of the New York City Board of Education will require stronger leadership than Chancellor Anker has given.

Impact of the Reorganization

Evidence on the impact of this ambitious reorganization is both incomplete and very mixed. The plan certainly should not be regarded as a great success; but neither should it be rated as a completely wasted effort.

Though a definitive assessment is not possible, given the short period that the reorganization has existed, some interim judgments can be made. Perhaps the most appropriate place to begin is with the recognition of what had to be changed in order for a public-sector organization like the New York City schools to work better. This would include the organization's structure, its personnel, its traditions, certainly its politics, its technology (both administrative and classroom instructional techniques), and its relations with other governmental organizations.

In the EDC-initiated reorganization, the main change was a structural one, supplemented by some improvements in management technology. There were few basic changes, however, in personnel, in agency traditions, in politics, or in relations with city government, and that has limited the reorganization's impact. Thus, the "insider-dominated," traditional bureaucracy that EDC found on arrival has essentially remained that way, to the point where personal loyalties still prevail in key agency decisions, thereby preventing more streamlining and modernization from taking place. Despite all that, however, some positive changes have occurred. Decisions on curriculum, staffing, budget, headquarters-district relations, and management problems do get made faster, with executive directors more likely to resolve them at their level than was the case before, thus freeing the chancellor to devote himself more to broader educational policy issues. He still gets unnecessarily involved in many crises, but less so than before. As one top EDC official reported: "Anker has people he can turn to now and can devote himself to critical policy issues—desegregation, accountability, funding, the status of the districts, and so on. Before, you might see him on TV, getting involved in the firing of cafeteria workers, and he doesn't have to do that now."

There seems, in addition, to be some slight improvement in headquarters-district relations, though community school board members and district and school staff still complain vociferously about headquarters' failure to consult them or to provide timely administrative and educational support. Deputy Chancellor Gifford, for example, has developed procedures for monitoring the districts and has worked out a simpler and more "objective" budget allocation formula for them than existed before.*

Furthermore, Alfredo Mathew, the executive director of the Division of Community School District Affairs, has been able to resolve some local controversies without their having to reach the chancellor, and to do preliminary work in defining the issues in these controversies and working out alternative solutions. There has been much disappointment in the districts that he did not act as their ombudsman at headquarters and often played the role as the chancellor's "hatchet man," but he clearly took a big load off the chancellor. In that sense, both Gifford and Mathrew are doing what EDC had hoped the reorganization would accomplish, namely, enabling headquarters to respond more quickly to situations than it did before.†

The separation of business and management affairs from educational ones also seems to have helped. In addition to relieving the chancellor from having to tend to many administrative matters, the separation has facilitated a consolidation and modernization of business functions and afforded them more attention and expertise than before. The deputy chancellor's office has made many improvements as a result that would have been less likely had the reorganization not taken place. Budget data go from headquarters to the districts earlier than ever before, facilitating local planning. There is now an allocation formula for district budgets. Critical information in such areas as payroll, student and teacher attendance, absenteeism, scheduling, costs, and school performance has begun to accumulate.[6] Most important, the quality of management and policy research far surpasses anything the Board of Education ever did before. This is due

---

*Some headquarters staff disagree with this assessment.

†This is not at all to suggest, however, that headquarters has gone very far in providing technical assistance and support for the districts, as Scribner and other decentralization advocates had hoped for. I will discuss that point in greater detail below, in a separate section on EDC's community school district work.

mainly to the skills of Deputy Chancellor Gifford and his top staff, but the fact that there is such a deputy chancellor position, whose duties have been defined to include just these kinds of activities, creates a situation in which such skills can be expressed.

A further assessment of the reorganization involves looking at the new functional departments that it set up. One common headquarters view is that little change has in fact taken place.* The high school office had always been there, they maintain. The Division of Educational Planning and Support is quite similar to the old Office of Curriculum and Instruction, and even the Division of Special Education and Pupil Personnel Services is not that new, those functions having always been carried out by a headquarters unit. The only new units, they argue, are the Division of Community School District Affairs and the office of the deputy chancellor. "The thing EDC has done," reported a headquarters administrator, "has been to establish two important new offices and to fine tune the rest. Remember, though, that it only worked on the very top, and there's much more to headquarters than that."

One of the biggest changes has been a much more pronounced delegation of authority by the chancellor and concomitantly more autonomy for the executive directors in running their divisions. This seems to have speeded up decision making and increased the agency's responsiveness, as key actions are now taken at lower levels, with many problems never reaching the chancellor level. Such a development very well suits the personalities of key incumbents, in addition to constituting good management practice. "This is the way Anker prefers it," reported a knowledgeable insider. "He doesn't want to go around pounding the table and making decisions on these touchy local district problems. On the other hand, the executive director of community school district affairs is very assertive and tough. He knows the people locally. And it doesn't bother him that much to get embroiled in local controversies. The same thing in the high schools, special ed, and all the other units. Those executive directors run their own show, and they like it that way. Before, under Scribner, he told the head of high schools and all the other top people what to do. It doesn't work that way any more, and that's good."

Politics, Again, as the Main Constraint

Viewing the reorganization's implementation in the context of the central question of this study, the compatibility of a rational

*There was much merit in this view, with a few important exceptions.

efficiency model with the politics of the public sector, we see that those politics continue to affect what goes on. Reports a veteran headquarters administrator: "We really needed good management and a more sensible headquarters structure so badly; and it was good that EDC came in. But the controlling factor is politics. It's overwhelming here, and it washes away everything else. Much of it begins with the selection of the board members and the fact that they are paid. The borough presidents select them, with board members always having to respond to those political pressures. Since they're paid, and it's a job, they have a vested interest in staying, making it more likely for them to overreact to political pressures. With EDC's reorganization, the board then appointed many executive directors on political grounds. Until we get an unpaid board, it's going to stay this bad."

The Board of Education's succession politics is still another obstacle to management reform. Though some top school officials scoffed that the EDC's original four-deputy plan would make the succession politics of the agency even more fiercely contested than it had been, that has happened anyway. As one headquarters administrator noted: "There is greater Balkanization down there now than ever before, and there are at least three people fighting to succeed Anker. All you have to do is read the *Amsterdam News* to see how each of them is doing. It's hard to develop good management when you have all these people running for office, all this politics."

If the role of politics has been a key obstacle, the play of personalities has been another one. The reorganization plan's success depended on choosing strong people at the top, a key one being the chancellor. The general consensus at headquarters is that neither the chancellor nor the board has exercised strong leadership in implementing the reorganization.

The Central Board

A final part of the system hampering its management effectiveness and alluded to in the above discussion is the central board. Established in 1969 to help in the transition to decentralization, this Interim Board, as it is called in the Decentralization Law, became deeply involved in administration. Its distrust of the professionals and its tendency to establish its own committees duplicating what they were doing were quite marked.*

*As the authors of the New York State Charter Commission Report noted: "The Board tended to absorb administrative and professional functions and consequently became over-burdened and less able to accomplish its important func-

Very early in EDC's consulting relationship, the board president asked it to do a study of board functions and how well they were performed. The EDC report indicated, as had so many previous studies, that the board had become so involved in administrative detail that it had abrogated its policy-making function. EDC recommended that the board maintain its "connective role," relating the agency to various involved interest groups, which this board had done well. At the same time, however, it noted that it should not get involved in the details of each interest group's requests, but should let the professional staff tend to as much of that as possible.

Beyond that, EDC suggested, as had previous consultants, that the central board withdraw from too much involvement in such matters as labor negotiations, technical reviews of contracts and leases, and educational programs. It recommended that much more preliminary staff work be done on these matters before they came to the board's attention. Though the board has sometimes heeded this advice, many headquarters staff report that board members still "meddle in administration." Some of this so-called meddling represents an important outside check on the professionals' power, and a lot of it is required by law. Nevertheless, it does introduce long delays in decision making on important and even trivial matters. Furthermore, Chancellor Anker has exacerbated the problem. Rather than acting on his own on most issues and informing the board after the fact, as Gifford and some of the other top administrators have done, Anker has usually consulted with the board first. Being uninformed on the matter initially, the board would often set up its own committee to "get the facts." Decisions might then be delayed for months until the board was not only informed but able to reach a consensus on what actions it wanted to take.

The one pattern that comes through most clearly in looking back on the headquarters reorganization almost four years later is the central board and professional staff's pronounced lack of follow-through on it. Though EDC continued to prod top school officials on this, urging them in particular to streamline and clarify the missions of the new divisions and evaluate their effectiveness, that has been done only in a limited way.* A general lack of discretionary funds, time, and staff, the recent fiscal crisis, and other, related emergencies are undoubtedly factors, but there was much more to it than that.

---

tions" (p. 86). All central boards in the New York City School system, it should be noted, dating back several decades, have conducted themselves in this manner.

*The deputy chancellor did a major study on the management of the Division of Special Education and Pupil Personnel Services, and the Division of Educational Planning and Support did reorganize itself in the spring of 1976. These are only the beginnings, however, of administrative rationalization efforts.

The central board and two chancellors seemed to have other priorities in the context of all the problems they had to attend to. Certainly, the politics of the agency has been critical, in the sense that the top people have seemingly not had the power to push ahead on these matters—EDC not having developed a strong or broad-based enough constituency for such management changes.

One group with tremendous power which played a significant role in limiting the chancellor's, the deputy chancellor's, and the central board's leadership on most matters has been the teachers union. Though it did not take any explicit stand on the headquarters reorganization or on EDC, the union was a constant veto group with respect to any initiatives top school officials might take. Reorganization-related decisions that might even indirectly bear on increasing the powers of districts or increasing the vulnerability of teachers in terms of job security or outside demands for accountability and better performance were going to be vetoed or at the very least delayed. The principals' associations and other inside professional groups have played a similar role. The implications of all this for future EDC reform efforts in the agency and for assessing what it has already done will be discussed in a concluding section.

INDIVIDUAL PROJECTS

In addition to undertaking the headquarters reorganization, EDC also worked on numerous individual projects, most of them related to the functioning of particular business departments, including audit, personnel, budgeting, financial operations, supplies, construction, high schools management, payroll, public relations, relations with outside vendors, special education, management training, and others. Probably no other consultant in the history of the New York City school system has undertaken such a wide variety of projects.

While one could argue that undertaking so many projects spread EDC's limited resources much too thin, EDC's task force director felt that a deepening relationship could be established with the board through working on problems that it and the professional staff felt were important, and that even if no major solutions were forthcoming, at least some preliminary work could be begun. The risk lay in being too responsive to the board's needs, so that the potential benefits of working on a wide range of problems would be outweighed by the diffuse and uneven quality of the work.

Much of this project work began at the initiative of O'Rorke. As he reviewed the task force's activities when he arrived in early 1972, he could see the endless possibilities for management improvements and requested that the board indicate what projects it wanted done. Since EDC had already been working on some, this would just be an extension of that work.

Usually, one or at most two or three EDC people worked on a given project, collaborating with the director and staff of the division or department studied. The reports were then made available to the particular business unit, the board, and the chancellor. In some instances, implementation of EDC's recommendations began before any formal report was presented. In others, there was little implementation. One problem was that in many instances the EDC people who did the study had already returned to the private sector by the time implementation was well under way. While O'Rorke always provided continuity, it would have helped if there had been a more organized procedure for having outgoing people on loan available to help follow up on ongoing projects.

A comparative analysis of what happened on several of these projects should provide important insights into how and why change takes place as a result of management consultant efforts. What follows is a series of such case studies. They emphasize structural and procedural changes, and in a few cases those in costs and performance, that seemed to result from EDC projects. Though EDC made numerous claims of cost savings resulting from its work, the evidence for such claims was often limited. EDC, of course, faced the ongoing problem of demonstrating to its corporate members who were providing money and personnel for the program that it was in fact achieving bottom-line, efficiency results.*

The case studies to follow will indicate some successful projects and some unsuccessful ones, and attempt thereby to develop generalizations about the conditions for success in such efforts. As will be apparent, agency politics are usually the most critical variable bearing on their outcome.

Case #1: The Bureau of Supplies

The first case reports a quite extraordinary success, in which a single EDC person on loan had a big impact, long before his report

*Some board officials reported that they fully realized how EDC might feel under pressure from its corporate members to show "results," expressed in "efficiency" terms. They were grateful for EDC's assistance and did not begrudge some of its assertions about impact, even while remaining skeptical about their validity.

was ever completed. It illustrates the promise of the management transfer strategy when purely "technocratic" contributions by business can gain acceptance and have an impact, even given the politics of the public sector.

The business unit involved was the Bureau of Supplies, responsible for the purchase, storage, and distribution of all supplies for all schools and other units within the Board of Education, including the agency's many summer programs. Located in a rundown area of warehouses and light manufacturing in Long Island City, Queens, and quite distant both physically and administratively from school headquarters in Brooklyn, the bureau handled roughly 8,500 individual items for supply to some 3,500 ordering locations.[7]

At the time that the first EDC person on loan began working there, the bureau had three floors of a six-story warehouse that it shared with two other city agencies. There were only two available freight elevators, both of which occasionally broke down, paralyzing an operation already strained beyond its capacity. Even when both elevators were working, the bureau was so swamped with orders that shipments were unduly delayed or failed to go out. Its methods of assembly and storage within the warehouse were very archaic and inefficient by modern business standards. Operations were further complicated by a rigid truck delivery schedule resulting from a Board of Education contract with the Teamster's Union that permitted shipments to schools only on union vehicles, and only when there was a truck full for a particular borough. Moreover, the bureau had no information on past trends in usage or on its existing inventory, headquarters having denied it the use of a computer terminal.

As a consequence, much of the ordering from particular vendors for the schools had only a limited relationship to need, resulting in a serious oversupply of some equipment and a chronic undersupply of others, with the former tying up enormous amounts of capital and space. The only use of computers in this complex business operation was in relationship to school orders that were first sent to the bureau and then on to the data processing unit at school headquarters, where the information was placed on a disc file, waiting until enough other orders came in from the same district to fill a truck and justify a delivery.

The Board of Education's contracts with vendors were particularly constraining. The board followed the inefficient practice, long ago abandoned by many corporations, or ordering the total quantity of any item at the beginning of a contract and then further guaranteeing the purchase of 75-80 percent. As a result, the Board of Education ordered huge amounts of supplies it didn't need: it had inventories of 474 years of supplies of one item and 80 years of another. It typically also ordered a six months' supply of batteries that themselves had only a six-month life span. To make matters worse, the board failed to obtain discounts from its vendors for buying in large quantity. "A lot of vendors in New York City who could not compete with the same operations in the private sector are kept in business in New York," reported another EDC person, "precisely because they have contracts with city agencies like this one."

In brief, this was a complex business operation, but one that lacked the management procedures or staff to carry out its functions efficiently. It exemplified quite dramatically the need for management "modernization" that is so widespread throughout New York City government and its counterparts in other municipalities. Lest we seem to be making too invidious a comparison here between a city agency and the private sector, it wasn't very long ago that the warehousing practices of corporations were also quite primitive. Many have been substantially improved, however, in recent years.

Similar management improvements in government can come about, however, only through a full understanding of the latter's many constraints, some of which are reversible, others not. The bureau's relationship with school headquarters, as well as its own limitations, constituted key constraints in this case. Headquarters was primarily responsible for much of the overordering, the absence of usage data, limited computerization, rigid trucking and vendor contracts, and long delays in delivery after orders had been transmitted from schools to the bureau. In addition, headquarters' refusal to allow the bureau to hire competent people outside civil service lists also limited its capacity to institute needed management reforms.

Thus, when the first EDC person on loan arrived, staff morale within the bureau was very low. Its top officials felt that they needed budget lines for more staff, a better salary scale to attract good people, and computer assistance; yet they weren't getting any of those things. Instead, reported one top bureau official, "because we are just dealing with boxes and supplies, rather than people-oriented services like payroll, even though doing our work alone takes up thirty to forty percent of all computer time, we are always the tail wagging the dog and never get much help."

This bureau's past experience with consultants had been for them to document many of its problems, present a report, and then leave. The EDC person on loan acted quite differently. Though EDC initially asked him only to do a study, he didn't do that. A warehouse specialist who had worked his way up within Continental Can, he spent a few weeks talking with people at the bureau and at school headquarters and reading previous reports. He then decided that another consultant study was the last thing this bureau needed. Instead, he urged a "crisis intervention" program that included the adoption of new warehouse techniques that he felt were immediately applicable to the bureau's problems. "We had a lot of experiences with consultants who give you neat reports, long-range suggestions, Monday morning quarterbacking, and no help with implementation," reported a top bureau official. "The difference in the case of John was that he worked like an operating line manager, even though he gave us some long-range assistance as well. He provided us with immediate help, not just abstract recommendations."

At the time this EDC person arrived, the bureau had just moved its supplies into a new warehouse; he helped lay out the entire warehouse operation. (Had he come sooner, the move to a new warehouse might not have been necessary.) This included using a new "cube storage technique" and sorting out supplies so that those most in demand would be stored in the most accessible places. "In the old warehouse," he explained, "it was such a mess, stuff stacked everywhere, material lost, and when it was discovered, everybody was surprised to find it there. With the new warehouse, it is possible now to upgrade their methods, and they really wanted to do this." In introducing new storage procedures, he worked alongside the bureau staff and presented new techniques in a nonintimidating and noncritical manner. He also introduced the first systematic "inventory control system" the bureau ever had, and that helped cut down on the oversupply problem. "We tried many times working on this," reported a bureau official, "but he really got us going. He saved us at least $1 million on purchases that we would have made and didn't because of what he suggested to us."

Furthermore, he emphasized to bureau officials the great need for usage data on each school's annual consumption of different supplies. Traditionally, the bureau had data only on what the schools had ordered the previous year. "We had operated for a long time without any usage information or year or other time specifications," explained a bureau official, "and we kept overpurchasing because of that. We tended to purchase what we had purchased the previous year." After he convinced bureau staff that they had to have such data, he showed them how they could be compiled, which involved setting up a computerized information system that would include a terminal on the bureau's premises. The Board of Education computer and management information systems staff was then very slow in responding to this need, even though the EDC person indicated its urgency. Two EDC people on loan came a year after he left, in early 1975, and have indicated how such a system could be put in place.

Another of his contributions was to change the procedures for distributing supplies to schools. To cut down on excess inventory, as well as to introduce more flexibility, he suggested two shipments a year instead of one. "We now have a two-cycle requisitioning period," reported a bureau official. "John suggested it to develop a lesser amount of inventory and we had thought of it to shorten the delivery cycle, but the end result was the same, a lower dollar inventory."

Finally, he helped set up a "Commodity Management Unit," tying in purchases with information on existing inventory and past usage. This also cut down on the bureau's oversupply, as more realistic purchasing decisions began to be made. A key to all these improvements was, as I indicated, a computerized information system, and that is now being planned.

This is one of the few cases in which cost effectiveness data on the impact of an EDC intervention are available. Based on its weekly activity reports, the new "Commodity Management Unit" alone resulted in a cancellation of over $1 million worth of purchases in just the first eight months of its operation. Even more savings have probably resulted since then as a result of other management innovations that this warehouse specialist introduced. He found excess stock supplies, for example, valued at close to $900,000 in just a small (10–20 percent) sample of all items the bureau carried, and to the extent that the various new techniques the bureau adopted helped reduce that excess inventory, there was that much more savings.

Several factors made this such a "successful" consulting effort. Perhaps the main one was that this bureau's problems were basically not political or policy ones. They involved few intractable interests (except for the Teamsters Union and some vendors), making it possible to use efficiency criteria and management techniques. Furthermore, the problems of the bureau were relatively easy to define and measure and were consequently amenable to technical solutions. They involved issues of storage techniques, inventory control, distribution cycles, and the use of computerized information systems. Bureau officials were receptive to such improvements (in part because their bureau had a bad image because of its inefficiency); they welcomed the EDC person when he arrived and praised him and his work after he left. They knew that they did not have the staff or expertise themselves to do what he did.

Secondly, the technical skills of this person on loan well suited the bureau's needs. He was a warehouse specialist with much operational experience; though it was not in the public sector and therefore did not bring him into direct contact with the many types of constraints that this bureau faced, it was still relevant. Moreover, he became immediately aware of and accepting of these conditions—for example, civil service, headquarters resistance to computerization, and contractual obligations with vendors and truckers—and he developed many implementable ideas with them in mind.

Third, there was a similarly good match in background and personality between the person on loan and the bureau officials with whom he worked. John was a man of working-class origins with no college education, who was much more oriented toward "operations" than toward writing consultant reports. He belied, in this sense, the traditional stereotype that many white-ethnic municipal employees have of outside consultants as an elite group of upper-middle-class, college types who don't want to get their hands dirty. Furthermore, he had the interpersonal skills to go with his "favorable" background. He was flexible and unassuming in the way he approached the bureau's staff and as a result worked very amicably with them.

Finally, this bureau was physically separate from school headquarters, and there was probably less bureaucratic control than might otherwise have been the case. This probably contributed at times to the neglect by headquarters of its problems, but it may also have helped the bureau put some changes in place without a lot of higher-level review and delay.

The key to success, however, was the technical and interpersonal skills of the EDC person and his compatibility with the bureau's staff. The irony of his consulting contribution was that he found it very difficult to write up his final report, which, while interesting, communicated only the bare outlines of what he had contributed or of the dynamics of the process. For the bureau this was of no importance, since he had already made his many contributions long before the report was written. As one of them commented at the end: "You know, John came to work without a briefcase. He looked around, rolled up his sleeves, asked if he could see how the warehouse operated and what might be done to improve it. We didn't need any more briefcase guys with fancy reports."

It is important to note that although this consultant was providing "hands on," "operational" help, to use management jargon, in contrast to writing a traditional consulting report, he was also providing longer-term assistance. The modernization of procedures that he introduced would serve the bureau on a permanent basis. For that reason as well, this was one of EDC's most effective consulting contributions, and top officials in the school bureaucracy widely acknowledged it as such.

Case #2: Payroll Processing

Still another EDC project that had a positive impact was in the Board of Education's payroll operations. Payroll employed such primitive management techniques and was in such a state of chaos when EDC arrived as to almost defy description.* The progress that the Board of Education and EDC made in this area indicates the possibilities for substantive management reform, when the situation gets sufficiently critical and when outside consulting assistance is available. Again, however, a key consideration is the absence of any major "political" or "policy" problems.

When EDC arrived in 1971, there were roughly 90 different payroll classifications representing different job categories, with none of them computerized. New teachers often had to wait an average of six months to get their first paychecks, and 90 percent of those checks, when they finally arrived, were incorrectly made out. One reason for the system's deficiencies was the fiscal dependency of the New York City Board of Education, with the comptroller's office doing pre- and post-audits and issuing the checks. As with school construction, payroll information has to make its way through a tortuous sequence of steps and offices before a check is finally issued.

An even more serious problem, however, was the absence of adequate payroll information and of financial controls in headquarters' relations with the districts. Under the Decentralization Law of 1969, the districts had new powers to hire staff, which they exercised quite freely—so much so, in fact, that they overhired way beyond their budgets by the spring of 1971, giving the school system a $40 million deficit.† "The whole payroll and financial system was held together by chewing gum," reported a top Board of Education administrator, "and we went through many months of outside investigations before we developed a better, more efficient one."

The overspending and the payroll crisis were so severe that the Board of Education had begun these reforms even before EDC got involved. It hired an executive from NASA and the aerospace industry to be director of business and administration, and he immediately

---

*Top school officials correctly point out that they had already taken some initiatives on payroll problems before EDC arrived. They hadn't progressed that far, however, and EDC's contributions were important.

†As the State Charter Revision Commission's report indicates, personnel was the function of most interest to community school boards interested in providing jobs to their local ethnic constituencies. See pp. 44 ff.

worked on payroll problems, assisted by staff from Peat, Marwick, and Mitchell, a management consultant-accounting firm that had been helping the Board of Education institute budget and accounting systems since 1969. Together they developed a computerized teacher payroll system that included information on the name, rank, and school assignment of every teacher in the schools. They then developed procedures to prevent the districts from overhiring by requiring each district to have an assigned number of staff from headquarters and to hire against that number. The understanding was that if a district overhired, the new staff would not get paid.

Finally, they developed a system to provide up-to-date information on teachers who changed their status—e.g., retired, got promoted, or died. As an EDC official reported: "There was $8 million going out in 1971 or 1972 to people who did not merit it. They got something like half of it back, and this new system was designed to help on that."

EDC helped the board simplify and repair this payroll system rather than fundamentally redesign it. It also had a person on loan from Citibank do a study in 1972 and 1973; he made recommendations for improving the flow of payroll information along with the follow-up, monitoring, and overall control procedures within the existing system. Many of these recommendations were implemented.

EDC later recommended a complete computerization of payroll as part of a larger strategy of developing a management information system. The Board of Education has been slow in moving ahead on these later recommendations, partly for lack of funds and staff, and partly because its top administrators are not sure what they should do on these complex problems. Nevertheless, the payroll system is considerably improved over what it was at the start of decentralization and before EDC arrived. Again, as with supplies, the problems in payroll were largely technical, with no serious policy or political obstacles to effecting needed changes. There was the added incentive in payroll of improving teacher morale and responding to strong union pressure to pay people on time and in the right amounts.

Case #3: Office of School Buildings and School Construction

Still another case in which EDC was effective was in school construction, one of the more sensitive "nerve centers" in the agency. The Office of School Buildings—responsible, along with other Board of Education and outside bureaus, for all school construction—was where EDC began. Its studies of that office and later of the entire network of agencies that participate in school construction decisions met with a fair amount of success in effecting change; and the way in which this took place further illustrates some of the prospects for modernizing such bureaus in municipal government. While construction is much more "political" than supplies and payroll, given the many interests of citizen groups in having schools built or renovated in their areas, much of the work EDC did was so purely technical and involved such obvious potential cost savings that some immediate action on its recommendations was possible.

To provide some context for understanding EDC's contributions, the annual school construction budget until the recent fiscal crisis had been several hundred million dollars.* The Board of Education usually asked for much more than it ended up getting, in anticipation of slashes by other involved city agencies and elected officials. Two units, the Office of School Buildings and School Planning and Research, were most directly involved, with the latter doing the demographic research and work on school design and the former encompassing all construction and related functions, such as school maintenance and custodial services.

The Office of School Buildings is located in the same Long Island City area as the Bureau of Supplies, and is just as removed from school headquarters. At the time that EDC became involved, Chancellor Scribner was reportedly concerned about possible corruption or favoritism in letting out construction contracts, even though there was no direct evidence of wrongdoing. Indeed, the general reputation of that office and its director was quite favorable, though the city's construction administrator had expressed some concern about the slow pace of school construction projects.

The office did suffer, however, from severe deficiencies in staff, in organization, and in operating procedures that contributed to inordinate delays in the construction and renovation of schools. Such delays were common throughout city government, but their effects were particularly pronounced in the Board of Education. [8]

As a state agency, the New York City Board of Education had roughly 28 percent of the total cost of construction projects financed from Albany. The backlog of delayed projects had become so great by 1973, owing partly to limited staff in the office and to its failure to cope with required paperwork, that the city had reportedly lost over $53 million of state funds. Though this had not become a public issue, the board members claiming they were unaware of it,

---

*Given this crisis and gradually declining enrollments, there has been little construction in recent years.

top school officials agreed that the Office of School Buildings could use a lot of outside assistance.

As the EDC study indicated, the office had many administrative problems. A lack of clerical, stenographic, and technical personnel and the absence of an office "staff" group as such (instead, staff people were scattered throughout the organization) were the main ones. Because of these staff shortages, the directors of the different bureaus within the office (maintenance, design, construction, modernization) got too involved in operations and not enough involved in broader administrative and policy questions.[9] And the bureaus themselves were too fragmented, with, as the report indicated, "an overlapping of functions and separation of working units which should be merged to improve efficiency."

Two conditions contributed to these organizational and staffing problems. One was low entry-level salaries and an absence of "incentive increases," which together "reduce the quality or capability of entering employees" (p. 3). The other was rigid civil service regulations that allowed for the promotion of "unqualified" people by virtue of their having passed an examination (which often did not test for relevant skills) and conversely prevented the promotion of qualified ones. Furthermore, there was no "management development program" in the office to upgrade and improve existing personnel (p. 4).

These constraints were not unique to this office. In this instance, however, given the state aid situation, the overcrowding in some schools, and the uneven and inefficient patterns of school utilization, the constraints had a particularly severe impact.

The EDC report on the office, done by a New York Telephone Company executive, contained numerous recommendations for change, many of which were implemented. "McLaren, the Director, and his staff definitely wanted improvement," the executive reported. "I was located in his shop, so we had good relations. Maybe if I was located elsewhere, it might have been different." The main changes included: (1) a new consolidated central office staff, with its own director; (2) new deputy or assistant directors responsible for day-to-day administrative decisions, thus freeing directors; (3) new clerical staff; and (4) a consolidation of the office's bureaus into a simpler and less cumbersome structure. The changes didn't take place right away, but the office welcomed them, and the delays that followed were simply a result of the usual bureaucratic problems— e.g., delays resulting from the headquarters reorganization and from so many new headquarters staff having to review the recommendations. The EDC person who followed up on the report's proposals documented what happened. "The report was completed in February 1973. Then there was a letter from the Office of School Buildings Director, McLaren, to Anker in early March, indicating that he wanted to implement some recommendations right away. At the end of May 1973, McLaren wrote again to Anker, who said the reorganization would need the approval of the board. That would include the appointment of new staff as well. But McLaren never really got a direct answer. He went ahead anyway and appointed a director for staff and assistant directors for the bureaus of modernization, construction, and plant operations. Then McLaren wrote another letter to Anker on September 25, saying this is what I did and wanting concurrence for it and for Anker to go with the Board of Education to the city for approval of pay rates. Then there was a letter from Anker to all Executive Directors (including McLaren) asking them what their jobs were and how they planned to proceed. From then until November 1974, they waited for city approval for the lines and salaries. So it took from May 1973 through November 1974 to have it close to fully done and the people properly paid."

A particularly critical problem resulted from the fact that two Board of Education units partially duplicated one another's activities and were in constant conflict. The School Planning and Research Office had authority for all decisions up to the point where a contract was let for the building and actual construction began. This involved making demographic projections to determine what kinds of schools were needed where and determining school size and actual design, often with the participation of teachers and principals in the affected schools. The point of duplication was in design and, secondarily, in leasing. Thus, the design section of the School Planning Office and the construction division of the Office of School Buildings were doing much the same thing, and EDC recommended that they get together and eventually consolidate.

When attempts at consolidation didn't work, owing partly to resistance from the directors, EDC recommended that both staffs at least meet to make final design and construction plans for particular schools. They proceeded to do that more often than in the past, probably contributing to greater efficiency.

The problems of managing school construction in New York City far transcend these two offices, however, and even if each could be modernized and the two consolidated, there would be more important obstacles to overcome.[10] They result from the existence of so many participants, including community school boards and their staff; the City Planning Commission; the Board of Estimate; the mayor's office; the Bureau of the Budget; the Site Selection Board of

New York City, a critical interagency group; the Corporation Counsel's Office; community planning boards; and many others. As an EDC study on the school construction cycle pointed out: "The project will pass through almost one hundred separate steps—more if the design or sites are controversial—and be subject to the scrutiny of some 31 agencies or departments whose concurrence is required, resulting frequently in delays or compromises to the project. Of these agencies, 24 are outside of the effective control of the Board of Education. Six of these agencies have what is tantamount to veto power, and all have the capacity to delay progress (p. 7). We have a classical case in which the agency [i.e., the Board of Education] responsible for providing timely availability of satisfactory facilities lacks the authority to discharge its responsibility in a timely and efficient manner" (p. 5).

School building projects thus wend a most tortuous way through a fragmented intergovernmental production system whose complexity is so great that it seems almost designed for inaction. The EDC study documented in considerable detail the nature and consequences of this elongated decision process. It concluded that even accepting the legal and political requirements that bring so many participants into the process, decisions could be speeded up considerably, effecting quite substantial savings. As it noted: "There does, however, appear to be a substantial opportunity to reduce the time required, with substantial dollar savings and improved planning for needed facilities, through the development of more effective controls and the improvement of communication flows between various agencies involved in the lengthy and complex cycle. A reduction in the cycle, which now exceeds four years, of at least a year is potentially possible, with savings which could exceed $14 million, based on the projected 1974-75 Capital Budget of $200 million, and a current 7% per year inflationary cost increase. Additional savings would also continue to accrue on continuing projects in the 1973-74 budget" (p. 3).

EDC's main recommendation was to improve the existing computerized information system that provides monthly printouts on the status of each project and then convert it into an instrument of control. It would be used to indicate where the bottlenecks are and who is responsible, as a way of holding people accountable for any delays and then speeding up the process. "What we suggested," reported the EDC person on loan who worked on this, "was a very detailed implementation schedule that says who is on the hook when and indicates that the guy responsible is going to be held to account if he isn't delivering."

As was the case with the earlier study, there were many delays in implementing EDC's recommendations. "My report was submitted in May or June of 1974," reported the EDC person, "and nothing had yet been done in November. They are now painfully aware that inflationary costs in new buildings result from the delays, and I keep telling them that the longer they wait, the more it costs. They know that, but they are still slow in moving."*

This case illustrates perhaps most dramatically the many management pathologies of municipal government. Projects are reviewed by many participants, each of which has different agendas and interests. No mechanism effectively coordinates the participants or holds any of them responsible for delays. Authority thus remains highly fragmented, with no clear lines of responsibility. There is inadequate information and control so as to facilitate action. And long delays, escalating costs, and citizen alienation are the result.

This system does have some political rationality, as it allows many interest groups to be represented in the decision making process and provides for checks and balances. Furthermore, it allows for flexibility, as some areas may undergo rapid demographic changes that make past planning obsolescent or inadequate. The economic costs of such a procedure must be reckoned with as well, however, and some tradeoff between the two seems necessary. "A top person at the board told me the other day," reported an EDC official, "that it was good that there is such a long process in building schools. It gives them at the board a lot of flexibility. On that logic, I told him, you ought to build all schools prefab or in tents, so you could keep changing your minds."

Case #4: The Bureau of Audit

A business unit with management systems and procedures even more outmoded than those in supplies or payroll—and whose workings contained the basis for major scandals—was the Bureau of Audit. EDC had much less impact there than in supplies and payroll, mainly because Audit's functions were much more "politicized," dealing as they did with such sensitive matters as community school board expenditures.

*Given the huge budget cuts facing the Board of Education as a result of the city's fiscal problems, little construction is likely in the next few years, making the EDC report somewhat academic for the near future.

The New York City Board of Education, with an annual expense budget of over $2 1/2 billion, had virtually no internal auditing and had an accountant and former business teacher as the acting director of the auditing unit when EDC arrived.*

In this case, the EDC person on loan, an auditing expert from Ernst and Ernst, completed his study long before the bureau took much action to correct the serious deficiencies that he reported. His competent and "explosive" report was just as highly regarded among school officials as were the consulting activities of the EDC person at the Bureau of Supplies.† The Board of Education moved ahead very slowly on his recommendations, however, even though his study contained fairly scandalous information about the bureau's operations. We present this case, then, as an example of "failure," at least in the short run, and indicate some of the factors that contributed to that.

EDC had actually warned the Board of Education about the bureau's deficiencies long before this study, but the report itself, completed in August 1973, was devastatingly inclusive in its documentation and analysis.†† The main findings pointed to the absence of modern accounting and audit techniques; the poor training and limited professionalism of many bureau staff members; the limited control and supervision over their work; the limited scope of their auditing, excluding as it did functions within the agency comprising millions of dollars of assets and liabilities; the absence of good information on those assets and liabilities that might be the focus of such expanded audit activity; and the bureau's having an acting director who wasn't even a trained auditor. These were all compelling

*The fact that a nationally known accounting firm, Coopers Lybrand, did two outside audits on the Board of Education in recent years and failed to certify its auditing operations on both occasions is an indication of just how limited they were.

†This was so much the case that board member Joseph Barkan, a former business executive, issued his own sixteen-page "explosive" report on the bureau, thirteen pages of which were taken directly from the original EDC report; see Bureau of Audit: Review of Existing Procedures and Suggested Reorganization, by Donald Preston, Economic Development Council, August 15, 1973. Even the acting director of the bureau had very positive feelings about the EDC person and his professional approach to the study.

††It was based on interviews with all members of the Bureau of Audit, with people involved in accounting and other management control functions at the Board of Education, and with various Board of Education department heads and directors. In addition, selected reports and working papers of the bureau were reviewed.

indicators of the bureau's poor quality and, in some cases, perhaps even of fraudulent work.*

As the report indicated: "The accounting system does not have a double-entry record-keeping process, nor does it maintain general ledger control. . . . approximately 60% of the staff (exclusive of investigators) had limited or no previous auditing experience (my review of the working papers suggested to me that this percentage could be much higher. . . . many areas of the system are not being audited [e.g., Office of School Buildings, School Lunches, MIDP, Pupil Transportation, School Supplies, etc.]. In addition there are billions of dollars of assets and liabilities that are not being audited because there are no accounting records available as to their existence (e.g., fixed assets, supplies, encumbrances, etc.). . . . It seems quite evident from the background and current operations of the Bureau that decisions as to what and when an area should be audited are made by circumstances, or people outside the Bureau of Audit, rather than the product of a deliberate plan of operation. . . . I noted during my interviews that many auditors complained of poor or limited supervision, and in addition some of these people had no auditing experience. This causes a lackadaisical attitude in many. . . . Another frequent response I received during these interviews was the dissatisfaction they had with the lack of follow-up on their findings. The normal attitude towards the next assignment, because of this attitude, will be to ignore problem situations since they require additional work and nothing will be done anyway."

An evaluation of supervision and staff performance, done through the EDC person's review of a sample of the bureau's working papers, was similarly devastating: "I noted that the working papers, in general, did not indicate the signature of the preparer or reviewer, and the source of the information was rarely documented. The tick marks (related to erasures and deliberate changes and falsifications) were not explained, and many audit schedules were redundant and showed lack of thought. The working papers were generally disorganized, and it was difficult to follow the flow of work and the tie-in to the report. . . . I was informed by another audit staff that not all of their findings are disclosed in the reports, which is of ever more paramount importance. It was also their opinion that certain findings were suppressed by design and never reached the director or assistant

---

*Possible fraud was uncovered in interviews with some bureau staff members and from an examination of working papers and audit reports with erasures and other marks suggesting changes had been made. This was particularly so with respect to audits on community school boards and on individual schools.

director. This latter comment is beyond my ability to verify, but if true, would negate the effectiveness of an audit function."

A big part of the problem, as indicated in the report, related to the bureau's history. It had traditionally been used only to "put out fires." As the report noted: "These 'fires' will continue to erupt as long as the scope of their audits is so limited and a plan of overall coverage does not exist" (p. 6).

Though the report's well-documented criticisms were presented in a tactful way, considerable delay followed its submission. "We kept telling them that they had problems with the Bureau of Audit that are now near scandalous proportions, and that they are sitting on top of a volcano that is about to erupt, and yet they have delayed for two years on this," reported a top EDC official in late 1975.

The EDC report was very concrete and contained explicit and implementable recommendations for change, flowing directly out of its analysis. Furthermore, EDC and the person who had written the report indicated that they were available to assist in any phase of the report's implementation. But the fact that school officials knew that EDC was not likely to "go public" with its report and that it would continue to work with the agency in a "collaborative" way meant that it didn't feel under any pressure to move ahead. Even a lot of adverse publicity didn't have much effect, however. For example, when board member Joseph Barkan went public with the EDC report just after coming onto the board in April 1974, the fanfare over the issue died down a few days later.

Some personnel changes were made shortly after the EDC report came out, with roughly eight people in the bureau who had accounting ability transferred to the accounting department. Consultants from Peat, Marwick, and Mitchell located the people and helped arrange the transfer. A key decision on which the management reforms were to hinge, however, was for the bureau to get a new director. That decision was delayed for over a year, with EDC being rebuffed when it pressed for faster action as the board debated what the position should entail. First, there was a lot of discussion on whether the director should be a pedagogue or nonpedagogue (presumably an outsider). Later, with the new deputy chancellor and the director of personnel getting involved, new criteria were added. Both indicated that the director should have strong labor negotiating skills, and they drew up a job description reflecting that criterion. EDC insisted that such skills were unrelated to performing well in the position, and it seemed to eventually prevail. Interviews were then held with top auditors from the General Accounting Office (GAO) in Washington, and a person from Price Waterhouse, a big New York City accounting firm, was finally selected in late 1974. During that entire period, for about a year, the acting director was aware that he would be replaced, and neither his nor his bureau's performance, let alone their morale, could be expected to be very satisfactory under those conditions.*

In late 1974 the appointment was finally made, in the midst of a series of major crises likely to expose the bureau's inefficiency. Several community school districts were found to have overspent and to have engaged in other highly questionable practices with regard to staffing and contracting with outside consulting firms. Not long afterward, similar questionable practices were uncovered at headquarters, with respect to its relations with outside consultants as well as its auditing of the districts. Several investigations of headquarters' business operations then began, with the Bureau of Audit itself being the subject of at least two of them—one from State Comptroller Arthur Levitt's office and the other from HEW. In this atmosphere, and with some fanfare, the board appointed an "inspector general" to head up the Bureau of Audit.

From EDC's point of view, the board had delayed too long. In any case, the new auditor stayed for only seven months and then resigned. The general consensus of EDC people observing the bureau, as well as of many school officials, was that he was not given the kind of support by the chancellor and deputy chancellor that he needed, and when he saw that such support was not forthcoming, he left.

Administrative incompetence and bad judgment are, at best, only partial explanations for the inaction in this case, and one must understand the bureaucratic constraints that operated as well. The traditional practice of appointing a pedagogue or an inside civil servant to the position had first to be discarded. Then there was the city Department of Personnel, which was reluctant to allow the appointment of an outsider not on the civil service list.

The fact that the job description for the director went through so many headquarters officials for review and that it kept getting changed not only reflects the usual way things are done there, but suggests as well how particularly sensitive this matter was.†

This was a case, then, of an excellent EDC consulting report that was not acted on. Though EDC kept pressing for implementation, it

---

*There were many legitimate differences between EDC and the deputy chancellor on particular candidates, with the latter often feeling that EDC was bringing in people who were too old or not sophisticated enough in modern auditing techniques. EDC's feeling was that the deputy chancellor just didn't have any sense of urgency about this.

†There have been other directors since then, the most recent one being a former school official who was taken out of retirement. Many of the EDC recommendations have still not been implemented.

didn't have the leverage to get the board to act quickly on such a politically sensitive issue.

Case #5: The Management of High Schools

At the request of the High School Division, EDC also became involved in a study of New York City high schools, to see if it could come up with recommendations on how they might be better managed. It soon found from observations in several schools that principals spent an inordinate amount of their time, in some cases over 80 percent, tending to administrative details and political crises rather than providing educational leadership. The question was how to help the principals provide such leadership and manage their schools better, even within the constraints of existing budgets.

One of the main obstacles was the principals' resistance to delegating authority, a problem made worse by the increasing social ferment, in the form of student, parent, and community activist protest, against inadequate school programs. Having been under such outside pressure, many high school principals felt they had to keep close tabs on everything that was happening in the school and thus spent much of their time on crises. Many expressed little confidence in their assistant principals' (and other subordinates') ability to manage, further reinforcing their tendency to get into everything and provide little educational leadership. In management terms, their span of control was so great—with the typical New York City high school having several assistant principals, a dozen or more department chairmen, over a hundred teachers, and several thousand students—that they were able to do little more than react to immediate, day-to-day problems.

The issue, then, common to many social service and educational agencies, was one of helping practitioners with little training or experience in management to become better administrators. As the EDC report on high schools concluded: "It is clear from this study that most of the incumbent principals as well as most of their staff have come to their present positions from a largely pedagogical education and experience. Managerial training is neither a prerequisite for these positions nor are there any effective ongoing programs designed to supply these needs in the current system" (p. 31).[11]

Two on-loan people studied roughly twenty high schools of varying sizes, locations, and pupil composition as well as the high school office at headquarters in an attempt to find out more about this problem. They found that though most schools had a similar organizational structure, the management styles of principals differed. The vast majority had the nondelegative, crisis-management orientation already described, but there were some schools that were run very well. Their principals, it turned out, delegated authority and followed many of the other management practices that EDC was to recommend. As its study noted: "By way of example, the well-run schools have clear-cut assignments of responsibility with appropriate authority. The principal has clear job descriptions for positions reporting to him and conducts regular reviews with respect to progress or lack of it. While the principal is not aloof to the problems which surround him, they are usually *screened* by the appropriate subordinates before the principal is involved in the decision-making process" (p. 4).

Initially, EDC recommended a new position of deputy principal or senior assistant principal in each high school, to be responsible for all business and administrative activity (and reflecting the same separation between pedagogy and administration that it had recommended for headquarters). Under this kind of structure, the principal could delegate many business and administrative decisions to his deputy. Even in the case of politically sensitive issues—involving concerns of teachers, students, parents, or community groups—the principal's time might be spent more productively if his management staff summarized the main issues for him beforehand and even tried to resolve them. This would free the principal to provide educational leadership for the school.

These ideas are an integral part of management literature and practice and had already been tried in numerous demonstration programs. Bank Street College and the Rockefeller Brothers Fund, in collaboration with executives from Chase Manhattan Bank, had supported a program of establishing such a deputy principal for business affairs in several schools and districts throughout the New York metropolitan area. They had as one of their models the headmaster of British secondary schools, who was able to function as the school's educational leader by having just such administrative assistance.

The resistance EDC faced to this recommendation by high school principals, by their association, and by the High School Office at headquarters was so great, however, that the final EDC report all but abandoned it. The principals argued that limiting their span of control or delegating authority to a full-time business manager made little sense given the "hothouse" politics of inner-city high schools. Their view was that the principal had to be in control of the many situations that confront him and that he had to always be available to any participants with a large constituency or with reasonable complaints about the school. When EDC officials and other management experts pointed out how principals could be more responsive and more in control of their schools if they delegated business functions and had their staff summarize and screen grievances, they still questioned the applicability of this approach.

One reason for the principals' resistance was that the EDC people on loan doing the study evolved the concept of an administrative principal without ever consulting with the principals association or the High School Office. This turned out to have been an EDC project whose people on loan had worked in isolation both from EDC and from top school officials.

The final EDC recommendations, taking into account the principals' resistance to the original concept, involved programs of administrative training for principals, for their staffs, and for candidates for those positions; a yearly evaluation of their performance and provision of assistance to those whom the High School Office felt needed it; and efforts by the office and by the Board of Education to help principals deal with community and other external problems affecting the school as well. The main emphasis, then, was on management training for current principals and staffs and on requiring administrative skills of future candidates for those positions. Of particular importance was the recommendation that a "support team" be established at headquarters "to appraise the administration of each school at least once per year and recommend changes which would be helpful to the principal and his administration. . . . This team should also write an administrative operating manual which could be used by all high schools (p. 7).

The Board of Education is now moving ahead, through the High School Office, to institute a management training program similar to what EDC recommended.* It remains to be seen what impact this will have, but EDC has clearly been a catalyst in calling attention to the importance of improved management in high schools, a concern that may later be transferred to elementary and junior high schools as well. The EDC view is that "management effectiveness of the principal and his staff is a key determinant in high school effectiveness" (p. 5). The next few years may witness a test of that proposition in New York City.

Case #6: Management Information Systems

The area in which EDC worked perhaps most intensively was in the development of a computerized management information system

---

*The training program has been instituted only in Manhattan. High school superintendents from other boroughs did not express interest.

for the entire agency. From an administrative perspective, having the capacity to generate valid information on such key internal organizational functions as personnel, facilities, payroll, finances, and inventory and to better understand environmental forces is critical to any kind of well-managed organization. It bears on goal setting, planning, control, and operations and often affects key decisions on organizational structure as well. For some executives and management consultants this field has become something of a fad, but that is not to deny its widespread acceptance in business and public administration as increasingly important for good management.

It was in that general spirit that EDC undertook extensive efforts, starting in 1971, to assist the Board of Education in developing management information systems. Indeed, EDC recruited more specialists, put more effort into helping the board make changes, and experienced more frustration and resistance in seeking to implement its recommendations than in the case of almost any other activity it undertook.

To understand EDC's contributions, it is important to have some background on the Board of Education's past experience with regard to developing management information systems. As a top Board of Education administrator who had worked for many years on these problems noted: "Things have improved a lot in the past couple of years, even though we have a long way to go, but before 1970 or 1971, and even later, the Board of Education had no information system at all. It was like having a tin box that you kept taking money out of, and every once in a while, you noted that it was low, but you didn't have any reporting or information system to tell you just how bad it was or how close to catastrophe you were. The moment of truth came with the districts overspending in 1971, and after that a lot of basic work had to be done first at headquarters before we even got to the districts, because there was so much softness here; and we couldn't perform any kind of control or monitoring function for the districts, because we clearly didn't have the foggiest idea what was going on, either here or there."

Actually, there had been money to develop information systems since 1964, first through a grant from the Ford Foundation and later through a group from Stanford Research Institute. By most accounts, however, including some from within the Board of Education itself, millions of dollars were spent on this activity with amazingly little results. Part of the problem was the limited competence of many Board of Education administrators who were assigned to this task. "In the past," a board official reported, "we had used pedagogical people in these director positions to develop information systems, and the whole thing was a terrible swamp. We had a history of directors who were mostly ex-principals, and who stayed for a year or so and then left. The whole operation was very disorganized and we had no data-processing capability. When some competent people came from private industry in 1970, they had to deal with overcoming this history."

Literally every stage of EDC's involvement with the Board of Education focused on developing information systems as the key to management reform. The first group of people on loan in 1971, for example, immediately went into the districts to identify their data needs. They noted that most districts were generating very little usable information on their own, and that there was no overall plan at headquarters to correct this. At the central board's and the chancellor's request, and with headquarters floundering, EDC was asked to help develop such a data-processing capability at head-quarters.

A second EDC group then got involved in helping to develop an information system for running the high schools, which would include data on scheduling, grades, attendance, counseling, and the like. EDC heard about a program used in the California schools that did this, called the California Education Information System (CEIS), and some EDC people, along with school officials, visited California and brought the program back with them. They adapted it to New York City and soon introduced it into ten schools.

The implementation of that plan was, from EDC's point of view, painfully slow. The deputy chancellor, for example, expressed much skepticism to EDC about this California system and its applicability to New York City, citing an old RAND evaluation that was quite negative. EDC officials indicated that the evaluation had been done in the late 1960s and that the system had been improved consider-ably since then. The board found this argument compelling enough to urge the deputy chancellor to adopt the system, which he even-tually did.

EDC's main effort, however, was to urge an agency-wide manage-ment information system that would be computerized and set up as a separate data center. From early 1973, EDC kept urging the board to move ahead on this. Chancellor Anker refused to move on it until a deputy chancellor for business and administration arrived. When Deputy Chancellor Gifford did get appointed, EDC felt that he and his top staff still moved, by its standards, very slowly. Actually, Gifford and his staff have done considerably more than any of their predecessors, and they argue that they don't have the staff, the cooperation from the city with respect to recruiting new staff, or the budget lines to move ahead any faster. Gifford did get five people in to work on planning, and he appointed a top staff person to oversee the work. This person turned out to be more of a technician than a supervisor, and he was relieved of his duties after he failed to move the effort ahead very much.

There has been some movement, however, partly as a result of EDC's goading and partly through Gifford's initiatives. Unlike Chancellor Anker, who consulted his board on almost every major issue, Gifford simply went ahead on his own, putting $20 million into his budget in 1975 for this work without consulting either Anker or the board. Even with all of Gifford's assertiveness, there were delays, owing to many internal policy and organizational differences within Gifford's staff and between him and EDC on how the Board of Education should move on this and how a data center should be set up. EDC kept urging on Gifford and the board the concept of a separate data center that could service all major user bureaus, and it was only after almost two years of constant wrangling that Gifford agreed on that approach. "I have researched this very carefully," he reported, "as to whether such an MIDP department should be a separate service agency or integrated into some line function, and there are no easy solutions. We sometimes resent EDC's assuming that there is any simple answer and that they know what it is."

From EDC's perspective, however, the biggest problem was the board's failure (in EDC's eyes) to develop any consistent strategy on this important problem or to make it a high priority. EDC spelled a strategy out in a lengthy memo of March 4, 1974, and in numerous meetings with top school officials. It involved moving incrementally toward establishing an agency-wide information system for such major functions as payroll, supplies, facilities, students, personnel, and financial data and doing so in the context of a total plan. EDC recommended a permanent planning organization to work on this.

From EDC's point of view, its experience with the Board of Education with respect to establishing such a system has been one of continued frustration. While Gifford did bring in five new planning people and a project director at one point, there was considerable delay in establishing a separate data center and even more in developing any kind of coherent strategy. "Rather than deciding on a total system for the long term and then establishing priorities and putting it together piece by piece," explained an EDC official, "they are trying to do it all at once. Their project director never really got that concept of picking one priority system like payroll or supplies and developing it."

The issue of where the data center would be located within the bureaucracy has also been a source of delay and controversy. Over much of the first two years of its early development, MIDP was under the executive director of the Bureau of Business and Administration. Since he was also a big user, his needs prevailed over all others, and most of the center's resources went to serve his problems. EDC finally helped get it out from under him and operate as a true service bureau and separate data center, responsible to the deputy chancellor.

Relative to where the Board of Education was in 1970, then, when it operated "out of a tin box" with much "softness" at headquarters, there have been improvements. Under Gifford and EDC's leadership a planning staff was established to locate information needs for the total agency, generate data relative to those needs, set up an automated personnel data base, adapt the California system for New York City high schools, and get underway a long-range MIS planning operation. Though management systems and procedures at the Board of Education remain undeveloped in many areas, the agency is moving ahead more rapidly than many others in the city.

While some of this work began before EDC arrived, most of it can be attributable to EDC and to Gifford. EDC had proposed the new headquarters structure, with a deputy chancellor for Business and Administration, and Gifford's forceful style in that position moved things along more quickly than might otherwise have been the case. EDC's feeling that he reworked and claimed as his own many of its proposals did create conflict in his relations with them, but there has been movement toward improved management in the agency as a result of EDC's and his initiatives. If there were a way of institutionalizing this impetus, something that EDC has continually urged on the board, there might be some prospect for steady improvements over a long period.*

The issue in large part is one of building a core group of competent administrators and management and policy analysts within the agency as a countervailing force to the traditional staff, most of them ex-pedagogues and civil servants. The consolidation of business and management functions under the new deputy chancellor and the recruitment of trained administrators from the outside represent the beginnings of such a development. If EDC or an equivalent group remains there as a catalyst for management improvements, the prospects for a continuation and even an accelera-

*Gifford had periodically indicated to EDC that the two of them together could effect tremendous changes in the Board of Education; but he also periodically manifested extreme swings of mood and much inconsistency regarding EDC's usefulness and the alleged benefits of many of its management reform recommendations. He moved over to the Russell Sage Foundation in July 1977, and it remains to be seen whether EDC will find his successor, Ron Walters, a former top city official, any more receptive to its proposals.

tion of efforts already underway are quite good. The city's fiscal crisis, forcing agencies to increase efficiency, may well ensure that this takes place.

Other EDC Headquarters Projects

EDC had other headquarters projects that are worth mentioning as well, and that further indicate the potential of this management transfer strategy. One that has great significance in the context of City Hall's refusal to bring in too many outsiders into top management positions was a five-day management training program that EDC held with executive directors and middle-management staff of school headquarters in the spring of 1975. If this were done in a more sustained way and extended to community superintendents and principals, it might help improve management at many levels.* While most large corporations run continuous management and executive development programs and are aware of how change in an organization's environment makes executive skills rapidly obsolescent, such insight is rare in the public sector. Yet its environment is changing rapidly too; and those municipal agencies in which practitioners with little management skills have a near-monopoly over access to top administrative positions have a particularly compelling need for such training programs.

Another EDC activity related to the Board of Education's controversial Accountability Committee. This was a broad-based group composed of Board of Education, union, and civic group officials whose main task was to develop a system for measuring "school performance" or "productivity" and to then develop mechanisms for corrective measures (staff training, transfers, educational program changes) in those cases where productivity was low. In the context of its work on headquarters reorganization, EDC advised the board not to create another separate structure for this committee but rather to integrate it into the chancellor's office. Also, an EDC executive on loan wrote a highly sophisticated critique of an Educational Testing Service study for this committee, in which he urged a much more

---

*There has been little support from top school officials for continuing and expanding such training programs. One of the only supporters has been the Manhattan borough supervisor for high school principals, who has brought together his principals for training sessions. EDC has also arranged to have New York City school administrators attend management training programs held by its member corporations—for example, IBM, Union Carbide, Con Edison, and Western Electric.

institutional definition of accountability than ETS had developed.[12] He suggested through an analysis of the way in which the accountability concept had traditionally been used that it was important not only to note the many cases where student performance was poor but to carefully analyze why, focusing heavily on schools and teachers. As he wrote: "There is considerable difference between the 'acceptance of responsibility for taking effective action,' which is the position of ETS, and the responsibility for 'explaining *why* anticipated results were not realized,' which is the more generally accepted interpretation of accountability" (p. A-2).*

In addition, EDC worked on helping to improve needed support services for the Board of Education and the chancellor—involving in particular a reorganization of the legal staff of the board and the creation of a new public relations organization. Another major area of EDC study, one of the "nerve centers" of the entire system, was the Board of Education's Personnel Department. The second task force director, a personnel specialist from Western Electric, prepared an extensive report on the department in late 1971 together with a colleague from Bankers Trust. Unlike all the other EDC projects, this one focused heavily on policy questions. It suggested a number of changes in the headquarters Personnel Department to give strong central support to decentralization. They included helping the districts with recruiting; making testing and placement much more flexible, so as to give the districts more autonomy in this regard; loosening up procedures for teacher transfer and dismissal, to reflect district needs; involving the districts and community school boards much more in city-wide collective bargaining; and embarking on a major program to increase the number of minority personnel in teaching and supervisory positions. Other consultants and outside critics of the schools had made most of these recommendations before, but they were pulled together well in this report. It received little attention, however, because it supported the districts' desire for more power. Several board members and top administrators in the Personnel Department opposed most of its recommendations, and in the absence of their support, there was little prospect for much action. This thoughtfully developed EDC study on personnel, then, received little support within the agency because it advocated a

---

*EDC later backed off from completely endorsing this critique's conclusions, since they were so controversial and generated so much resistance from the teachers union and school supervisors. Several top school administrators and board members criticized EDC for not having the courage of its convictions, but they had failed to press vigorously on reforms as well.

controversial policy position, rather than just concentrating on administrative issues.

Other EDC projects as of mid-1977 include further work on developing a computerized management information system, a study on budget and fiscal controls throughout the entire agency, and one on the board's outside relations with vendors, from the perspective of what cost savings may be effected by getting more vendors to bid, by paying bills to them more promptly, and by getting lower prices when buying in volume. It is unclear what EDC's role will be after these studies are completed. One earlier agreement was that EDC would report to the board once or twice a year its evaluation of how well the agency was doing in its modernization efforts and would provide further assistance when requested.

COMMUNITY SCHOOL DISTRICT STUDIES

As we indicated at the beginning of the chapter, Scribner's letter of invitation to EDC indicated that the critical problem facing the New York City Board of Education was decentralization and that the main purpose of any management improvements should be to make it work. Despite its extensive work at the headquarters level, EDC recognized quite early the importance of developing much better management capability in the community boards and districts as well. The central board and top headquarters officials, with few exceptions, had not effectively provided such assistance.

The districts always felt that headquarters rarely if ever consulted with them on critical decisions affecting their operations.[13] There was no effective ombudsman-type mechanism to allow complaints to filter up to the central board and the chancellor, since Anker and the board, as we indicated earlier, had reversed Scribner's and EDC's plan for the Division of Community School District Affairs to play this role.

Another mechanism set up in the early 1970s and still in operation is the Board of Education's Consultative Council, a forum of community school board members, their superintendents, and headquarters officials which meets twice a month to discuss pressing issues. Though the council has had some productive meetings, it is generally an adversary confrontation, with headquarters officials often just announcing new policies that have not been developed in any consultation with the districts. Many community school board members and district officials don't even bother to attend.

This is not to say that headquarters has done nothing to try to improve the management of the districts. When decentralization first began in 1970, the central board hired a management consultant firm, Cresap, McCormick, and Paget, to help train community school board members.* Many community school board members, however, looked on the consultants as white, middle-class outsiders who knew little about the day-to-day realities of the New York City schools, particularly in ghetto areas. Some board members felt that this was a "consultant rip-off" program and that more blacks and Puerto Ricans with community experience should have been doing the training. After a year or two, attendance at the sessions dwindled so much that the program was discontinued.

The Board of Education also brought in McKinsey to help improve the management of community school districts. It did a preliminary study in 1970 of District 14 in Brooklyn, a predominantly Hispanic and black district, and wrote several papers on the management requirements for successful decentralization. Its main thesis was that the central board should introduce management systems in a "bottom-up" fashion, starting first at the district level and deciding what functions headquarters should perform only after district needs had been ascertained. As we indicated earlier, McKinsey's political problems with then-Comptroller Beame and the City Council in connection with its role as a consultant for the Lindsay administration probably contributed to the central board's not offering it any major consulting contracts.

Still another effort at upgrading the management of community districts involved a minority consulting firm, Optimum Computer Systems, Inc., working with a black superintendent and his board in a predominantly ghetto-area district in the Bronx. They worked there for about a year and a half, developing management information systems, computerized data, and the like, but that district became embroiled in such severe political controversy, involving relations between the superintendent and the teachers union over his decision to hire more Spanish-speaking counselors off the civil service lists, that he and his board, though they won their case in the courts, were voted out in 1973. The new board not only terminated its relations with Optimum but refused to even honor its predecessor's contract, thereby failing to pay for over $100,000 worth of work. This later became an unprecedented case of a minority firm suing a minority district for failing to honor a contract, a case that is still pending in the courts.

*The firm had done a management study of headquarters in the early 1960s, urging major reforms. It became one of many such studies that gathered dust.

The only other significant management training activity before EDC got involved was through the New York City Regional Center for Planning and Innovation, a headquarters unit that had been funded for several years through Title III of the Elementary and Secondary Education Act (ESEA) of 1965. That office had money to help community districts develop more effective management processes and had worked with five districts in the 1971-72 academic year. It got cut out of such activity after that, however, because of headquarters politics, and EDC then became active.*

EDC is thus the most recent of a long line of parties that have been interested in improving the districts' management. When its task force director realized that the regional office was not going to be permitted to do that job, he announced at a Consultative Council meeting in early 1973 that EDC was available to provide management assistance to the districts. School officials wanted EDC to do the work out of headquarters, but EDC argued against that. "We told Anker that that would be the worst way we could be introduced," reported a top EDC official, "and instead we did it the hard way, by going in only on invitation and maintaining our independence from headquarters." Thus far, EDC has worked with five districts. In every instance, EDC was invited in and did not impose itself in any way.

EDC's strategy was roughly the same in each district. Its people on loan would interview up to thirty or forty people in the district—the superintendent, principals, assistant principals, board members, district staff members, and civic groups people. They also interviewed administrators at headquarters to find out how productive their relationships with the district were. EDC was generally well received, since it was usually invited in by the community school board president, who then asked educators and civic groups in the district to cooperate. The fact that EDC was identified as having worked to reform headquarters, that it sent competent on-loan people who showed much empathy for district problems, and that it avoided being identified with anybody at headquarters helped in establishing its credibility.

Some educators and liberal parent groups initially regarded EDC with suspicion, reflecting their negative views about how "efficiency-minded" businessmen deal with the public sector. They feared that EDC might be more interested in cutting costs and in dropping "redundant" staff than in improving the quality of educational services by helping bring in new resources. EDC acted in a way

*Some top headquarters officials, including the deputy chancellor, did not regard management as an area that the Regional Center should get into, a reflection of turf struggles within the system.

that overcame those fears, however, and the fact that most districts continued to work with it and implemented many of its recommendations meant that it at least partially overcame this problem.

The recommendations that EDC made for management reform were roughly the same in every district. They included: (1) separating pedagogical from business and administrative functions; (2) consolidating all educational programs and functions in one place and all business ones in another; (3) integrating the schools more into the district office, so that they could receive the support services (educational and administrative) they needed; and (4) establishing new, middle-management positions in the district office when important functions were not being performed. These recommendations were quite consistent with the general strategy EDC followed at school headquarters, where it had recommended the same division between education (under the chancellor) and business (under the deputy chancellor), and in the high schools, where it initially made the same suggestion. At any rate, they were well received in most districts, and EDC has developed, over three and a half years, perhaps the only locally based program in the entire New York City school system for helping improve district management. The fact that it did not try to impose any changes unilaterally from headquarters or "downtown" and that it worked locally with the districts contributed to its success.

The first place EDC worked in was District 24 in Queens. Referred to by one EDC person as "strictly Archie Bunker territory," it was a predominantly white, middle-class district with few of the problems of poverty, pupil achievement, and ethnic controversy that beset so many others in the city. Though this district was in no way representative of typical inner-city problems, being much more peaceful than most, it was good strategy for EDC to go there first. The community school board chairman had invited EDC in; and the fact that it allowed for an instant early "success" was important.

EDC went into the district in May 1973 and conducted roughly fifty interviews with local school officials and parents and another fourteen with headquarters staff. It also examined many documents pertaining to the district's budget and administrative operations. In less than three months, EDC presented an eighty-page report to the community school board chairman. It made recommendations along the lines mentioned above, including (1) a new position of deputy community superintendent for business and administration, thereby reducing the number of district supervisory staff reporting directly to the community superintendent from eight to three, and allowing him to get out to the schools to try to improve educational programs there; (2) a consolidation of the district's business functions, including the merger of reimbursable (state and federally funded) and tax levy (city-funded) programs; (3) new, middle-management directors and supervisors, directly responsible for these newly consolidated functions; and (4) a new encumbrance system to keep track of district expenditures.

The results were quite positive, with this board implementing most of EDC's recommendations. A new deputy position was established, and it improved educational leadership in the district. "There has been great improvement since those changes went into effect," reported one of the EDC people on loan, a year after EDC submitted its report. "We reduced this huge span of control and helped get the superintendent out on the firing line. He's not buried in the district office, having to deal with all the nitty-gritty. That's not where his strengths really lie, anyway. Now he can delegate all that stuff to the deputy, and he goes out to the schools. Sometimes he doesn't get to his office until lunch. He is out observing schools in the morning, which is where he belongs."

In addition, the district office now has a series of new middle managers overseeing key functional departments, including curriculum, pupil personnel services, staff personnel services, and business affairs. This has led to much more consolidated administration and has further freed the superintendent to tend to educational matters, including the evaluation and training of staff, the development of new programs, and the like.

No readily available data exist indicating that these changes are associated with improved pupil achievement or that cost effectiveness as measured in some other way has increased; but it is the consensus of the EDC people and those out in the district that these changes have helped. Also, the district's community superintendent, who was later selected for a top headquarters position in charge of providing business assistance to the districts and still later became the director of the Bureau of Supplies, established a very close relationship with EDC and has continued to consult with them quite actively.

A case where EDC was less successful, primarily because of local ethnic politics, was District 7 in the rapidly ghettoizing Grand Concourse area near Yankee Stadium in the Bronx. This was a district composed of two-thirds Hispanic and one-third black students. Its problems were indicated by the fact that 30 percent of the students in elementary schools were not speaking English or were doing so only haltingly; student mobility and dropouts were very high; and roughly 75 percent of the students were reading one or more years below grade level. EDC arrived in November 1973, just after the appointment of the third community superintendent there in just a few years. A new board had also been installed that July, with five new members, and considerable internal conflict existed around patronage appointments and the control of new programs. Many board members rarely attended regular meetings, except when staffing issues were being discussed. [14]

EDC immediately reported to District 7 what it had done in District 24. The District 7 people indicated that they had many of the same problems, and EDC thus ended up making similar recommendations. It indicated first, for example, that the superintendent's span of control was much too large, involving her in too many operating details, and it recommended the appointment of a deputy superintendent; this would free the superintendent to visit schools, work with the community board and local groups, and provide the kind of leadership that the district needed so badly. It also noted that the schools were isolated from the district office, and suggested that by freeing the superintendent to visit schools and by organizing the office with new middle managers, that office could begin to provide needed services. It pointed out the fragmentation of educational programs and curriculum development, with no focal point of responsibility existing below the level of superintendent, and it recommended in that regard a consolidation of such programs under a single director of curriculum and teacher training who would have two supervisors under him—one for tax levy programs and one for reimbursable ones. Finally, it recommended a consolidation and strengthening of supportive services and business-management functions within the district office.

Though many of the EDC recommendations were similar, then, to those in District 24, and were made in response to the same problems, most were not implemented in District 7. Indeed, the board and superintendent never responded to the EDC report. "We made many calls, asking what had happened and holding them to their past promises," reported an EDC official, "but they refused to answer. I'm afraid that except for our own personal education, not much was accomplished there. We ran into a situation that was very polarized, with serious ethnic conflicts." A year later, when some of the conflicts had apparently simmered down, the district did begin to consolidate its tax levy and reimbursable programs, but that was done by the board on its own, without much direct contact with EDC.

EDC has since gone into Districts 2 and 6 in Manhattan and District 32 in Brooklyn and done much the same kind of work. District 2, encompassing the East Side of Manhattan between 14th and 98th streets and the West Side up to 59th Street, is ethnically diverse, containing heavy concentrations of Spanish and Chinese students in its southern portions and many middle- and upper-middle-class whites farther uptown. A consolidation of several earlier districts, this one evidenced no clear organization of any kind in its district office. Again, EDC made the same kinds of recommendations; to separate business and educational functions; to consolidate tax levy and reimbursable programs; and to establish a new group of middle managers for particular functional areas, with those in education reporting to the superintendent. The report was submitted in July 1975, and much of it has been implemented.

One of EDC's most dramatic successes has been in District 6, the Washington Heights-Inwood area in the extreme northwestern tip of Manhattan, which has a predominantly Hispanic and black population. It has undergone rapid ethnic change in recent years and has an outspoken community board. Their response to EDC's report on how to streamline and rationalize their district office operations was one of deep appreciation, and they have implemented many of the recommendations.

EDC's ultimate objective is to develop a model and some strategies for management assistance to districts, based on these experiences, that may work city-wide, depending on particular district problems and characteristics. Recent studies including EDC's indicate that this is a great need and that filling it has implications for many other agencies as well, since New York City government is now undergoing decentralization as the result of the referendum of November 1975 on the City Charter Revision Commission's recommendations. Furthermore, very little is now being done at the district level to improve local management.

A basic issue of strategy is involved in assessing the future of this work. The deputy chancellor, who, incidentally, has tremendous power and can determine to a large extent how much impact EDC will have on the Board of Education, takes the view that developing better management procedures and information systems has to be done from the "top down" rather than from the "bottom up." "When I first arrived," he reported, "I thought I could go out to the districts and do what McKinsey had done in District 14. But they were not set up in the districts for that, and we have nothing at headquarters, so I had to work here. I believe you have to start from the top to create a viable center, and then after we have rationalized headquarters and developed some standards and procedures, we should drive information down. Then and only then can we help the districts develop their own management capability."

While EDC does not disagree with his approach and has tried to work with him on it, its work in the districts was a potential threat to him. "Either he or somebody in his office indicated that they didn't think much of our community school district work," reported one of the EDC people on loan to that project. "They were saying that first we went into District 24 in a middle-class area that didn't need it. Then we went into District 7 in an ethnically polarized area that couldn't use it. So we struck out twice. What they were really saying was that they didn't want us upsetting their relations with the districts or giving the districts any support in making unnecessary demands on headquarters. I can understand their feeling, but we were providing an important service that they hadn't gotten around to providing and probably couldn't, because headquarters was still defined as the enemy. There's a saying around the districts that even if the ten commandments came down from headquarters the districts would find them unacceptable."

CONCLUSIONS

This has been a case study of a significant effort by a business group to reorganize and introduce modern management methods into the biggest school system in the nation. EDC contributed 50 person-years to this program, amounting to over $1 million worth of executive talent and many more services in kind over a six-year period, and the project is continuing. There was some unevenness to EDC's work, but basically it did some good studies and reports, introduced timely recommendations, provided valuable advice for the chancellor, the central board, and many top headquarters and district staff, and conducted itself in a nonpartisan, objective, and collaborative manner. Moreover, its task force director, Edward O'Rorke, showed much political astuteness—pressing the board when it was not acting on proposals it had seemingly adopted, providing constructive counseling and criticism, and maintaining high standards of integrity. He and EDC faced enormous political problems in getting through many reforms, however, that are essential to review in assessing the impact and future strategy implications of EDC's work in this agency.

The main problem was one of finding a client inside the agency with both the power and the commitment to management reform to make it likely that changes would in fact be implemented. The initial invitation came in a letter from Scribner, but the central board always claimed credit for having invited EDC in. Even in the early stages of EDC's involvement, the board was at loggerheads with Scribner over what some of its members felt was his overzealous and naive advocacy of decentralization, as well as over what many of them felt were his limited administrative skills.

Over time, it became apparent that the central board and, in particular, the board's president was EDC's main client. None of its presidents, however, could necessarily swing the votes of the entire board, and all of the board members had many other pressures to which they had to respond, not just those from EDC for management improvements. They were selected by the borough presidents and were in that sense political appointees who had to be responsive to pressures from their sponsors. Those sponsors rarely considered improved management a high priority. Moreover, EDC itself was unable to mobilize a strong enough constituency for good management to counterbalance such political interests.

EDC also worked with Chancellor Anker, Scribner's successor, and Deputy Chancellor Gifford. Anker, a forty-year insider with strong loyalties to old-line colleagues and tremendous political survival skills, moved slowly on EDC reform proposals, rarely taking the initiative and always consulting his board, the teachers union, supervisory associations, and any other powerful interest group that he felt had a stake in the decision. This was in many respects the only way he could function in such a political bureaucracy, and yet the more of these groups he consulted, the slower the agency moved on implementation. EDC had little control over that political process, even though its periodic threats to leave and O'Rorke's highly skilled and tireless pursuit of management improvements certainly did have at least some impact. No other management consultant had ever followed up on its recommendations with anywhere near the determination that EDC did, but the obstacles it faced were often quite overwhelming.

The agency client with whom an EDC alliance seemed to have the greatest potential for management reform was Deputy Chancellor Bernard Gifford. Gifford was keenly aware of the fact that he had not been EDC's choice for that position, but he and EDC nevertheless worked closely on many projects. He had other interests, however, besides responding to EDC, and they had many disagreements as to appropriate strategy. As the chief school official in charge of management and administration, he had his own agenda of priorities, developed in the context of all the political and financial constraints that he saw operating. At times he and EDC collaborated very well and at other times they clearly did not, with each being quite critical of the other's judgment and talents. Such strong disagreements existed with respect to a wide range of EDC- and Gifford-initiated projects.

A fairly consistent EDC strategy in many situations was to go over Gifford's head to the board president and other board members when he was not moving ahead on its recommendations. They enjoyed many short-term victories, but Gifford's increasing influence within the agency and in the city does not bode well for this strategy.*

The result of all of these difficulties in finding a client was that EDC had limited leverage with the agency. Perhaps it might have had more had it actively cultivated the support of community school boards or of various civic groups, but it didn't do that either. It didn't see such coalition building as part of its consultant role, and most of its studies were not publicized, in keeping with its prior agreement with the board to maintain a relationship of confidentiality.

Also, the kinds of reforms that EDC recommended were of little concern to most civic groups, with the exception of such organizations as the City Club, the Citizens Budget Commission, and the Citizens Union, which had always been interested in governmental reform. Thus, at an annual meeting of the United Parents Association, a citywide organization claiming to represent as many as 400,000 parents, O'Rorke, an effective public speaker, gave a presentation of EDC's reorganization plan and of its management projects. As he and others present reported, the large audience seemed thoroughly bored with the topic. Such good-government proposals often have difficulty generating constituency support.

This is not to say, however, that EDC's work in the Board of Education was all in vain or that it had no significant impact on the agency. If that were the case, its work would hardly merit the detailed analysis just presented. Indeed, one of the main implications of EDC's work is that when business provides management assistance to city agencies on limited projects and on problems that are mainly technical in nature, through the use of on-loan people with relevant expertise who are skilled in relating to public-agency staff, and in bureaus and divisions whose functions are not permeated with political and policy controversy and with vested interests, it can have a positive impact. Agency staff members will welcome its assistance, and the new management systems it recommends may well get implemented and may result in important improvements in agency efficiency. EDC's work in the Bureau of Supplies, in payroll, and in construction illustrates that. Even in the community school districts

*Gifford's popularity within the agency had become so great by late 1976 that he was constantly mentioned as the logical successor to Anker, who was near retirement. Anker stayed on, however, and Gifford moved on to the Russell Sage Foundation.

there were positive results, though the districts were always a focus of much political controversy.

By contrast, when a consultant group undertakes more diffuse management-reform projects in large, politically turbulent agencies, as with EDC's work in headquarters reorganization, it will be much less successful. There are too many vested interests at stake, the consultant and those inside the agency who want change may not have the leverage required to override resistance or arrange the necessary trade-offs, and the problems may be much too complex to be handled effectively. This is not to say that even the EDC headquarters reorganization was a failure. We have already discussed the improvements that resulted. Just the establishment of a deputy chancellor for business and administration, as well as of the various executive director positions, improved the agency's capacity to plan and expedite matters more quickly and more responsively. The political and fiscal problems the agency faces, however, are so complex, and the power of status-quo groups inside the system so great, that EDC could not be regarded as having made major changes in headquarters.

What did take place was the beginning of a serious effort to streamline the headquarters bureaucracy, and if this process were to be continued in the future, it could have an important positive impact. Stated more generally, EDC has begun to help change the agency's *structure* and *procedures*, but has failed thus far to develop the leverage needed to change the *people*, the *traditions*, and, most important, the *politics* of the agency, which limit how far the organizational reforms will be carried and the impact they ultimately have on agency performance.

As for EDC's future role in the Board of Education, several recent developments indicate how it may increase its leverage, and they have implications for management reform-oriented groups in other cities in which similar efforts may be undertaken. Since late 1975, EDC has worked with the central board to review its priorities in the context of the city's increasing fiscal crisis. EDC's timing was good in this respect, in that it took this propitious occasion—when the agency was under increasing pressure to cut administrative overhead costs and improve efficiency—to once again urge it to move ahead with the reorganization. That meant setting up standards for a review of programs, developing guidelines for establishing priorities, and identifying essential and nonessential programs and then trying to act on that information.

The question remained, however, as to how EDC might develop the necessary leverage to get the Board of Education to do those things. In the past it had worked alone, not mobilizing any broad-based constituency other than its business members, lest it jeopardize its privileged consultancy relationship and be pushed out. The costs of that strategy, however, were that EDC ran the risk of being co-opted, which often happened.

Two recent developments may possibly alter this situation. One is the existence of powerful new agencies—Big MAC and the Emergency Financial Control Board—that have considerable leverage over agency decisions and have been critical of the schools for inefficient practices. The other is a new coalition of sixteen civic organizations, the Educational Priorities Panel, that has been doing much research on the Board of Education's budget priorities and has been publicizing inefficient practices. For EDC to pursue these matters alone was very problematic, but with the political support of such powerful outside groups it may have more success.*

The other potential new development that may bring some of EDC's recommendations to more fruition is the increased interest in New York City in changing the entire system of governance of the Board of Education, as a way of improving its management efficiency and responsiveness. EDC officials concluded that one of the reasons for the limited implementation of its proposals related to the way the entire agency is set up. It has existed in an ambiguous relationship to City Hall, in the sense that while it is legally an independent state agency, it is fiscally dependent on the city. The mayor, the comptroller, and various city overhead agencies (Bureau of the Budget, Department of Personnel) have strong veto powers over school decisions, making the agency less responsive to citizen interests than might otherwise be the case. In brief, top school officials have limited power to make important policy and administrative decisions. More generally, there is a pattern of divided authority between the Board of Education and the rest of city government, with no clear mechanism for ensuring accountability.

A change that EDC has pressed quite vigorously and that has gained the support of increasing numbers of powerful citizen groups is to effect a much closer integration of the Board of Education with City Hall through having the school chancellor selected by the mayor and made directly responsible to him. He would thus function almost as a cabinet member in city government, thereby limiting the political isolation of the school system from other city agencies and increasing the possibilities for more productive collaboration with

---

*We will discuss in the concluding chapter the issue of orchestrating the EDC collaborative strategy with the more adversarial, consumer-advocacy one pursued by such outside, political groups.

them. This new arrangement would also include a policy and advisory board to the chancellor.

EDC came to this view only as a result of seeing how the agency was so slow to act on its management reorganization proposals. From EDC's perspective, all the deep frustrations and political resistance that it faced in its many years of dealing with the Board of Education might well be minimized in a new, more responsive structure. If EDC's main contribution were to help set the stage for such changes by indicating how the old structure was unable to mobilize itself, it would make the past six years of EDC activities in the school system worthwhile. It remains to be seen, however, whether such a reform impetus can be maintained.*

In the meantime, EDC has developed one other new mechanism that has promise for improving the schools' performance. It has set up an Education Council that brings together a wide range of public and private organizations whose main concern is how the schools prepare youth for local employment. All the main vocational and career education programs within the Board of Education, along with manpower training agencies and many business, labor, and civic organizations who share this concern, are members. EDC hopes to have the council improve programs by having all these agencies share information, do evaluations, and engage in joint planning. Interagency coordinating councils have not been that effective in improving the delivery of public services, but it is conceivable that this one may improve some programs. At the very least, it will bring together educators and employers to discuss how the schools can better develop and coordinate their programs so as to prepare youth for work.

From EDC's point of view, all of the problems discussed in this chapter were necessary preludes to business becoming involved in these more productive recent efforts. Whether that will, in fact, happen remains to be seen. In the meantime, the above comments on where EDC had its greatest and least impact should serve to guide future efforts by management consulting groups to improve the management of big-city school systems or, for that matter, of many other human service agencies as well.

*Mayor Beame presented such a new system of governance for the Board of Education in June, 1977, following closely on EDC's reorganization proposal, and he held hearings on it. By September he had backed away from it, in view of the proposal's limited public support. Strengthening decentralization through legislative and administrative changes to increase the power of community school districts is another reform strategy that might improve the schools' performance, but EDC has not pressed hard for this approach.

5. The High School Project

We wish to stress again that despite the notable achievements of the past decade of research, product development, evaluation, and dissemination, the schools are much as they have always been, and not always by choice. We attribute this in part to the whole way R&D has been thought about—as an external activity whose results will inevitably be found useful by operating agencies.

Building Capacity for Renewal and Reform, National Institute of Education, December 1973

THE POLICY CONTEXT: WHAT TO DO ABOUT INNER CITY HIGH SCHOOLS

One of the first urban agencies that American corporations tried to help, following the ghetto riots and student protests of the 1960s, was the high school. Many business executives realized that the high schools of the inner city were not producing an employable population to meet their manpower needs. As we have discussed, this may well have been an important reason for business and industry leaving the city. Furthermore, those corporations that stayed were being double and triple taxed for the failure of the schools. They paid corporate-income and other taxes that provided over 50 percent of the city's funds for public education. They paid, too, for correctional and welfare agencies, the need for which was at least in part a consequence of the schools' failure to adequately train the city's large minority populations. Finally, they paid for the basic educa-

112

tional programs that they had to develop for those graduates from inner-city high schools who had such minimal competence in reading, mathematics, and other basic skills that they were not employable and were unable even to take an occupational training course. Certainly in New York City and in other inner cities as well, the equivalent of a parallel school system existed to educate those youth whom the public schools and manpower training agencies had failed. As the school problem became more severe in the late 1960s, exacerbated by ghetto violence and crime, corporations tried to deal with it.[1] Various school–industry partnerships were developed, the most publicized being those of AT&T, some of whose branches (e.g., Ohio Bell, Michigan Bell, New York Telephone) were tied to the inner city and hence had to rely on its manpower pool for many of their employees.[2]

These were exceptions, however, and though corporations are the biggest consumer of the schools' "product," those in inner cities have done little to help improve public education. They have been involved in partnerships, vocational advisory councils, and the like for many decades, but few of these relationships were on any significant scale, and probably even fewer produced needed changes in the schools. A big part of the problem was that educators and businessmen distrusted one another. The former regarded employers as seeking to impose narrow, vocational curricula on the schools so as to meet their own manpower needs, or as trying to make the schools more "efficient" in an equally narrow administrative sense. Businessmen, meanwhile, regarded the schools as out of touch with local labor-market conditions and badly managed as well.[3] Inadequate relations between schools and industry had existed for many decades, and with the tremendous influx of rural blacks and Puerto Ricans into the inner cities and the vast changes in inner-city economies, the problem became even more severe in the 1960s.[4]

The problems of high schools, moreover, go deeper than this, having become the subject of intensive study by no less than five national commissions over the past few years. Before discussing EDC's programs, it is worth reviewing, at least briefly, what these commissions had to say.[5]

The argument of all of these studies is that the large, comprehensive high school, of which there are so many in New York, has not improved public education, as its proponents had hoped. Because of its size and incremental adding on of functions (from vocational, citizenship, and sex education to driver training and drug therapy), it has become more difficult to manage and more bureaucratic. This has been reflected in a standardization of curriculum and of rules governing student conduct, in impersonal relationships between students and faculty, in centralized decision making, and in an organizational rigidity. These conditions, so the argument continues, limit program diversity, student options, student participation in school governance, and meaningful student-adult relationships in the school. Given the trend toward more schooling, larger schools, and extension of the age of compulsory education, adolescents are increasingly placed in a passive, dependent role that is forced on them through a repetitive round of required schooling, in protest against which a youth culture emerged in the 1960s.

A further characteristic of high schools reinforcing this passive student role is their institutional isolation from the economy and from the wider community. Given the closed nature of formal schooling, students are seen as having few opportunities for economic independence, for civic and citizenship activities outside the classroom, and, more generally, for development through *doing*.[6] They experience in the process an isolation from significant relationships both with adults and with younger children which may also limit their development. Finally, youth are confined to this limiting environment and dependency status at just that time in history when they characteristically develop a capacity for independence, service, and adult responsibility much sooner than in the recent past.[7]

Based on such a diagnosis, at least two broad types of recommendations have been made. One relates to *making changes within high schools*, restructuring them into smaller units and thereby offering students more choice, more diversity, more specialization, and more power to shape school decisions.

A second involves *establishing closer linkages between high schools and such outside institutions as work places and community organizations*. This may involve a variety of arrangements, including cooperative education, work-study programs, public service activities, internships in outside agencies, and the like, all involving students moving back and forth into and out of the traditional classroom. Such arrangements are assumed to contribute to more student learning than schooling alone can provide, by allowing youth to play more active, adult-like roles.

Even before all these commissions had been set up, prototype programs existed that incorporated some of their ideas, several having started in New York City. Some of the most significant included an internship program in which up to 1,000 high school students spent a semester working and observing full-time in a city agency; the New York Urban Coalition's efforts to restructure an entire inner-city high school into separate mini-schools and then develop a strategy for helping other schools throughout the city to do so; some Satellite Academies that involved cooperative education and work-study programs in clerical and health occupations; and the Economic Development Council's partnerships with several high schools and junior highs.

A comparison of the EDC partnerships with these other programs, all of them viewed in the context of the critiques we have discussed of American high schools, is helpful in assessing how well the partnerships did and the assumptions on which they were based. The most significant comparison for our purposes is between EDC's partnerships and the Urban Coalition's mini-school program, mainly because those are the two biggest programs in New York City high schools that involved business supporting institutional change. They are prototypical programs of national significance, having both been designated by the National Institute of Education as exemplary cases of trying to build a capacity for renewal at the local school level, and therefore meriting financial support and evaluation.* Each involves a consortium of large corporations working as consultants to particular high schools and attempting to mobilize business resources and expertise to help solve school problems.

The two programs differ markedly, however, in many respects. As we will discuss below, EDC concentrated on activating a process of participative planning and self-renewal in schools, without trying to impose any preconceived organizational designs or educational programs. Its strategy was to let change ideas get initiated by key school participants—students, educators, and parents—and simply try to help create a group problem-solving situation within which such a process could take place. The particular actions taken by the school might or might not involve a restructuring of organization and program.

In contrast to the five commissions, EDC had no initial substantive proposals. What it had instead was a strategy of facilitating planning so as to encourage a process of organizational and program development in schools in which a demand for particular innovations would emerge from the schools themselves. EDC set the process in motion and then brought in resources to support implementation, institutionalization, and replication of those innovations that got initiated.

In sharp contrast, the early Urban Coalition strategy involved trying to bring to inner-city schools a particular model, based on its staff's diagnosis of what was wrong with those schools. It was a

*Actually, the Urban Coalition has moved away from its earlier mini-school program to support many of the same kinds of school-based renewal efforts that EDC has initiated. But at the time of its original funding, it was still involved mainly in mini-schools.

diagnosis, incidentally, quite similar to that of the commissions, stressing the negative consequences of school size. The Coalition recommended restructuring the schools into smaller units, each with more accessible services and learning opportunities, provided in a more humane setting than before. In that sense, its mini-school program represented an important prototype of a strategy that all five commissions had recommended on a national scale. It lacked in its early stages, however, the participative planning orientation that was to emerge as the strength of the EDC approach.

Viewed in the context of EDC's economic development focus, its high school program reflected its concern with trying to protect the city's tax base, which it saw as threatened by the middle-class flight to the suburbs and by the business exodus. Both reflected dissatisfaction with the schools. In addition, top EDC officials were also concerned about giving minority students a chance that they might not otherwise have to be educated and trained for regular employment.

The chapter reviews EDC's high school programs from this policy perspective and from a related one of how outside consultants may help effect change in public-sector agencies. We stress in particular the evolution of the program as a function of EDC's increasing awareness of how the schools work and of its own strengths and weaknesses.

The main part of the chapter analyzes how partnerships proceeded in three high schools in which EDC was deeply involved. It is presented as a series of analytical case studies.

Several issues emerge in an assessment of the program. The most basic one is how an internal research and development (R&D) process can be developed in inner-city high schools and how successful EDC has been in promoting that.* Another relates to unleashing the talents and energies of teachers. The EDC high school program concentrated increasingly on changing the status of teachers from that of functionaries to one of more autonomous professionals. It emphasized the importance of giving more recognition and resources to teachers to enable them to develop new programs that would

*By R&D is meant an institutionalized process of introducing change that has become quite common in American industry in recent decades. Many large corporations now have large research and development departments, to create new ideas, develop and test them, and finally put them into operation. A good description and analysis of how such departments work is contained in William Foote Whyte, *Organizational Behavior*, chaps. 26 and 27, Irwin Dorsey, Homewood, Ill., 1969. See also Simon Marcson, *The Scientist in Industry*, New York, Harper, 1960; and William Kornhauser, *Scientists in Industry*, University of California Press, 1962.

better meet the needs of their changing clientele than traditional ones did. Stated more sociologically, it involved a concerted attempt to change these schools from a "bureaucratic" to a "collegial" or "professional" organization.

Finally, this effort at energizing a self-renewal process in New York City high schools is taking place in a context of ethnic change and severe financial constraints. All these schools had experienced a vast influx of minority students from poverty homes, creating new curriculum and instruction needs. They were still primarily staffed, however, by white, middle-class educators who had in the past taught academic courses for college-bound students. Furthermore, though EDC developed the program on the assumption that more resources alone were not the main answer to the schools' problems, more funds were needed to get the process going in each school. At a time of such fiscal crisis, it was going to be difficult to sustain this program in many schools, let alone spread it to others.

This EDC program differs in important ways from the school headquarters project and the one on the courts that will be described in the next chapter. First, it was not done through a task force, as those others were, but rather through a more decentralized structure. Second, much of the staff work was done through a consulting agency that EDC contracted to, and not just by EDC and its on-loan people alone. And third, EDC was not engaged to nearly the same degree in a management transfer program in these high schools. Though its work did involve an attempt to transfer a research and development process from business to the schools, the emphasis was not primarily on improving management in those schools.* Instead, it was on unleashing teachers to develop innovative programs and on providing them with the necessary resources. The innovative programs related, then, more to matters of curriculum and instruction than to the management and delivery system of the school. Nevertheless, the issues raised in chapter two concerning public-sector characteristics that may limit the transfer of management practices apply also to this program.

---

*Some management improvement projects were undertaken, however. Three systems analysts spent three months at Monroe High School to design an information system for student records, scheduling, and the like. They proposed a central unit in the school for this, which is now in its third year of development. Also, two systems managers spent a year each (one following the other) at Brandeis High School to design an attendance and class-cutting information system that has been in operation since 1975.

EDC'S INITIAL ENTRY INTO THE SCHOOLS

EDC's involvement in the high schools began early in its existence. Throughout 1967, top EDC officials stood by watching while the controversy over school decentralization raged, and they wondered what employers could do. In 1969, for example, of the estimated 80,000 students leaving the high schools, only 30,000 received academic, commercial, vocational, or technical diplomas, while 30,000 dropped out and another 20,000 received only General Diplomas.*

Furthermore, student protest hit New York high schools particularly hard in the late 1960s, and racial and ethnic clashes among students as well as attacks by students on the school establishment were causes of great concern to business and to EDC, as well as to educators themselves.[8] One of the things that really shocked the city's business leaders was Superintendent Donovan's announcement in late 1967 that his goal for the next school year was to have every high school graduate reading on an eighth-grade level. As a result of this and other experiences, EDC officials began to realize the enormity of the school problem. But they knew very little about the schools and had no idea what to do.

The first thing EDC did was to bring in several outside experts on the New York City school situation and to conduct its own informal survey of business–school partnerships elsewhere. These activities began in June 1968 through EDC's newly formed Committe on Public Policy, which decided on education as its first area of concentration. Paul Busse and Roland Delfausse, two top EDC staff people, took the initiative, doing much preliminary interviewing and investigation, and then two EDC members, Dr. John W. Riley, Jr., a sociologist and vice-president of Equitable Life, and Joseph T. Nolan, a vice-president of Chase Manhattan Bank, took over. After interviewing experts and prospective consultants in late 1968 and looking at business–school partnerships in various cities, they encouraged EDC to bring in a newly formed educational research and development organization, the Institute for Educational Development (IED), to advise it on these matters. The early committee and staff work of this EDC group was critical in enabling it to move ahead on this new program soon after IED appeared.

This was a case, then, of one consultant (EDC) hiring another consultant (IED). The two of them were to work together produc-

*General Diplomas indicate little more than that the student has been in attendance. Neither employers nor colleges regard them as having prepared the students for work or for further education.

tively over the next several years. The initial contact was between George Champion and IED's president, Dr. Sidney Marland. Champion lived in Darien and had known Marland when he was superintendent of schools there.* Marland's associate, Donald Barnes, a former banker, vice-president of IED, and a strong devotee of organizational development (OD) and group dynamics techniques for changing organizations, emerged early as a key figure in the entire EDC high school program.†

Initially, EDC didn't know whether to begin in particular schools and districts or at headquarters. Barnes presented EDC with many possibilities. Since the high schools were closest to the economy, which was obviously what interested business the most, just concentrating on them had some appeal to EDC.†† Meanwhile, IED did an inventory of the main business–high school "partnerships" elsewhere, following up on earlier EDC staff work, to see if any lessons might be learned from those experiences for EDC in New York City.9 From that inventory and from Marland's and Barnes's other projects and experiences, they made several suggestions on strategy that EDC accepted. First, they said, it should go into the schools with a low profile and not try to take credit or get publicity for its efforts.§ Second, it should not try to impose any preconceived programs or designs on the schools, but should rather let them emerge from whatever relationships got established. Third, EDC should not expect fast results, certainly not for several years. Finally, it should expect more failures than successes, just as often happens with R&D programs in the private sector.

After gaining EDC's acceptance of those ground rules, Marland got it entree to Superintendent Donovan and other top school

---

*The fact that Marland had worked with business leaders while superintendent in Pittsburgh and, before then, in Winnetka probably helped make it possible for him to do so in New York.

†Barnes was particularly effective as a group leader in the "participative planning" sessions that were held at each partnership school, as well as at conceptualizing what the strategy of the partnerships should be. Organizational development refers to the use of social science findings and techniques to help organizations adapt better to their environment.

††Albert Shanker, president of the UFT, indicated to EDC in late 1968, at a private meeting to which they invited him, that from his point of view it would be best to intervene at the elementary school level. By the time students reached high school age, he argued, they were so deficient in basic skills that it was too late to help them.

§Michigan Bell's public relations staff had issued a press release after that corporation had begun a collaborative effort with a Detroit high school, de-

headquarters officials, including the high school office, to arrange for EDC's working with individual schools.*

These school officials arranged in late 1968 for EDC to meet with several high school principals, two of whom—those at James Monroe High School in the Bronx and Brandeis High School in Manhattan—seized the opportunity to work with EDC. Both were competent, innovation-minded, highly receptive to EDC's participative approach, and able to bring their school and its many constituencies along with them. Also, their schools had all the typical inner-city high school problems: overcrowding, high absenteeism and drop-out rates, serious retardation in reading and math, many students unable to use English effectively in regular school subjects, widespread use and dissemination of drugs, high rates of pupil suspensions, little student knowledge about work, future careers, and their requirements, and considerable apathy among students, parents, and teachers.

As soon as EDC arrived in the schools, IED conducted under Barnes's leadership what it referred to as "feasibility studies." This involved bringing all the main participants in the school, including the principal, teachers, students, parents, community organization officials, and EDC representatives, into a planning committee. The principal appointed either a teacher, a guidance counselor, or an administrator as school coordinator, and Barnes usually moderated.[10]

EDC and IED then did what they called a "needs analysis" of each school, encouraging the participants to identify what they saw as the main problems. They then established goals based on that; tried to rank them in order of importance; developed preliminary ideas about programs to achieve those goals, including procedures for their implementation, and talked about who would be responsible for what tasks and how they would get the necessary resources. "There were no closed doors," reported an EDC official. "The minutes of the meetings were circulated, and that helped a lot in further establishing our credibility."

There was considerable emphasis on "consensus seeking," and the main interest of EDC (as a result of IED's advice) was to get this process going in each school. As one social science–trained business executive on loan to EDC explained: "We were trying to create an

---

scribing the program. This had a very negative repercussion among some black community leaders, who then interpreted the program as just another attempt by a "white racist, establishment corporation" to improve its image.

*Marland and Donovan were colleagues, and IED had already had contact with New York City school officials through an earlier project on school decentralization.

R&D process in those schools where none had existed before, and to turn the school from a nobody-wins to a joint-payoff or everybody-wins situation."

Participants in these meetings felt good about the experience, indicating that communications within the school became more open after the partnership began. Implicit throughout was EDC's and IED's interest in working within the system and in avoiding any open, "Ocean Hill-Brownsville-type" confrontations.* EDC and IED were missionaries for change, but they were OD-type missionaries rather than militant reformers engaged in any kind of confrontation politics with the educators. [11] For EDC, the main purpose of these exploratory meetings was to see if business could establish a relationship with the schools and if, indeed, it made any sense to try.

The kinds of topics aired in the meetings were things the participants felt were wrong with their school and things they wanted changed or improved, including: overcrowding; poor school security; the need for reducing drug use; strengthening remedial reading and math programs; special classes and materials for non-English-speaking students; intramural and other student sports programs; more information about work, and more pre-employment counseling and work-study opportunities; a reduced clerical and administrative workload for teachers; better student-teacher communications; improved relations with community organizations, including employers; and better school management. For EDC and IED, the most important aspect of the sessions was the group problem-solving process that got energized rather than the substance of what was discussed.

The question was where to go from there. After four months of such feasibility studies, conducted in early 1969, IED wrote them up and presented them to the Education Subcommittee of EDC's Committee on Public Policy and to the schools. After the schools concurred in inviting EDC in—reviewing the decision with all their major constituencies—the Education Subcommittee recommended to the EDC board that it go ahead, at an estimated cost of up to $100,000 per school. The schools informed EDC of their decision in the spring of 1969, with the partnerships to begin the following September.†

---

*Ocean Hill-Brownsville was a ghetto area of Brooklyn where teachers and community groups came into bitter conflict in the fall of 1968 over an experiment in school decentralization.

†EDC emphasizes that it only became involved in these partnerships by invitation. As noted in its NIE proposal: "EDC required that the invitation come not only from the school principal, but also the faculty, the parent association, and the student government organization." NIE proposal, p. 4.

The process then went well enough in each of these schools that EDC and IED repeated it a year later, at the Board of Education's request, in Bushwick High School in Brooklyn and George Washington High School in Manhattan.† Both had the same kinds of problems that Brandeis and Monroe had, and George Washington was in desperate need of outside assistance. A few months after EDC did feasibility studies in these schools, it entered into partnerships with them as well. It was thus involved in four schools by the fall of 1970.

COMPONENTS, GOALS, AND STAGES IN ' THE PARTNERSHIP STRATEGY

EDC wanted to help develop better schools through this participative approach, but it was to struggle for many years, as did so many other reform groups, in trying to best achieve this. In retrospect, at least two strategies were rejected. First, the partnership schools were not to be "demonstration" schools, in the sense that the goal was to effect systemic changes in the school as an end in itself.

Second, these were not meant to be primarily experimental schools, though the program was certainly geared to improving them. But a broader goal, even in the early stages, was to identify methods of developing more effective programs in "need" areas, and then replicating them throughout the system. Beyond that, there was the hope that the entire approach might be useful to other school systems. IED and EDC thus regarded the schools mainly as trial sites or proving grounds for developing new educational programs, through a process modeled after what passes for R&D in the private sector.

The R&D strategy had two components. One was the process itself, conceptualized in the early stages as "participative planning" and later as "self-renewal"; the changing nomenclature was significant in describing the program's development. The second was the new products or educational programs that this process helped generate.

Stage One: Gaining Entree, Establishing EDC's Credibility

Notwithstanding the fact that EDC only gradually evolved a clear sense of what it wanted to do, we can in retrospect discern at least

†Actually, the board had requested that EDC go into ten schools, but EDC's board decided to proceed more deliberately and more intensively in fewer ones.

three main stages in the program's development. The earliest, continuing through the first few years, involved trying to establish an R&D process in the schools through "participative planning," and to develop new programs that groups inside or associated with the school saw as relevant to meeting critical needs. EDC had first, however, to establish a relationship. Some educators initially distrusted EDC, expressing the conventional liberal stereotypes about business—its profit-seeking outlook and its traditional concern for cost savings in government. These educators felt that EDC had little to offer them except more resources—which they were, of course, happy to receive, as long as there were no strings attached. Thus, one of the only ways EDC could prove itself in this early stage was to demonstrate its good will by providing money, equipment, jobs for students, and other resources that the educators said they so desperately needed.

Some school staff saw EDC, then, as an outside "Santa Claus"— an expression actually used by EDC and some school people. The more EDC provided such resources, the more it would gain the educators' acceptance.* Over the first year or so, EDC responded willingly to such requests, though even then mainly for projects related to the school plan that had been developed in the feasibility studies.† To illustrate: EDC brought in volunteer executives as tutors in one high school; it had an R&D budget to pay for consultants, for supplies, for rent in temporary facilities, for student trips, for sports team uniforms, and for curriculum and instructional materials used in remedial and "enrichment" programs; and it made available summer and part-time jobs as called for in the school plans. It also raised additional funds for larger projects—a career education program in one school, a remedial reading project in another, and an attendance program in all four.

These were all things that seemed to improve morale in the schools, and they may even have marginally improved student performance as well. But other outside groups could provide such resources, and if that was to be EDC's main contribution, the partnerships would hardly constitute a significantly new effort at change.

One other short-term perspective also dominated at this stage. Many of the early people on loan took the assignment because of a strong social orientation. "Several of the early people on loan were

---

*This tendency to see the infusion of more resources from the outside as a solution to agency problems was characteristic of many city agency officials, and posed problems wherever EDC worked.

†In the first year, however, EDC was not as insistent in scrutinizing whether the request fit the plan, because of its immediate need to increase its credibility.

oriented toward social service or were minority people themselves," explained one of their colleagues, "and they wanted to help these kids any way they could—get them tutors, jobs, or anything else they needed." Again, this practice was good in and of itself, but unless it fit into some larger change strategy, few positive, long-term effects would result. Some students would obviously be helped, but the school as an institution would not be enhanced. "After a while, I started telling some of our good-willed people on loan who were so eager to help these youngsters that they would make a more lasting impact by working with faculty and supervisors on programs that could lead to longer-term improvements in the school," reported a top EDC official. "I told them that I want to help the kids too, but what about those who will be there next year and the year after that? Unless we do something to help improve the school itself, the students will benefit only as long as we are there. And we can't stay there indefinitely. Furthermore, out of 3,000 to 4,000 students, how many can we reach directly? Very few, in any systematic way."

Over time, EDC gradually redefined its role. The tendency of some educators to view the infusion of more resources alone as a way of solving their problems made progress fairly slow; but they began to accept the notion that more resources was a means, not an end, and that the basic idea should be to apply problem-solving and management methods to improve the schools within existing resources. The educators gradually shifted to the concept of reallocating already available resources in accord with their own change strategies of how best to meet students' needs.

Stage Two: Developing Model Programs and Replicating Them in Other Schools

As the educators became more receptive to this R&D role, and as EDC began to more clearly envision an organizational development strategy, it moved into a new mode. This involved developing new educational programs through the participative planning process described above, with the intent of making them self-sustaining within the school and of replicating them in many other high schools throughout the city. Though a lot of EDC's early work was on developing model programs, that goal became much more explicit in late 1971, after EDC had gained greater acceptance. EDC and IED officials increasingly saw the four high schools at this time as testing sites. They often used the R&D language of industry in describing what they were doing, referring to their having gone through the early stages of product development and testing and getting ready for an intensive marketing to reach as many schools as possible. Even though the educators' acceptance of this more long-term goal was uneven, there was enough of it after a couple of years to allow EDC to continue.

A critical turning point was EDC's request to Chancellor Scribner in April 1972 that he provide release time from their regular assignments for teachers in the partnership schools to work on developing new programs. EDC and the schools had been successful until then in starting a planning process and in generating through it many new and needed programs. But the pace of generating such programs and having them implemented became painfully slow, after the early excitement of the experiment and of having EDC involved began to wear off. EDC and the schools began to feel enormously frustrated at their limited progress, even with well-intentioned teachers, and they realized that there was no way to make a significant dent in the schools' many problems without released time. EDC was also concerned about the imbalance between its commitment of personnel and that of the Board of Education.

Scribner did provide released time for the equivalent of two full-time teachers for each school, an arrangement that began in the fall of 1972. "That was a big breakthrough for us," recalled a top EDC official, "and it helped things move much more than ever before."

A wide range of educational programs consequently got developed. They dealt with career education; school administration and management; English as a second language; remediation in basic skills (math, reading, English); student motivation; and health. Many research and development projects got started on these matters, and we will be describing them below.

All of the projects dealt with critical student needs that had been inadequately addressed before the partnerships began. At first glance, they appear to be simply a series of individual programs, potentially beneficial in and of themselves, but initiated within a system which itself would have to be changed before any new programs could work.

While this is a reasonable view, and one that many school critics have taken, it doesn't lead anywhere. It argues that an incrementalism strategy like the partnerships cannot succeed, since the existing structure is so defective, and that that structure's major overhauling is needed instead. The last chapter analyzed extensively EDC's school headquarters task force projects, which were designed to do that. As we indicated there, the system-wide, structural change strategy also moves slowly over the short run. The question, then, is what to do in the meantime.

Perhaps some combination of the two might begin to work, and that was the direction in which the partnerships evolved. Instead of attempting to initiate the usual kind of incremental program change within a particular school, the partnerships began generating change with headquarters involvement.

The emerging goals of the partnerships in this second stage were to institutionalize a problem-solving process in four schools, develop self-sustaining model programs, and then replicate both the process and the programs in other schools. This might make the programs available to many more students and help develop an effective replication procedure as well. It might even contribute to improved headquarters–school relationships, as it became evident that existing ones hampered innovation in the schools.

That was, at least, the goal. The replication process, however, was uneven. School headquarters had never functioned as a service agency to provide technical assistance to individual schools, and it was slow to convert to that role in this instance. As long as EDC was just working in a few schools, it could be effective. When the issue became that of helping many more schools develop a research and development process and self-sustaining programs, and then having the school system replicate them elsewhere, headquarters participation became much more important.

Historically, school headquarters had functioned to enforce rules and procedures on schools, not to support new programs. EDC thus had to engage in the same organizational change process at headquarters that it had started in the schools, so that an effective replication mechanism might exist to make its programs available on demand throughout the system.

Actually, two main headquarters units had to be involved—the Division of High Schools and the many curriculum bureaus. As for the former, EDC reported that it had always been very supportive and had in recent years established an office to monitor and support innovative programs. Since the early 1970s, the High School Office had made funds available for the replication of several EDC-initiated programs. "The bureaus, by contrast," reported an EDC official, "were a mixed bag. Some supported and facilitated replication, while others were indifferent."

It turned out, however, that headquarters was not the main problem. "We learned that we couldn't count on replication, even within the partnership network and even if headquarters support and funds were made available," reported an EDC person. "Inducing change in schools, we found, takes more than a program and resources. After much analysis and reflection, we concluded that each school needed a process to shape its own future and that ownership of projects was essential."

Stage Three: The Self-Renewal Phase

It was on the basis of EDC's discovery in this second stage that change on a city-wide basis required creating a strong demand for it in each school that EDC moved on in late 1973 and 1974 to what it called a "self-renewal" strategy. The renewal process seemed to be working in each of the four partnership schools, but EDC was puzzled about how to spread it. The problem was not so much the bureaus and how some of them might slow down replication, but rather that demand had to originate in the schools themselves.

EDC's high school program director, Dr. Floyd Flom, and his program review committee first proposed the transition to the new strategy in an evaluation report they prepared for EDC's board in April 1973.[12] The principals of the four partnership schools also participated and reluctantly accepted that part of the plan calling for the removal of EDC's corporate on-loan people from the schools, to be replaced by a "renewal coordinator" chosen from the teacher ranks to direct the effort. Then in June 1973, Donald Barnes of IED and the teacher coordinator at George Washington High School prepared a document further supporting the shift, which described the participative planning process at the four schools.[13] It was a preliminary "how to do it" manual, indicating how a school could get such a process underway and drawing heavily from EDC's success at George Washington. That new stage represented, in EDC's words, "designing a replicable model of self-renewal processes for urban high schools," and the proposal to do this that was submitted to NIE in the spring of 1974 redirected the program. It did not, however, deal directly with the problem of headquarters' replication capabilities, partly since the proposal needed strong headquarters endorsement to be acceptable to NIE. At the same time, EDC was developing strategies to get more headquarters cooperation, and some of the changes that the EDC school headquarters task force had been able to effect seemed to produce more support than before for carrying out the program. For one thing, the Division of High Schools had much more autonomy to make decisions without having to defer to the chancellor.

The main components of the third stage, as outlined in EDC's proposal to NIE, involved: (1) the design of an improved self-renewal process in the four high schools; (2) getting it institutionalized there, without the necessity of EDC's continued full-time involvement; (3) installing it in up to six additional high schools; and (4) testing and refining it over the next three years "until it becomes a fully-replicable, appealing, convenient, low-cost operational model of self-renewal that can then be used more widely in New York City as well as nationwide."

EDC designed this self-renewal strategy to overcome two limitations of the partnerships. One was their dependence on EDC's keeping business people on loan at the schools. The other was the danger of the schools' becoming so dependent on EDC's presence that they might never develop on their own.

Several assumptions were basic to the new strategy. One was that many teachers were capable of developing new programs, but most weren't afforded the opportunity or resources to do so. That is, New York City high schools had an abundance of talent, but the system had never systematically engaged that talent at the school level to meet the needs of the changing student body. EDC thus discovered from its partnership experience what New York City educators and knowledgeable outsiders had long known: that creative teachers felt they had rarely been encouraged to innovate.

A second assumption was that the considerable talent in the system must be given the resources necessary to develop new programs. For teachers, this requires released time from the classroom and associated administrative tasks for developing and implementing new programs. (Teachers in New York City schools often have an enormous amount of administrative paperwork in addition to regular classroom assignments, giving them very little time or incentive to develop new programs.)

A third and related assumption was that by giving recognition to talented teachers and providing them with resources, the renewal process could help create a demand for new programs at the local school level that had not existed before. EDC's model for self-renewal was designed, then, to give recognition and resources to teachers interested in program development, in the hope of thereby stimulating increasing interest in such development over time. If teachers began to see that there were resources and time available for innovation, more of them might begin to engage in such activity.

EDC also spelled out the institutional arrangements and procedures necessary to allow teachers to function effectively in such an innovative role, based on its five years of experience in the partnerships: a full-time renewal coordinator with an office and an assistant; at least two and preferably more full-time positions to release selected teachers from instruction one or more periods a day for developmental programs; a school renewal planning committee, simi-

lar to the participative planning committees set up under the partnerships; and a later program review committee to guide implementation
after a plan had been developed. Other critical components included
a special renewal development budget and available consulting services from school headquarters.

This approach might then succeed to the extent that the educators were able to generate on their own a continuous self-renewal
process that, in turn, produced needed educational programs. As a
top EDC official explained: "The whole thing is developing their
own internal capability. We simply could not stay there forever. It
would be too difficult to justify economically. Even if we had only
one person from industry for each high school, that would still
require 96 people from industry. We couldn't get commitments for
that many, and we are convinced that people in the schools can do it
better than any outsiders could do it for them."

EDC is thus attempting to generate a model of self-renewal that
differs from the original partnerships mainly in that the process is
not dependent on the presence of several full-time people on loan
from EDC's member companies. As of September 1976, the model
was being tried out in sixteen inner-city high schools. EDC has made
available OD consultants from both industry and academia on a
once-a-week basis and as needed in each school, to work with the
principal, renewal coordinator, and other school staff members and
to act as an internal consultant and change agent.

IMPACT OF THE PARTNERSHIPS

It is too early to assess the impact of the self-renewal strategy. One
can, however, review in some depth the past experience of EDC in
the partnership schools. We will do so first by taking particular
schools as our units of analysis, indicating what resources EDC
brought to the situation and how they contributed to school
improvements.

We will not report on EDC's experiences in all the partnership
schools, but rather concentrate on three: Monroe High School in the
Bronx, Bushwick in Brooklyn, and George Washington in Manhattan.
Though these schools had many common problems, EDC's intervention in each school was distinctive enough to merit separate analysis.
The emphasis at Monroe was on the professional development of
teachers; that at Bushwick was on career education; while at George
Washington, EDC played a critical third-party mediator role in a
violence-ridden situation and then moved on to help initiate key

educational programs. Many interesting programs were also being developed at the fourth partnership school, Brandeis in Manhattan, which had, incidentally, one of the most highly acclaimed principals in the city. But no single theme or strategy was followed there that would give an analysis of the Brandeis case any broader significance. The same could be said of EDC's involvement in the two junior high schools.

The partnership program had several components. From 1969 through 1974, when the self-renewal phase began, $3.7 million was spent on the project.* This involved the services of 55 separate on-loan people, serving a total of 64 person-years. Thirty of the 55 people were black and 4 others were Hispanic. (Fourteen were women.) These minority people, particularly the men, constituted role models for the students. This was a dedicated group who found much satisfaction in the assignment.†

Each of the four partnership schools had an EDC office, managed by a teacher/coordinator from the school along with a director from among the on-loan people. In the first couple of years, there were usually four to five on-loan people at each school, with the number decreasing as EDC moved into the self-renewal phase.

The people on loan functioned largely as project managers, following through on particular programs that were part of the school's overall plan. That plan had, in turn, been arrived at through the participatory process already outlined.

The high school program had a different kind of structure than the other EDC agency projects, which were run through task forces. The EDC director (to be distinguished from on-loan directors in each school) was Dr. Floyd Flom, a former professor of political science and an executive at General Electric, who brought to the project a strong interest in Management by Objective (MBO) approaches to organizational problem solving.

Flom, in turn, formed an advisory council consisting of four high-level corporate staff people who were all themselves either educators or academicians. They constituted a group of "corporation intellectuals" who helped EDC and Flom constantly review the entire project, evaluate results in each school, and provide assistance as needed. Each also took on responsibility for supporting and

---

*This included EDC, Board of Education, and foundation contributions. Another $1.4 million went into self-renewal from July 1974 through June 1976.

†Many lived in the city, and some were so committed to this work that they would often talk with one another about their experiences, trying to see how the program could be expanded.

monitoring an individual school, including recruiting on-loan people and directors.

A final component was EDC's paid consultant, the Institute for Educational Development. It helped in gaining EDC entree to Superintendent Donovan and then into the high schools themselves. It also did research on business–school partnerships. And it later served in an active staff capacity, helping to run the participative planning sessions in the schools, doing studies on national curriculum developments, bringing in many new educational programs and university consultants, helping develop proposals, and evaluating individual programs.

Flom and EDC had thus brought together an array of outside consultants and staff, and his role was largely one of organizing and orchestrating their work. Since his and their roles were developed through the project's participative management approach, the EDC structure for the high schools project was more decentralized than were the task forces. Broad policy decisions were made by Champion, Flom, his council, and IED, but the on-loan people, teacher coordinators, and educators at each school had much flexibility to pursue what they regarded as the highest-priority issues facing them.

Monroe

One of the first schools EDC became involved in was James Monroe, located in a transitional area in the mid-Bronx. Historically, Monroe was a community high school, with many of its present teachers as well as their parents having been students there and having lived in the area. It had served a white, middle-class population, largely Jewish and Italian, but had changed markedly in the 1960s.*

The main change was a steady increase in black and Puerto Rican students from poverty homes. As recently as 1958, 85 percent of the students were white. By 1969, the school had changed to one almost evenly divided among black, Puerto Rican, and white students. In 1975, there were only 5 percent whites, with the majority of students Puerto Rican. The school and the area around it, then, were

---

*The school boasts many graduates who are now city-wide and national celebrities and has their pictures prominently displayed on the first floor. It had a fiftieth-anniversary celebration in the fall of 1975 with many of these people attending, thereby renewing the sense of community pride and identification with the school that had waned in recent years, with ethnic changes in the area.

obviously in a state of rapid transition when EDC arrived in 1969. The school had a very high student transiency rate and one of the highest teacher turnover and transiency rates of any high school in the borough. Expenditures per pupil were among the lowest, and the school also had a serious problem of overcrowding, housing close to 4,500 students with a capacity of only 2,000.

At the same time, Monroe was clearly not the worst-off high school in the Bronx. Its distinguished history, along with the fact that it still had some very good staff and programs and that its immediate neighborhood was not yet an impacted ghetto like the South Bronx made it possible for EDC to have some impact.

Key Variables

Through a set of fortuitous circumstances, all of them relevant in terms of their implications for effective replication elsewhere, EDC had a significantly positive intitial impact on the school.* Those circumstances included: (1) the first two *EDC directors*, who were both highly personable and established close relationships with faculty, students, and other participants in the school; along with some outstanding *early EDC staff*; (2) a deep involvement by *Citibank*, led by *Dr. Norman Willard*, a psychologist and management development expert who started a major teacher development program and brought in many of his own staff and other bank resources; (3) *a strategically located office* (near the students' and teachers' cafeterias), with a warm and open atmosphere (refreshments and phone always available, along with counseling for students and educational materials for teachers); (4) a highly effective *office manager* of Puerto Rican background who had been president of the parents association, was very influential in local school and community organizations, and lived in the area; and (5) a small *core group of dedicated teachers*. Other, less important conditions were the *teacher coordinator*, who, though not very dynamic, had good personal relations throughout the faculty and identified strongly with EDC; the support of the local union leadership; and the *acting principal*, who gave EDC the freedom to pursue innovative projects, even though he did not publicly back them at first.

---

*I use the term "initial" because the program was to sag quite appreciably after a few years. A summary of the Monroe experience that contains many insightful observations and interpretations of what went on in the first three years of the partnership appears in *EDC-Monroe, A Three-Year Evaluation*, by Dr. Robert S. Lee, February 1972. Lee is a social psychologist who spent a year on loan at Monroe from IBM. The comments to follow draw heavily on his paper, as well as on other documents and interviews with key participants.

The first EDC director at Monroe was a charismatic black law-yer from Equitable Life who developed instant rapport with many minority students. He also reached those teachers who were still trying to develop new programs. One of the most important things he did was to recruit the office manager mentioned above, who had enormous influence in school affairs, interceding with school officials to gain acceptance of new programs, securing local jobs for Monroe students, through private employers and community organizations, and informally counseling many students with per-sonal problems. Her student contacts and the many school projects that she organized and ran—such as concerts and athletic events—enhanced the entire program. She became, in effect, another proj-ect director and was the only person who provided continuity at the school level.

Many of the early EDC staff on loan at Monroe were minority people themselves, and that also helped. "We were living witnesses for a lot of those kids," reported one of them, "who had made it ourselves and had come in from industry to help."

A critical figure from the corporate world was Dr. Norman Willard, a member of Flom's advisory group. Monroe was Willard's school, and he and the bank were deeply involved there. He helped put together a proposal for federal (U.S. Office of Education) fund-ing of a teacher development center there that became one of the school's main long-term innovations.

Willard also recruited the second EDC director for Monroe, a young staff person in his department at the bank who was very competent in management training and organizational development and had the same strong commitment of many other on-loan people to helping minority youth. He and Dr. Robert Lee, the social psychol-ogist from IBM, were two of the most effective on-loan people EDC had recruited; and they, along with the first director, Willard, and the office manager, were critical to the partnership's early successes.*

Perhaps most symbolic of the spirit that prevailed at Monroe during the first two or three years of the partnership was the role of the EDC office. It became a focal point of continued developmental activity, functioning as a communications center within the school and providing assistance to many students and teachers. The commu-nications and guidance functions were filled in a spontaneous and unplanned way, indicating how strong a need there was for both that the school itself had not met.

*Monroe teachers kept contacting this second director for advice on school programs and strategy long after he had returned to the bank, indicating what a critical supportive role he had played while he was there.

The Monroe office functioned particularly well as a research and development laboratory, something the school had never had before. "R&D in the New York City schools is impossible," reported an on-loan person at Monroe. "The R is terrible where it exists, and the D is done by publishers. The people closest to the problem, the teachers, are given no freedom. Their prep periods are just kaffeeklatsches. Within the schools there is always a small minority, say 20 percent, who can develop lots of new programs, but they have no support. We were the only people in the building whose full-time job was trying to figure out how to make the place better. The principal, department chairmen, and teachers didn't have time, with all their administrative tasks and [their] being caught up in the petty internal politics of the schools. We knew something about how to manage an improvement, how to do strategic planning and engage in continual re-examination of programs."

The informal integrative function of the office was also critical to improving the school's performance. As one active parent reported: "Before EDC arrived, most communication within the school was not fruitful. The newsletter of the principal was just teacher talk and nothing that had meaning to parents or students. There was little communication across departments and very little between parents and teachers, let alone between students and the school." The EDC office did help change that in those first few years, through new programs that provided something for people to talk about. As Lee wrote: "The EDC office has been a much needed source of professional stimulation. . . . Through EDC [the teachers] have become aware of new ideas in education—there have been people they could talk to, books, journals, educational games, workshops, and seminars. . . . here they have found a variety of educational resources. . . . The EDC office has been a catalyst—a major source of information about what is going on in education outside of the school—in business, at universities, and in other schools in and around the city. It has also been an informal communications channel linking together teachers, students, parents, and the administration. The principal, for example, pointed out that he often obtained feedback from the EDC office on things that he didn't know about from other sources. In this way, EDC has helped to knit the school together while at the same time it has made it easier for teachers to learn about and try new ideas."

Professional Development

A main theme in the Monroe partnership was the professional development of teachers. Under the leadership of Willard and his colleagues, EDC decided that efforts at long-term development there would be most effective if they concentrated on teachers. The office manager and EDC people on loan did not give up on serving students, and the informal counseling and guidance activity continued, but there was much more effort to help teachers develop new methods and curriculum. "The operation became focused around teachers," reported one business person on loan, "with the general approval and consent of the principal. 'If you can sell it to the teachers,' he said, 'I will go along with it.' And we were able to do that."

The teacher development program started with a weekend seminar on "problem solving" in the spring of 1971, attended by twenty-two teachers, the former principal, Willard, several training staff people he brought with him from the bank, and Flom, the program director. Referred to as the "Willard weekend," the seminar was publicized in advance in the school and drew roughly 10 percent of the total teaching staff.

The central theme of the weekend sessions was that the teacher's role might be similar to that of a manager in the private sector and that the concepts and skills used by the latter might apply to effective classroom management. "We demonstrated to them that their role was much like that of the first-line supervisor," reported a Citibank staff person. "This did not make them management, quite, but close to it. So the Citibank people went through all the usual management training stuff about setting behavioral objectives, behavioral modification, motivation, allocation of time, planning, controlling, organizing, evaluating, all this sort of thing."

The teachers responded very positively to the sessions, and some even began to apply the concepts and techniques discussed. "They saw the relevance of much of this for classroom management," reported one of Willard's staff who was an EDC director, "and they really began to use it in their own classes. It was a conversion experience for some of them." The fact that the approach made the teachers feel more like autonomous professionals and much less like the functionaries the system had always defined them as was one of the main reasons it was so successful. Willard and his group were suggesting a new organizational model for the schools that, if implemented, might have far-reaching effects on teacher performance.

This was in April 1971, and though it was near the end of the school year, teachers made many requests to the EDC group in the school for further training and back-up support. "Twenty teachers came back to us," reported the director, "and began to ask how they could begin to write behavioral objectives for their classes. 'Now that you stimulated us over the weekend, give us the tools we need to make it work,' they were saying. One of them even said to us: 'You know, I feel just like an AA. I have gone to all these sessions and I agree with the approach, but when I get back there in the classroom I'll be all alone, and I don't have a chance in hell of actually doing it. I am so isolated.' "

These insights—(1) that teachers felt professionally isolated from recent developments in education and from one another;[14] (2) that they felt like functionaries on an assembly line rather than professionals; (3) that some felt they got little support for innovation from their department chairmen; and (4) that the supervisory training techniques of the private sector were applicable to managing the classroom—led to the idea of establishing a teacher (professional) development center at Monroe. That summer Willard, with one of his top staff people; Oscar Dombrow, the former Monroe principal; and Flom, put together a proposal for funding such a center, got the necessary Board of Education signatures, and took it to the Office of Education. They received a $300,000 grant for the project, $100,000 for each of the first three years. There was some initial planning at the school in the 1971-72 academic year, and the program got underway in July 1972, when the money arrived.

Four teachers were selected as the first group to be trained and to run the center, and the circumstances of their selection revealed strong teacher interest. Monroe teachers elected ten colleagues from a larger list of applicants, and the principal selected four from among the group. It was the largest teacher turnout for an election ever recorded at Monroe, with roughly 195 of the school's 225 teachers voting. With the phasing out of the EDC office under self-renewal, the center, referred to as the Educational Applications and Assistance Group (EAAG), eventually became the main R&D unit within the school.

School Morale

Another contribution of the partnership was a series of specific morale-building activities that markedly improved the atmosphere of the school. They included reviving the school newspaper, intramural and team sports, assembly programs, outings, and other extracurricular activities. A visit to the school by the Harlem Globetrotters, a concert there by Tito Puente, and weekend geology field trips were among the more dramatic of these activities. In addition, EDC sponsored a widely used tutoring program for students, helped expand participation in the school's evening community center for adult education, and stimulated some increase in parents association membership, even though it was difficult to get high attendance at meetings.* "All these were small, nonthreatening things that did not

*Parents of high-school-age students tend to be much less active in school affairs than those with younger children.

add up to a program," reported one of the active EDC people on loan to Monroe at this time, "but they helped a lot in developing a better school spirit and more warmth."

Perhaps most typical of the feeling toward EDC and the partnership in this early period was a graffiti on the wall near the first-floor elevator that read "EDC is all together." EDC had thus gained strong acceptance within the school by helping start some important new activities that gave hope to staff members and students for the first time in many years. One EDC person on loan referred to the "lifeboat effect" of this process, whereby a small cadre of roughly twenty teachers began, with EDC help, to reinforce one another in their search for better programs.* Lee even described the school as having a "hothouse plant" atmosphere at this time (1970–72), so numerous were the innovative programs that were generated. To be sure, only a small proportion of staff members were involved, but a process of innovation seemed to have begun.

While the above descriptions might seem like mere hyperbole on the part of a "true believer" participant in that process, an improved school climate was generated and many new programs did take place.† They included an anti-drug program in which students, under the guidance of a teacher released full time to serve as drug coordinator, provided counseling assistance for their peers;†† the use of simulation games in social studies classes and in other subjects; the development of an English as a Second Language (ESL) program for the school's many non-English-speaking students, with EDC's office becoming a "second home" for them; the tutoring; an Operation Call-Up program in which paraprofessionals phoned parents in the evenings to discuss the absence of their children from school; various remedial reading and math programs; and some programs in vocational and career education. These programs reflect a significant short-term accomplishment in that they provided more educational services in a school whose rapid demographic changes had created many problems.

There was some question, however, as to whether these improvements could become institutionalized, given the many constraints that the school continued to face even after the partnership had begun.

---

*The "lifeboat" metaphor refers to the fact that innovative teachers were finally receiving support from colleagues and supervisors within the school for their work.

†No systematic baseline data on school performance exist to assess the program's impact. And EDC's goal was not to change the entire school.

††The program had such positive effects on some drug-using students that it soon served as a model for a city-wide program in many other high schools.

System-wide Obstacles

Many of the debilitating constraints that had contributed so much to the school's low morale at the time the partnership began, however, continued to operate. One was the school's accelerated changes in pupil composition, from roughly one-third black, one-third Hispanics, and one-third "other" (mostly white middle-class) in 1969 to virtually 100 percent minority, most from poverty homes, by 1975. The weight of the increasing number of such students, who required so much extra assistance that many teachers and department chairmen were not prepared to provide and didn't have the resources to provide, continued to cast a pall over the school. Unless EDC could do more than develop some programs and improved school spirit, it would be difficult to sustain the innovations and optimism that clearly prevailed in its first few years.

Another problem was that EDC began to see the futility of having the school perpetually dependent on its resources and presence to sustain these innovations. Starting in 1972, it began phasing down its staff involvement in each school, as released time became available. The EDC office that had begun with five people on loan had only three by 1973.

Then there were many institutional obstacles to maintaining an innovative climate and programs at Monroe. As Lee wrote in 1972, "The system tends to turn off the idealism, the hope, and the spirit of its teachers. Many of them become coasters who put in their time with minimal effort. In their experience, nothing seems to work. Inevitably, the students are blamed for the failure of the system. . . . The resignation mentality that so often develops in teachers leads to a lack of hope which, of course, precludes both drive and concentrated effort."

Beyond that, the structure of the entire system—its rigidity, its protectionism, its functioning for the convenience of those who ran it, and the absence of any adequate management or merit system—made it difficult to sustain the improvements that the partnership had helped establish. EDC succeeded in spite of this, but when its support waned, these constraints began to limit the development work that had gone on. Some of Lee's observations described the process well:

> Because the school system is extremely inflexible, it is very difficult to succeed with any program, no matter how educationally valuable, if that program requires any deviation from established structures and procedures.

> Frozen institutions tend to be run for the convenience of those who run them. We saw many examples of this—the keeping of fixed desks in the classroom, prep (mini-school) teachers doing clerical work they would otherwise have to do at home rather than helping EDC run simulations and

learning how to do this themselves as agreed upon, etc. Schools are administered, not managed—there is no focus of energy and talent on the major
problems. Instead, there is almost an exclusive concern with keeping things
going and avoiding trouble.

There is, in effect, no results orientation and no concept of investing time
and money in terms of anticipated payout in student learning. . . . The
system is unable to drop traditional programs that are obvious failures. It is
also unable to exploit its own successes. . . . New Programs are often tried,
but without adequate resources, planning, or teacher training. . . . This leads
to the dropping of the program with the feeling that "we tried that," when,
in actuality, the new programs never had a chance and very well may have
worked out brilliantly, given the proper conditions.

These perceptive comments by a strong advocate of the partnership
approach indicate how difficult it is to sustain an adaptive, innovative climate in an inner-city high school.

One disappointment was the early experience of the teacher
development center. Though it had received a grant of $300,000
from the Office of Education, a retrenchment in that agency's
budget led to a termination of the grant after the first year's
$100,000 was received. The executive director of the division of high
schools then provided roughly $50,000 for several years thereafter,
allowing Monroe to have two teachers working there full-time,
instead of the four that would have been there under the Office of
Education grant. However, the budget crisis of 1975–76 forced even
this allowance to be eliminated in September 1975.

Several problems developed in the first year of the center, hampering its progress. One related to who had power and authority over
its operations, and another to the limited skills of the teachers
involved. None had had any previous training in running such a
professional development center. Though they were widely
acclaimed within the school as outstanding teachers, they needed
much guidance in order to effectively assume this new role. "They
feel they have no direction, no educational design or philosophy, and
they would like to have one," reported an EDC person on loan.
"They come down to the bank (Citibank) to see Jim (a former EDC
director at Monroe), but Willard is ultimately responsible for keeping
the thing together. He was the person who conceived it. But he
doesn't want to interfere too much, because it is, after all, the school's
program and not his."

Still another problem was that the department chairmen had not
been involved in the selection of the center's teachers and had no
authority over them, and hence did not see the center as "their
thing." The fact that the center was developing new programs to do
what they were supposed to be doing also bothered them.

The picture we get of the Monroe partnership, then, is one of much early promise and hope, followed by a period of decline, as EDC resources diminished. After the first few years EDC was searching for a different mode of operations, not only at Monroe, but in all of the partnership schools. Even during that period of decline, however, from late 1972 through the beginning of the self-renewal stage in September 1974, EDC was still involved with the school, and some positive things were happening. The teacher center recovered from its early floundering, owing in part to the intervention of an evaluation group from the City University, who pressed the center's four teachers to clarify their goals. "This evaluation team was very tough on the four teachers," reported Willard, "telling them that their goals were much too soft and vague. Reluctantly at first, they let the group in, and now they are grateful. It has helped them a lot."

Soon, as word got around Monroe and other Bronx high schools that such a center actually existed, it began reaching more teachers. It had an ERIC (Educational Research Information Center) library of newly developed programs that teachers found helpful. It sponsored a course at Pace College on classroom management techniques for teachers and on methods for finding out about new programs. It developed some reading, math, and guidance programs at Monroe; and despite its slow start, it had begun to replace the EDC office. (As EDC steadily decreased the number of people on loan, its office was being phased out.) Most important, it had worked out an arrangement through which each department chairman who had not been involved in its formation was assigned one of the four teachers for research and development support. As a result of a big turnover among chairmen, with the newcomers more willing to collaborate; of the new principal's increasing reliance on the center for educational assistance; and of the increasing skills (administrative and educational) of the center's teachers, it began to assume an important role within the school. It conducted workshops on new programs and techniques, many of which it was initiating, and they attracted more teacher interest than in the past.

The ESL program was another important innovation that had survived. Established under the guidance of a Puerto Rican EDC director who persuaded dissatisfied Hispanic students to present a 2,000-signature petition instead of picketing the school to express their dissatisfaction with instruction, the program was pulled out of the Speech Department and expanded to serve increasing numbers of students and then set up its own office, with its own coordinator and Spanish-speaking guidance counselors. The office became a home within the school for many Spanish-speaking students, and its coordinator, one of the few Puerto Rican staff members in the school, was widely acclaimed as having done a very effective job.

Moreover, the main efforts of the last EDC director, who served in 1973, were to institutionalize as many programs as possible so that they could run on their own, without any further assistance from EDC. This has apparently been the case with Operation Call-Up, the intramural program, the drug program, the ESL program, and the teacher development center. EDC's success in 1972 in getting a commitment from the Board of Education for two full-time teacher positions for development programs, in addition to the two teachers at the center, further helped boost morale among school staff, at a time when it had declined.*

In contrast to EDC's consulting at school headquarters and in the courts, most of the substantive improvements at Monroe did not involve management transfer. The entire project was a management transfer one, however, in the sense that EDC had brought to the school an R&D process quite prevalent in business.

The particular theme at Monroe was teacher development. One of the main insights of Willard, his staff members, and other people on loan was the dedication and talent that they had found among teachers. "I came out of this thing with a lot of respect for many teachers," reported one on-loan person. "After working with them, I feel that many are receptive to and desirous of change and do care. That came after our weekend program and was the basis for our developing the proposal for a center."

In conclusion, though there was a noticeable decline in spirit at Monroe after the euphoria of the first couple of years, it emerged once again in the self-renewal stage with some of the same hopes as before. As of early 1975, the teacher development center had become a research and development arm for the school as well as a resource for high school teachers throughout the Bronx. It has changed its mission, however, from one of generating individual projects on its own to that of serving as a catalyst, stimulating others to develop projects. It has conducted many workshops for Monroe teachers, helped them in proposal writing, and trained them to search for better curriculum and instructional materials. As an active teacher at Monroe reported in early 1975: "I can only tell you that we have now generated a sense of excitement about getting educational improvements that is spreading throughout the school. Though the teacher center was slow in starting, it is now getting many

---

*Most of the time allotted for these two positions was for the ESL and remedial reading programs, both of which met critical student needs.

teachers and other staff involved. It is true that the initial excitement that came with the EDC involvement wore off after awhile. But we have it again even without EDC's presence in the school, and what EDC has done here is more than just another program. One of the biggest problems before was that classroom teachers felt left out, felt that nobody cared about their ideas and problems. We've given them hope. The principal is now more on top of things in the school. And the department chairmen are very involved in the renewal activity. We are now more integrated into the school than the teacher center was originally. The principal has now made us central to the entire planning and program development in the school. I have a lot of hope for what we can accomplish here in the future."

Bushwick

After EDC had been at Monroe in the Bronx and Brandeis High School in Manhattan for a year, the Board of Education asked it to move into ten more schools. EDC was very reluctant to expand the program that quickly, but it did add two more schools in September 1970. The criteria for selecting the schools were that they had the typical inner-city problems that Monroe and Brandeis faced and that their principals wanted EDC in. Four principals were interviewed, and Bushwick in Brooklyn and George Washington High School in Manhattan were selected. "We had a meeting at IED," explained the Bushwick principal, "and four principals were there, with all their high schools under consideration. I made my case on how much help our school needed, and maybe I talked faster and more convincingly than the others, because they chose us over them."*

Located in northeast Brooklyn, opposite the Lower East Side area of Manhattan, Bushwick, like Monroe, has always been a community high school. Indeed, 97 percent of its students in the 1970–71 academic year come from within the district, which represented one of the highest local enrollments of any high school in the city. It had traditionally served a stable working- and lower-middle-

*EDC's choice of Bushwick was largely due to its being located in Brooklyn, according to an EDC official present at the meeting. Another criterion sometimes mentioned at EDC was Bushwick's accessibility by public transportation from midtown Manhattan: it was located just a few blocks from a subway stop. George Washington was picked over the other two schools, Evander Childs in the Bronx and Haaren in Manhattan, because it was by far the most troubled school of the lot. Childs, by comparison, had more of a middle-class student body, and Haaren, an all-boys school, seemed less typical in that respect of New York City academic high schools with which EDC was involved.

class German, Irish, and Italian community but had other ethnic groups (Poles, Slavs, Czechs) as well, living primarily in small one-, two-, and three-family stone houses.*

Some time in the fifties, the Bushwick area experienced the same kinds of ethnic succession that the area south of Monroe had, with decaying housing and a very substantial influx of blacks and later of Puerto Ricans and Haitians. The ethnic composition of the school kept changing as a result, and by 1970, when EDC came in, the student body was only 18 percent white, as compared to 45 percent Puerto Rican and 37 percent black. Since then, the proportion of whites has decreased to 6 percent, while that of Puerto Ricans has increased to almost 60 percent.

Reflecting in large part these changes in its student body, Bushwick had the usual array of problems mentioned above. Like Monroe, it was a "respectable" middle-class school that had changed rapidly in ethnic composition, but did not yet appear to have either the very negative reputation or the severe pathologies of some of the city's ghetto high schools.†

Bushwick did have one neighborhood problem when EDC arrived: namely, its isolation from the surrounding community. This resulted from the fact that Bushwick was a minority school in a transitional area that still had many white (lower-middle-class) shop-keepers and elderly residents. As one EDC on-loan person to Bush-wick reported: "The first thing I did when I arrived there was to walk around the neighborhood. I went down one side street and saw these old women, some of them scrubbing the sidewalks and some just sitting out on the stoops. A couple of blocks away you would see some of the rundown houses where the newer Puerto Rican families lived, and around the corner was the ninth-grade school annex, with all those black and Puerto Rican kids. I wasn't surprised to find that these old people feared the kids."

Indeed, both the shopkeepers and the older white residents felt some apprehension and hostility toward minority students, who perhaps reflected for them the area's decline and whom they hoped might be contained in a custodial manner, much like the white students of a previous era. Regardless of whether these feelings were

---

*Bushwick was once one of the best-known of Brooklyn's many ethnic communities, with big German breweries and small machine shops as its hallmarks, along with a quite famous semiprofessional baseball team—the Bushwicks—that was widely acclaimed throughout the country.

†Such as, for example, Boys High in the Brownsville area of Brooklyn; Benjamin Franklin in East Harlem; Morris in the South Bronx; and Franklin K. Lane in East New York.

based on racist attitudes, generational differences, or some combination of the two, they contributed to the limited relationship between the school and the community.

Several critical incidents illustrate how this hurt the school. Some relate to its ninth-grade annex, a converted office building located several blocks from the main school. The annex was acquired because of the school's overcrowding, but it took a long time before the Board of Education could get it, and there were problems of community apprehension after it opened.* "You get the feeling right away," one EDC person on loan reported, "that the business people and the older whites in the neighborhood felt the annex students were an alien breed in their community, and these people easily took offense at any little incident. When the annex put out its garbage like any other institution would, since the students had to eat lunch and there had to be garbage, right away you could hear the complaints about 'those' people and 'their' garbage."

Another incident involved attempts to secure a community facility for a mini-school for roughly 125 chronic truants who had been unable to "make it" in the regular school. Elsewhere in the city outside mini-schools had been set up, but that didn't happen at Bushwick. Efforts to secure such a facility involved continuous confrontation with community groups and agencies. One effort involved a vacated Metropolitan Life Insurance Company office in neighboring Fort Greene. "We were just ready to occupy it the next week," reported the mini-school head, "when community leaders turned against us, including a priest and, believe it or not, a junior high school principal, whose school was nearby and who I guess thought our kids would be a bad influence on his."

A second attempt involved a day care center in Bushwick that school officials found out was to become available. "Even though many of our mini-school students were working there as volunteers," reported the mini-school director, "the head of the center refused to allow us in"†

EDC's entry into Bushwick followed much the same course as in the other partnership schools. The principal played a very active role in getting EDC in, and the faculty voted on it, after IED and EDC had conducted participative planning sessions over the 1970-71 school year. In contrast to the other schools, however, several

---

*EDC helped Bushwick exert pressure on school headquarters officials when the latter seemed to be delaying acquisition of the building.

†Bushwick finally got access in 1975 to a recently vacated Catholic school in the community. By September 1975, however, budget cuts had eliminated the mini-school.

teachers were very vocal in their opposition. They were concerned about a business "takeover," about the possibility of changes that would threaten their jobs, and particularly about their being evaluated by efficiency-minded executives who knew little about their school. A few stated that they opposed it because they disliked the principal. If he wanted it, they didn't want him to have it. The majority, however, were either neutral or favorable, and the principal pushed it through.

One of the things that then happened at Bushwick, similar to what went on at Monroe, was the conversion of many skeptical teachers by their more receptive peers or through their observation of and contact with the EDC on-loan people. The program review committee, for example, kept getting new teachers in attendance at its monthly meetings. As one teacher recalled: "When EDC's coming in was first broached, about ten teachers were strongly against it. Most have since changed their minds, and one even wrote a proposal through EDC. They changed their minds partly because of what EDC did when it came in, and mainly because of what those of us who were in favor of EDC told them about how it was helping the school." EDC won the teachers' confidence by providing resources (released time, money, curriculum development materials) for those who wanted to develop new programs and acknowledging their capacity to do so. Though it monitored their activities, it did so in a supportive way, giving them a lot of freedom to pursue projects on their own. This meant a lot to many teachers, as a recognition of their professional worth.

One characteristic of Bushwick that distinguished it from Monroe was the style of its principal. Beginning in 1970, Monroe had two acting principals, both former department chairmen, and though they were receptive to EDC and supported many of its programs, neither exercised much personal leadership while serving in that acting capacity. The second was a dedicated person with much empathy for the students and respect for his staff, and once appointed as principal, he supported innovative programs more actively. Still, he ran the school in an informal and relaxed manner.

By contrast, the Bushwick principal was a very dominant figure in his school and exercised strong leadership, having been principal there for five years before EDC arrived. As a result Bushwick was a well-run and well-organized school, with a minimum of disruption and chaos. The principal appeared to some school staff members, students, and outsiders, however, to be authoritarian in his leadership style, and he was certainly much more so than his counterparts at Monroe.

For all his authoritarian style, however, the Bushwick principal ran his school in a way that made it quite receptive to innovation. He had high standards along with a desire to have his school be a showcase, and that made him eager to accept EDC's help. He also supported his small cadre of dedicated and competent teachers, who, like their counterparts at Monroe, became key figures in developing the new programs that EDC supported. Moreover, the fact that he ran a structured and well-managed school meant that new programs were likely to be implemented efficiently. He was also quite entrepreneurial, coming up with some new program ideas on his own. He thus contributed to making Bushwick one of the more effective of the four partnership schools.

Key Variables

There were several positive factors in the Bushwick experience, in addition to (1) this principal and (2) some outstanding teachers who engaged in much of the early developmental activity. They included: (3) a well-organized, dedicated, and perpetually cheerful teacher coordinator who was liaison to the EDC staff and was its link to the school; (4) some effective EDC directors and people on loan; (5) the active involvement of a top staff person from IED; and (6) the establishment and continuation, at the principal's suggestion, of a program review committee that met every month to assess current projects and give constant impetus to the development of new ones.

Like Monroe, Bushwick had a small but important group of outstanding teachers who formed the nucleus for the developmental activity that was generated there. As one black business person on loan commented: "The thing that was particularly impressive about Bushwick was the many dedicated teachers there who were eager to work with the kids. The students felt that the teachers cared, and there was no sense of resentment that they were almost all white teachers in the school."

Each of these teachers took on responsibility for a particular program. Thus, one became the EDC coordinator, another was the head of the mini-school, another worked on developing the main career education course, and still another became the career education coordinator for the ninth grade.* Several reported how isolated they had felt before EDC arrived and how much of a boost it had

---

*This reflected the pattern in all four partnership schools of on-loan people being project managers taking on responsibility for one or more parts of the school plan, in collaboration with teachers who did much of the curriculum development work.

been. One of the most competent, the director of the mini-school, who lived in the area, commented: "I felt alone here for a long time before EDC brought us together. We always felt we were encroaching on the rest of the school, with other teachers not having much feeling for our kids and giving us little support. But EDC brought us together. Also, they helped come up with many new ideas and a lot of support."

The teacher coordinator was also important. Having served in that capacity since the second year of the partnership, she was a good administrator and constituted a strategic link between EDC and the school, especially with the principal. Moreover, she provided a strong element of continuity, much like the Puerto Rican parent and office manager at Monroe, as EDC directors and other on-loan people changed over time. She played a particularly prominent role in managing the program review committee, which was so critical to the partnership's success.

The EDC directors and people on loan provided a significant input as well. The first director was a black personnel supervisor from Irving Trust, under whose leadership many EDC-stimulated programs began. He was particularly sensitive to the needs of minority students and to improving the school's community relations, especially with business. The second, from Metropolitan Life, conscientiously pursued many programs. He had excellent relationships with teachers and department chairmen and helped pick up the school from its relatively slow start. He, in turn, was succeeded by a black accountant from General Motors who had been on loan for over a year at George Washington, and who did an outstanding job there and at Bushwick. He and his successor, a black psychologist on loan from IBM, both lived nearby, and both combined an extensive experience in business with an understanding of minority-student and local school problems. The psychologist was a specialist in vocational and manpower training, and she was able to help develop local jobs as related to career education programs within the school. In brief, Bushwick had many competent people on loan, often with expertise in fields important for the school's development.

Then there was the active assistance of the top staff person from IED, Dr. Virginia Newton. Assigned as its consultant to EDC, she was particularly involved at Bushwick because of its career emphasis, attending most of the program review committee meetings and helping the school on other projects as well. She also brought in Teachers College faculty members and a graduate student who were specialists in counseling, to help develop a career education program. A specialist herself in guidance and vocational education, she provided much advice in these fields.

Finally, a key to Bushwick's effectiveness was the early establishment, at the principal's suggestion, of a planning committee that met every month to review R&D efforts to implement various components of the school plan. It included teachers, students, department chairmen, the principal, and EDC and IED representatives, and was also open to other outsiders. With its monthly meetings usually attended by fifteen to twenty people, it soon became the main vehicle within the school for program development. Program directors and teachers involved in new programs would report on their work at these meetings, and the fact that they would be reporting to their colleagues on a scheduled date was often an incentive to them to get more done, so that they could report more progress.

Such a monthly planning meeting was not established in the other three schools. Once the first feasibility study and plan for school improvement was completed in those schools, the participative planning group was dissolved and the partnership program was placed under a school council, usually called the school consultative council, where progress reports and program reviews were conducted. (It did not engage, however, in the systematic program review and planning that the Bushwick planning committee did.) For whatever reasons, some having to do with the Bushwick principal's strong management and planning orientation and his more structured approach to running his school, a planning committee continued to meet at Bushwick and helped it maintain and increase the pace of change there.

Career Education

The main new program at Bushwick, paralleling the emphasis on teacher development at Monroe, was career education. Though never well defined at that time, either in Washington or at the state and local levels, the term usually referred to an infusion of job-related materials and experiences into academic as well as vocational courses.

This emphasis at Bushwick resulted from a combination of circumstances. First, Bushwick staff members were aware that many students had little desire to be in the school and little understanding of why they were there or why they should study, which contributed to high dropout rates and poor preparation for work. Also, a school guidance counselor had emphasized during the participative planning sessions the need for a course on careers, and that need became part of the school plan. An EDC on-loan person at Brandeis and available to Bushwick as a resource person immediately assisted in developing such a course, having already set up training programs for the disadvantaged in the private sector. Finally, EDC's director of its high school program had a strong interest in following up on this developmental opportunity, because this was the first time a partnership-school plan had called for a career curriculum. He was convinced from his prior inner-city school experiences in Philadelphia that many minority students saw little connection between schooling and obtaining desirable jobs as adults.

Data on the performance of Bushwick students indicate the strong need for a career education emphasis there. In the 1970-71 school year, over 600 of its 2,500 students, mostly tenth and eleventh graders, dropped out. In addition, two-thirds of the 460 graduating seniors received general diplomas, widely regarded among parents, civic watchdog groups, and even many school officials as inadequate for future employment. In the eyes of some, such diplomas were mainly certificates of attendance.

As an EDC report of early 1972 correctly indicated: "They [Bushwick students] have had little or no work experience; little insight regarding opportunities available to them; and very minimal knowledge of the requirements and responsibilities that business will demand of them. Most of these youths are from black and Puerto Rican, ghetto and fatherless homes with essentially no knowledge of the 'world of work.' "[15] These were students, then, who were undeveloped in what occupational psychologists refer to as "vocational maturity."[16]

One of the things that thus emerged from the participative planning sessions at Bushwick in the fall of 1970 was recognition of the need for better preparation of students for jobs. A guidance counselor suggested that ninth-grade "general" students especially needed a course on career opportunities in business, where they could get some "hands-on experience" and begin to find out what work was all about. Through the involvement of a Bushwick business education teacher and strong EDC support, one course and later a school-wide program evolved. EDC provided many resources: university faculty and graduate student consultants in career education to help the teacher develop such a course; summer pay for the teacher and a consultant to complete the course development work; funds for curriculum materials; minority people from industry, to discuss their experiences with students; released time during the school year, for the teacher to further refine the course; typing and clerical assistance; the cooperation of employers for student visits and field trips; a career resource center, with a large inventory of occupation-related material; and an evaluation scheme designed to measure the effectiveness of the course. The graduate student who helped develop the course also did her doctoral dissertation on its impact on the Bushwick students.

The first course sought to introduce incoming "general track" ninth graders to jobs in business, providing them with information about work and with skills and habits that would help them in applying for jobs (e.g., interviewing techniques, dress guidelines, etc.). Called Careers and Business, and subsequently—at EDC's suggestion and to avoid the appearance of attempting to track the students into business only, changed to Careers and You—it was taught by two business education teachers without advance preparation.*

Finally referred to as Looking Into Future Employment (LIFE), the course exposed students to information and experiences related to work. It involved visits to work sites, classroom visits by "living witnesses"—minority people, some from the Bushwick area, who were successful in the corporate world; and the use of resource-center materials on careers. It was originally taught in the 1971-72 school year by a business education teacher to 400-odd non-college-bound annex students with mixed results, primarily because the teacher was not able to spend time with EDC in developing the course. That teacher withdrew, and an English teacher agreed to develop the course for tenth graders for evaluation in the fall of 1972. The decision to change from the ninth to the tenth grade was based on the fact that ninth graders were not ready for such a course and that tenth graders were closer to taking on jobs or seeking further education and would see more relevance in the materials.

In the summer of 1972, the English teacher worked full-time with the Teachers College doctoral candidate to develop the course. It was first offered as an English option. With the LIFE course in operation and evaluated favorably, the principal immediately saw some broader implications in this course and indicated that he wanted to convert the course in the ninth-grade annex into an entire program that would infuse all subjects with occupational information.† The staff of the ninth-grade annex then prepared a Career

*Interest in the school and at EDC in continuing the effort led to the selection of a teacher to work with a Teachers College doctoral student in developing the course along lines spelled out by Dr. Jean Jordaan of Teachers College, who was retained as a consultant for the program. By this time, Jordaan and two of his colleagues at Teachers College had tracked the careers of a group of tenth-graders for over fifteen years and had developed out of this some curriculum ideas about the information and business needs of students to facilitate self-guidance. The teacher, however, had little time to spend with the consultant, given her full teaching load during the week; so after school and on Saturdays were the only times available.

†Subsequently, when word got around about the Bushwick career education programs, people from other New York City schools visited and requested

Exploration Program (CEP) in the spring and summer of 1973 and began implementing it that September. As the coordinator of the program indicated: "Every department has rewritten its curriculum to center on the teaching of basic skills around career exploration, work attitudes and responsibilities, practical application of skills in service to school and community, field trips, and guest speakers in areas related to the working world."[17] By dividing the semester into six and nine week mini-courses, "all students were to be introduced to career opportunities in all the departments: English, social studies, math, science, home economics, industrial arts, accounting, secretarial studies, and art." Another component of the program was group career and educational counseling for all ninth graders by one guidance counselor assigned full-time to the program.

Studies were done of the effects of both the LIFE course and the Career Exploration Program on Bushwick students. The first was done as a doctoral dissertation by Asma Hamdani, the Teachers College doctoral student who had helped the teacher involved develop the course. The study applied concepts and scales related to vocational growth and maturity and was done in the fall 1972 term on four tenth-grade classes of boys and girls who were taking the course and were enrolled in the general educational curriculum. Program (course) effects were assessed by administering two scales originally developed by Super and widely used in the field—a Career Maturity Inventory Attitude Scale and a Career Development Inventory.* In addition, attendance and lateness data were gathered and a Student Exploratory Activities Form was administered about two-thirds of the way through the term. Finally, the Career Maturity Inventory Attitude Scale was readministered four months after the program had terminated. Follow-up data on attendance, lateness, and career exploration activities were also collected.

The findings indicated significant gains on the part of the students on all of the vocational maturity measures, as well as improved attendance, less lateness, and increased information-seeking activity. Follow-up data indicated that all these improved gains were still in evidence four months after the course ended, with the exception of

---

materials. To help the teachers in Bushwick, EDC's director interested headquarters' Bureau for Curriculum Development in the Bushwick program. He then made funds available for the teacher to work at the central board in the summer to produce a course description and teaching manual that was subsequently distributed to all New York City high schools.

*In the absence of a comparable group of tenth graders who could be used as controls, the scores on a variety of vocational tests of untreated ninth graders were used to determine whether any possible changes in student attitudes and behavior could be attributed to the program and not to maturation.

occupational information seeking. Even on that measure, however, students exposed to the program were still engaging in more exploratory behavior four months later than those who had not experienced it.[18] As Dr. Hamdani indicated, after having observed the students over several months: "The course did mobilize the students and generate a lot of interest. It got so they wanted to come to school and talk to other students about it. There were new people coming in as staff, there was money coming in, and this new program was a stimulus to students. It was a way to hook them and get them involved."

The analysis by Teachers College professors Jordaan and Lin of the ninth-grade Career Exploration Program indicated that it also increased the maturity of students' vocational attitudes, though to a lesser degree than Hamdani found in the LIFE course. They also found that the career education program was more effective with tenth rather than ninth graders.[19]

The career education activity at Bushwick contains important lessons on how to effect changes that are applicable to other types of programs as well. The idea of moving from a single course to an entire school-wide program was critical, and the principal was responsible for it. Desirous of making Bushwick, in his words, "a model career education school, the career education center of the city," the principal was seeking to affect many more students within the school and to get more outside visibility and funding than a single optional English course could provide.

Since 1972, an expanding career education program has been in operation for the entire ninth-grade annex, and it is now being extended to the upper grades as well. Through EDC's assistance, the school got some state funding for the program under urban education monies, but thus far, it has not attracted any more outside funding for it. Nevertheless, the principal has continued to support and even expand the program. As he indicated in June 1973, when the school was unable to attract more outside funds: "We really lack money, staff, and space for career education and some of our other new programs, but they are so important we're going to pay for them any way we can." Following up on this commitment, the principal appointed a teacher as full-time coordinator of the Career Exploration Program in the annex and assigned a counselor to those students as well. Still another teacher had already been assigned to further develop the LIFE course.* Thus, though EDC provided resources at

*These assignments were made possible by EDC's success in 1972 in getting headquarters to provide funds for released time for teachers in the partnership schools.

the beginning, the school eventually took on full responsibility for the program, and EDC applied its resources to other school projects.

Bushwick's limited relations with local business unfortunately hampered its career education program, in the sense that very few local jobs were available (though jobs were not an essential component of the program). The program's coordinator at the annex held many meetings with neighborhood businessmen, and one of the last EDC people on loan worked closely with the Brooklyn Chamber of Commerce. Bushwick did have an internship program in which students worked in community agencies; but neither the coordinator nor the person on loan were that successful in getting local business cooperation. That still remains a problem.

Other activities at Bushwick that the planning process and the partnership either helped initiate or gave support to included a strengthened ESL program with curriculum materials in many different subjects for the school's increasing numbers of Spanish-speaking students, and a new remedial math program, Peer Mediated Instruction (PMI), designed to upgrade the basic skills of the school's many disadvantaged students. The principal supported all of these activities, to the point where, as he indicated: "When the money and space weren't there, especially for the mini-schools, we just took it out of our own hide, so committed am I to these important programs."

Mini-schools have been established in high schools throughout New York City. While EDC was not committed to that concept as the sole means of improving education, it did support efforts at setting up such schools when that was established as a priority in the early participative planning meetings, as was the case at George Washington High School and Bushwick. The Bushwick mini-school was particularly important, since the principal was chairman of the Board of Education's committee on mini-schools, and his mini-school director at Bushwick also served on that committee. It was likely that what they did at their school would gain high visibility for others and perhaps be tried there as well.

The school plan at Bushwick did not endorse the mini-school program. Rather, the Office of High Schools of the Board of Education suddenly announced one Friday early in the 1971-72 school year that Bushwick would have one, to begin the following week. The principal appointed as its director a male English teacher who lived in the area and who had been effective in a similar program dealing with marginal students. EDC gave him considerable support in finding an outside facility, in the development of curriculum materials, and in getting the rest of the school to accept his students. The purpose of the mini-school was to provide an alternative educational setting for Bushwick's truants or near-truants. The attendance and school performance of many of these students improved significantly, and several graduated from Bushwick and found employment.

Another priority program that Bushwick's plan called for and that the partnership helped strengthen was ESL. It was already in place when EDC arrived, but the planning committee called for a more comprehensive effort, to be expanded to include many departments, including history, geography, science, math, and English. EDC was helpful in securing released time for teachers to develop curriculum materials and in actually bringing in such materials from the outside, including from George Washington High School's well-regarded curriculum unit in American history for non-English-speaking students. EDC thus provided additional resources to help those teachers already skilled and deeply involved in the area to be able to do more. Recently Bushwick was named as one of ten pilot schools for a bilingual program, and it has received outside support for that through federal funding.

One of the most promising new programs in which EDC played an important role was Peer Mediated Instruction (PMI) in Mathematics. With funds obtained from Dr. Gordon Bowden, AT&T's director of educational relations and Flom's advisor to Bushwick, EDC retained Professor Peter Rosenbaum of Teachers College, who had developed the PMI technique for reading instruction in company training programs at AT&T. Later PMI was introduced into the public schools in Jackson, Mississippi, with AT&T assistance. The EDC director at Bushwick, knowing about the PMI reading program at Brandeis (developed the previous summer), went to the math department chairman, tactfully pointed out that his department was the only one in the school not involved with EDC, and asked him if he could use any help in teaching remedial math to his slower classes. PMI had never before been used with math, but the two went together to visit Rosenbaum at Teachers College, and this led to the incorporation of his PMI technique into the school math program. The technique involved pairs of students using programmed materials and checking each other's work, with first one grading the other and then a reversal of roles. The work itself was simply a series of math problems that covered basic concepts and skills, the technique being essentially a drill method, but one conducted in a way that students found quite stimulating. Indeed, the entire exercise took on a game-like quality. Some of the most withdrawn and failing students often experienced heightened motivation and performance in the PMI situation.

Evaluations of the program indicated big gains for the PMI students that might otherwise not have taken place. The computational and problem-solving skills of Bushwick students exposed to the technique were compared with those of an equivalent Bushwick student population who had not been so exposed and who had achieved similar scores in those skills before the course. Rosenbaum then found that the PMI instruction had such a positive effect on both skills that the speed of their acquisition by the PMI students far exceeded the average rate of growth in these same skills for the same students prior to their entry into the program and that the PMI students gained significantly more than the non-PMI ones. As he concluded: "The Bushwick data suggest that the Fundamentals of Math classes incorporating Peer Mediated Instruction progressed in mathematics skill at an encouraging rate during the fall term, a rate that exceeds the average rate of learning for the population on which the Metropolitan Achievement Test was itself standardized. . . . In both Computation and Problem Solving, it is highly likely that Peer Mediated Instruction will prove an especially efficacious approach to such systematic instruction."[20] The program has now been expanded to include many more students, and it involves algebra classes as well.

During the 1973-74 and 1974-75 academic years Bushwick kept up its development of new programs, in addition to expanding career education, ESL, and PMI math. For example, there was a week-long career fair at the school in May 1974, in which students were exposed to information on various occupations. Business, government, and social agency people were present, and many students attended. While no formal assessment was done, informal surveys conducted by the career education coordinator suggested that students felt that the experience gave them a lot of information about different prospective careers.

One of the most significant developments was the school's success in increasing attendance at parent association and program planning committee meetings. By the spring of 1974, as many as twenty-five parents attended parent association meetings, with committees having been formed that had never existed before. The school also attracted new community leaders to the monthly Consultative Council (school-community) meetings. Some of the distance and tension that had existed between the school and the community when EDC first came seemed to have abated.

Finally, there was a noticeable increase in the number of teachers actively involved in new programs, which contributed to the Bushwick partnership's success. As an on-loan person reported: "So much of the success at Bushwick was due to the desire of the teachers there to make things work. They worked with the kids after school and had a more positive attitude than I sometimes noted at the other schools. There were many teachers at Bushwick who had been there for a long time, old Irish and Jewish teachers and department chairpersons as well. This was a faculty that identified with the students. EDC's coming in simply unleashed the talents and energies that had been there before and that now had the support necessary to be used more productively. That was the key to success at Bushwick."

George Washington

The partnership school that constituted the greatest risk for EDC, by virtue of having many more problems and far more severe problems than did Monroe or Bushwick, was George Washington High School in Upper Manhattan. It had at one time been an elite, "showcase" school, and was sometimes even referred to as a "country club" high school. It served an upwardly mobile, middle-class, and predominantly Jewish population and had a long and distinguished array of graduates (Henry Kissinger, Arthur Miller, Jacob Javits, Lauren Bacall, Dr. Kenneth Clark, Marvin Kalb, Edwin Newman, William Shea, and Rod Carew are among its more illustrious alumni), some of whom went on to Ivy League schools and to eminent careers in business and the professions. Like Bushwick and Monroe, George Washington had been very much a community high school; in 1970, 93 percent of its students were from the immediate school district. The area has changed markedly, however, over the past several decades. In the 1930s it was predominantly Jewish, with many refugees from Nazi Germany settling there. As their children graduated from high school, however, many of these Jewish families moved out. During the 1940s and 1950s Irish and Italians moved into the area, but they were a fairly transient group. By the 1960s, the area had a large Greek, Puerto Rican, Haitian, Dominican, and black population, and the school reflected that. When EDC arrived in 1970, the school was predominantly Puerto Rican and black, with whites constituting only 24 percent of the total student body, in contrast to Puerto Ricans (46 percent) and blacks (31 percent). By 1972, whites had dropped to 14 percent and Puerto Ricans increased to 57 percent, and those trends have continued.

This academic high school thus had to develop an entirely new program for its minority students. The year before EDC arrived, school staff members had become polarized between those who wanted to keep it a primarily academic school for college-bound students and those who saw the great need for remedial programs. Some teachers transferred out in 1972, when a new high school opened in the North Bronx, but many remained to try to keep fighting a rearguard battle to maintain George Washington as an academic high school. The teachers union had a particularly strong chapter there, and they fought this battle quite vigorously. Even in 1975, the nostalgia for an academic curriculum still lingered among some staff members. This was so despite the school's changed student body, almost 70 percent of whom have severe language and learning problems, and despite parent and student resentment over the school's past failure to develop programs to meet the needs of the new ethnic groups. The old type of academic curriculum was clearly unsuitable for George Washington's new students, and EDC became a force to support those educators who wanted to accommodate the curriculum and the school's limited resources to its new student population.

To say that George Washington had problems when EDC arrived would be putting it mildly. In addition to the usual conditions of overcrowding (4,400 students in a 3,200-seat school), high absenteeism and dropout rates, and low achievement, the school was torn apart by violence, both inside the building and spilling over into the community and the subways, and had acquired considerable notoriety as a result.

As Samuel Kostman, the school's principal since 1970, reports: "By 1969, George Washington had become probably the most notorious example of urban high school violence and educational deterioration in the city."[21] The following description, put together by Donald Barnes of IED and Raymond Connolly, the teacher coordinator, indicates how bad the situation had become: "When EDC's representatives first visited the George Washington building, an imposing Georgian structure on the heights above the Harlem River at Manhattan Island's northern extremity, the situation of the school was, by any standards, precarious. Police were stationed at the gates and doors and throughout the halls; the street was crowded with patrol cars; barricades and riot helmets were prominently in evidence; several hundred students sat and stood on the lawn near the front entrance. Four principals had served in the school during the previous year and a temporary principal was trying to keep order until a permanent successor could be found; the parents were divided into militant factions, aroused by sensational reports in the news media; an exclusive group of dissatisfied and disaffected students whiled away most of the days in the cafeteria; neighborhood merchants closed their stores when George Washington's students left in the afternoon; and the threat and reality of violence against any person, young or adult, pervaded the campus. Police action, or even the mere presence of uniformed officers, seemed to heighten the tension and escalate the prospects for more violence."[22]

George Washington, then, was the most extreme case of institutional breakdown encountered in any of the four partnership schools and would undoubtedly be classified as extreme in relation to almost any inner-city high school. The ethnic changes in the student body were of such magnitude, they had happened so fast, the students brought in so many problems and learning difficulties, and the school had so failed to respond, clinging nostalgically to its academic programs of the past, that it had moved into a condition of advanced anarchy.

There was serious debate within EDC as to whether it should go into such a conflict-ridden school, but the decision was made that it should do so as a critical test of the partnership strategy. The argument of those who wanted to go in was that if George Washington, with all its well-publicized troubles, could be turned around, then any school could be. Conversely, if EDC failed to succeed there, that would not invalidate the strategy, since conditions there were so heavily weighted against success to begin with.

To further illustrate just how bad conditions were when EDC arrived, the school had completed a three-month period in which it was officially closed about 20 percent of the time, because violence of some sort seemed to erupt within a day or so of each opening. As an EDC report of 1972 indicated: "Two weeks after school opened again in September 1970, an in-school riot overflowed onto the streets and into subways and some 34 subway travelers were reported to have suffered injury from rampant students."

EDC began participative planning meetings in the fall of 1970 with most of the main participants in the school—the acting principal, teachers from both factions, several students, and EDC representatives—but no parents. A parent group seeking to represent student interests, though invited by letter, was still picketing and handing out appeals to students to boycott the school. They eventually joined after Flom of EDC met with them in Harlem, asking them to give EDC a chance to improve conditions in the school.

This planning group identified five critical problem areas that had to be dealt with as rapidly as possible: (1) a cafeteria that was a meeting place for truants and problem students and was where much of the violence started, in addition to being a purveyor of consistently bad food; (2) a breakdown in communication and cooperation between students, parents, teachers, the school administration, the community, and school headquarters; (3) a serious language problem for over 50 percent of the students (now over 60 percent), most of them Spanish-speaking, that prevented them from doing well in school; (4) an equally serious security problem; and (5) a widespread use of drugs.

Even before these issues could be addressed, however, the school had to find a principal, which it did soon after EDC arrived. Over the next several months, and in active collaboration with this principal, EDC played a remarkably effective mediator role, helping to resolve many of the conflicts that had so torn apart the school before. Even the most dissatisfied and militant parents, who had been in severe conflict with the teachers union and the school administration, were effusive in their praise for EDC's work. Mrs. Ellen Lurie, leader of the parent group that felt that the administration and the teachers were failing to respond to students' needs, had this to say about EDC at George Washington: "My daughter and her friends found your office a wonderful relaxed place to drop in where a very receptive adult ear was available to each and every student. I think that is very high praise. . . . your project helped George Washington so much because you made your decisions on the scene, based on the day-to-day reality. So many programs are written from a distance . . . and lose so much—sometimes everything—because they are based on theory and not reality. . . . I sincerely hope you will continue your program."

Immediate action was taken on many of the problems noted above. Thus, EDC arranged for a study of the cafeteria by a General Motors Commissary executive. The study contained many recommendations on how the cafeteria could be improved, including the removal of its director. Students and teachers acquired a lot of confidence in the new principal when he implemented the recommendations despite the possibility of a union grievance. They included changes in personnel, in operating policy, in menu (to accommodate the ethnic tastes of minority students), and in methods of providing security in the cafeteria. As one EDC person on loan recalled: "George Washington was like a little UN, with its many different ethnic and cultural groups, which is what the neighborhood was. The cafeteria was one place where all these groups were thrown together, and in that close proximity, a lot of bad feelings and disagreements could come out. The new dietician arranged for dishes for the Spanish, Haitian, Greek, and Southern black students that were cultural dishes they had had from infancy. It really helped."

The same fast action took place on the security problem. A security specialist from an EDC bank did a study and made many recommendations related to the recruitment and training of security personnel for the school. The principal's rapid implementation of these recommendations as well probably helped a lot to markedly improve the security situation at George Washington. Thus, in September 1971, I.D. cards were introduced at George Washington, which became one of the first schools in the city to use that security device. From October 15, 1970 through March 1972, the school was only closed two half-days, and it has not closed at all since September 1971. It has remained a quiet school since then.

The security problem was also eased by the establishment in March 1971 of a mini-school, George Washington Prep, for students who had failed to attend classes and had participated in many fracases. A separate facility was obtained, and the program had para-professional street workers and teachers to tend to the many needs of these students. At first, EDC paid for rent, for start-up expenses, and for some staff salaries and course materials, until the Board of Education underwrote those costs. Early results were impressive. The average daily attendance of the prep students improved from 15 percent to 90 percent, in contrast to 70 percent attendance at the main building. Furthermore, 60 percent of the students in the mini-school were passing subjects in 1972, in contrast to their 10 percent passing record in the previous year.

The plan helped George Washington move quickly on its language problem as well. The school had procrastinated for many years on developing programs for non-English-speaking students, because of jurisdictional rivalries between the English and Speech Departments as to who would take control. "Since neither department was able to handle the situation of these non-English-speaking students adequately, it was clearly a disaster," an involved George Washington teacher reported. "There was a lot of friction and tension between them and it was obvious that something had to be done. There had been discussion for two to three years, but no action."

EDC arranged for a study and finally achieved a consensus among the participants that a separate English as a Second Language (ESL) Department, with its own chairman, should be set up. It took a lot of prodding by EDC to get the principal to move on this, since it involved working through the political conflict between the two departments. The principal prevailed, however, and a separate department was set up. IED then did a broad study of ESL programs in the Southwest and made the results and other materials available to the new department. Most important, there was an extraordinarily able substitute teacher within the school who was a specialist in this field, having lived and taught in France for many years. He became the acting chairman, and the curriculum he and his staff developed soon became a model nationally as well as for other high schools around the city.

There were other early programs as well. The most prominent included a Career Opportunities Resources Center, where students and teachers could find out more about work; a number of vocational programs in health careers, radio electronics, and automotive trades; support for the school's first football team in many decades, which later expanded into many other sports and intramural teams; a diagnostic reading laboratory with federal funding; and a variety of smaller-scale activities, such as a health fair and attendance programs.

The career center was one of the most significant of the new programs, providing students with materials, information, and equipment relative to career opportunities. Guidance and counseling were offered there, with thirty to forty students moving through the center every day. Most of the school's vocational programs were tied into it. One involved forty to fifty students interning in nearby Columbia Presbyterian and Jewish Memorial hospitals, a program that was developed in large part as a result of EDC efforts. (Unfortunately the school could not get continued funding for student stipends, and the program no longer exists.)

The athletic programs also helped many students at the school. For years, the school's beautiful stadium and playing fields had gone underutilized. Out of the plan came a proposal to start a football team, though without funds or needed equipment. The school raised money for uniforms and travel expenses for a football team, and that was such a success that the school itself financed other team sports.* Intramural sports also picked up, having received impetus from a similar program at Brandeis. School officials and EDC people on loan were in wide agreement that school spirit improved markedly as these sports activities got underway, and it is likely that attendance may also have gone up as a result.

One change at George Washington that distinguished it from Bushwick was the deep involvement of the local Chamber of Commerce. An explicit goal in the school plan called for rebuilding relationships between the school and the community. Local businessmen, through the Chamber, provided money for football uniforms and jobs for students, and worked actively to help secure a gymnasium. They even made the principal an honorary member of the Chamber, bestowing on him a special citizenship award at one of their annual dinners. These businessmen didn't want any more student riots and hoped instead to stabilize the area. They saw the partnership and the programs it spawned as a constructive development.

---

*"The football team, in particular, recruited some of the bigger boys who were ring leaders of gangs," reported an EDC person on loan, "and we kept them too busy to fight. This became a way of constructively channeling the enormous energy of these kids."

To meet the remedial reading needs of students—a priority in the plan—IED's Dr. Virginia Newton assisted in writing a proposal to establish reading labs. The proposal was funded under Title I and two such labs were set up in February 1973, to serve over 300 students. They did diagnostic and remedial work on reading disabilities and adjustments of students, and after some difficulties with the design of the lab and the curriculum material, they have helped many students.

Stages of the George Washington Partnership

The George Washington partnership had two phases. The first involved EDC in extensive mediating activities, with the intention of developing enough peace in the school so that it might at least begin addressing itself to educational problems. On this score, all participants agreed that EDC had been highly effective. The changes in the cafeteria, the improved security system, the availability of the EDC office for students and staff, and the establishment of George Washington Prep all took place during this early stage and helped curb much of the conflict and violence.

After the school had been relatively quiet for a while, EDC and school officials turned to developing educational programs. The career center, the reading labs, and the ESL department were examples. EDC people on loan and many change-oriented teachers felt that things did not go nearly as well in this second phase. There were some teachers and some department chairmen who strongly opposed the program changes and wanted to keep George Washington an academic school, emphasizing college-bound programs. "George Washington had a climate of unionism like I had never seen," reported an EDC person on loan. "It was one of the stronger union high schools, and when the union said let's have a meeting, everything in the school could stop. Many of the union teachers were our toughest problem." Yet, many teachers were sympathetic to developing new programs for the disadvantaged students. "GW had a terrific turnover," reported another person on loan. "There were some old grads who came back and wanted to save the school and the new kids. There were others who had hung in, and they too gave us support. We supported each other." The school was thus polarized between more traditional academic and more remedial-oriented teachers, with the partnership plan calling for changes.

Department chairman were also a potent force in favor of maintaining the status quo. Meanwhile, the principal, a decent, highly intelligent, and dedicated person who wanted change but was also committed to maintaining academic standards and minimizing conflict among his staff, had to move deliberately on implementing new programs. Some activist teachers and on-loan people felt that he was at times a traditionalist, who was not as forceful as they would have liked. Given the circumstances of his school, however, he has exercised strong leadership; and he has given numerous testimonials on the value of having EDC in his school.

It remains to be seen, then, how much George Washington will continue to change in response to the needs of its new minority students. At present it has a strong coordinator who is oriented in that direction, having served in the position since 1971, and it has increasing numbers of teachers who have a similar commitment. They may give the principal the support he needs to develop new programs.

COMMON PATTERNS IN THE PARTNERSHIP SCHOOLS

The variations apparent in the EDC experience in the partnership schools were due to factors already considered—the principal and his style; the outlook of teachers and department chairmen; the coordinator; the EDC people on loan, especially the directors; and the school's general demographic experience. Some important common features were also noticeable, however.

A key one was the participative planning style of EDC and IED. It was consistently successful in the early stages of the partnership in establishing some consensus about school needs and program priorities and getting a lot of developmental activities underway to meet such needs. The many elements of that style that have already been discussed all helped: EDC's not imposing any preconceived agendas, not having any simplistic solutions, making the minutes of all meetings available, keeping meetings open to all participants, and bringing in a skilled discussion leader (Donald Barnes of IED) who encouraged honest communication among all parties. EDC's providing many resources—people on loan, R&D funds, curriculum and instructional materials, work sites for jobs and vocational programs, educational consultants from universities—as well as their building support and cutting through red tape at school headquarters further helped to maintain a relationship of trust between it and the school and keep the innovation process going.

In brief, EDC made at least two contributions. First, it initiated a participative planning process leading to research and development within these schools, which was later supplemented by released time for teachers and other new resources as well. Second, it played a mediator role in schools with much internal conflict—among students, teachers, departments, supervisors, and parents and between the school and outside groups, namely, employers, community organizations, and school headquarters. It played a continuous role as the link among all these participants, and that improved the school's capability to effect change.

The EDC office played a particularly critical role in this regard. We mentioned it as so important in the early stages of the Monroe partnership, but it was also critical in the other schools. Over time, EDC created many other such offices, which became "communities" for people inside the school and centers for developmental activities. The teacher center and ESL offices at Monroe and the Career Opportunities Resources Center and EDL reading laboratories at George Washington were examples, as were the mini-schools at all three schools.

Giving competent teachers an opportunity to create new programs was a particularly important component of EDC's successes. The professional isolation of teachers from stimulating contact with outside educational developments and the system's failure to adapt to changing clienteles were major causes of the poor performance of these schools at the time the partnerships began. The demoralization of teachers and their sense of futility about change were still other critical factors in their poor performance. The partnership tried to overcome these problems by giving teachers recognition, resources, and status that they had never received before.

This last point has broader implications for restructuring schools. When EDC intervened, the work situation of teachers was similar to that of unskilled factory or clerical workers. Lesson plans were highly rationalized, as were curriculum and instructional procedures; teachers were required to punch in and punch out on a time clock, and they were essentially treated like low-level functionaries. The system had in this sense attempted to routinize and monitor their job as much as possible. The union, while a force for increased status for teachers, reinforced some of these tendencies. Union work rules, standardizing the working conditions of teachers, encouraged a functionary mentality. Many union-oriented teachers in these schools, for example, were unwilling to give of their time in a way that was required in an innovative school.

EDC, through the partnerships, was attempting to transform this production-line setting into a more professional atmosphere that had teachers involved in identifying school and student needs, establishing goals, and actually developing educational programs to meet these goals. In the process, the teachers had more frequent and richer contacts with their peers and with students. In the language of organization theory, a bureaucratic, authoritarian, Theory X-type organization was gradually being changed into a more collegial, participative, Theory Y one.[23] All key participants in the school, and teachers in particular, became involved in a diagnostic exercise designed to identify student needs, establish goals, develop programs, and work on their implementation. The schools became more actively engaged in a "search" process to better meet these needs.

Viewed in more general terms, this was an attempt to combine an organizational development (OD) and a research and development (R&D) process. The organizational development aspect of it was the participative planning method that EDC and IED used to get people in the school oriented toward planning and change. OD, however, is neutral with regard to the substance of what change is needed, and that is where research and development came in. As needs were identified and priorities established in each school's plan, IED did extensive research on practices in schools and industries all over the country to determine what the "state of the art" knowledge was. On the issues of drug prevention, remedial reading and math, and English as a Second Language, for example, IED brought back to New York significant information about what had been done elsewhere. Donald Barnes and an associate published a book on their survey of drug prevention programs; and Barnes brought in through a Teachers College professor a Peer Mediated Instruction program for remedial math and reading that had been tried in Jackson, Mississippi, and at AT&T. He also brought in extensive materials on bilingual programs from the Southwest. These were significant contributions, and the particular examples could be multiplied to include many other educational programs as well. Where such "state of the art" knowledge did not exist, EDC and IED encouraged the schools to develop new programs on their own, as in the PMI math and career education programs at Bushwick and the EDL one at George Washington. They did so anyway, since programs brought in from the outside had to be adapted to fit particular local conditions.

The most basic assumption behind the partnership program was that supervisors and teachers know the problems and are usually the most competent people to deal with them, if they are only given the proper resources and incentives. One factor affecting EDC's success, then, was the extent to which it could find such supervisors and teachers and provide the resources they needed. Many successful partnership activities were a function mainly of having a teacher in the school, with the backing of a supervisor, who would develop and carry on the program long after EDC was gone. Conversely, those programs that were not sustained suffered from a lack of supervisory support and teacher participation.

6. The Courts Task Force

A key aspect of the nation's urban crisis that hit New York particularly hard in the 1960s was the accelerating increase in crime. If the problems of the schools were complex, those related to crime were perhaps even more so. Any attempt at diagnosis and effective deterrence involved dealing with not one but several agencies. Solutions were also hampered by the lack of knowledge about the causes of crime as well as by the lack of societal consensus as to the appropriate goal in dealing with it. Should it be mainly one of punishment, deterrence, rehabilitation, or society's moral vindication against those who violate its rules?

EDC was deeply concerned about this increase in crime in New York and about its wide-ranging impact on the city's economic base and quality of life, and was determined to do something about it. It formed a Public Safety Committee for that purpose in 1968 and has been involved ever since in attempts to improve the criminal justice system.

The immediate concern of EDC officials was that the city's increase in crime would further speed up the already accelerating exodus of corporate headquarters and manufacturing plants from the city. They spent over a year casting about for some way of interceding. After first exploring the Police and Corrections departments as targets for management assistance and doing some fairly extensive work in the former, EDC finally settled on the criminal courts. The organization problems there were particularly acute, requiring much management improvement that business was potentially equipped to provide; EDC had good initial access there; and most experts on the city's criminal justice system, including the mayor and his staff, saw the courts as in a state of chaos and in desperate need of immediate assistance.

Since 1969, EDC has done a series of management studies of New York City courts and related city and state administrative agencies. The result has been a voluminous body of reports on these agencies, documenting for the first time and in considerable detail how they work and the sources of their breakdown, and containing numerous recommendations for change. Some of the recommendations simply crystallized an emerging consensus or gave legitimacy to needed reforms that innovation-minded insiders or such outside agencies as the Legal Aid Society had suggested before, but could not get implemented.[1] EDC, as a prestigious business group giving its stamp of approval to such management reform recommendations and presenting them in an "objective" and systematic way, thus made their implementation more likely than if others alone had suggested them. In this sense, EDC played an important third-party, consultant role in the New York City courts. Like most consultants, EDC and its reports got "used" by court officials to justify things they wanted to do anyway. EDC, in turn, relied heavily in some cases on the insiders for information, diagnoses, reform ideas, and support for actual implementation. It also introduced many new perspectives on its own.

THE IMPORTANCE OF THIS CASE

EDC's work in the courts has national implications, and for several reasons. First, as with its Board of Education projects, those in the courts probably represent the biggest effort of any business group in the country to bring management skills to bear in attempting to modernize that institution. Since 1969, EDC has provided 35 man-years of consultant assistance to the courts and other criminal justice agencies, valued at roughly $900,000. It has, in addition, secured several outside grants, including a recent one from the state administrator's office of $138,170.

Second, the New York City Criminal Court, where EDC began its work, is an important type of urban, high-volume, "lower" court that had been neglected in the past. There had been a few in-depth studies of the court's management, dating back to an excellent Citizens Budget Commission report in the 1930s, but little reform had ever resulted. The court's breakdown in the late 1960s, however, was so marked as to require that management improvements be made.

Third, EDC's work in the courts reflects an important national trend, namely, the increasing attention being given in recent years to improved court management and modernization. A wide variety of organizations, including foundations, bar associations, government agencies, academicians, and commercial management consulting firms, have funded studies or developed programs in this field. The studies and programs of these organizations—the Institute of Judicial Administration (supported by many of America's largest corporations, including EDC member companies), the Institute of Court Management at Aspen, and IBM's judicial data processing systems unit are significant examples—include recommendations to reduce court congestion, improve judicial performance, and rationalize court management and personnel practices. EDC's court work is thus part of an emerging management modernization strategy and has significance in that context as well.[2]

Fourth, just in terms of New York City, EDC's involvement in the courts in 1969 was part of what appears to have been a major public policy decision to begin modernizing the criminal courts and to consolidate the recommendations of many different groups. The virtual breakdown of the New York City criminal court system at that time created a serious crisis for the city, and EDC played a key role in helping to deal with it. EDC was one of the first nonjudicial, civic groups to have ever become so intimately involved in management reform of the courts. Unlike such other municipal agencies as the schools, the courts have never had active citizen constituencies for management reform.* Deep-rooted traditions related to the sanctity of the judiciary may well have a lot to do with it, even though some judicial appointments, particularly to lower courts, represent prime examples of municipal patronage. In any event, this EDC involvement represented an important break with past court reform efforts, and has significance from that point of view as well.

Finally, this is an important case because it constitutes one of the most successful management transfer efforts that EDC undertook. That can be understood only in the context of the complex and often byzantine nature of the courts and the wider criminal justice system. The analysis to follow points up the complexities, in particular, political ones, that accompanied EDC's projects every step of the way, from gaining initial entry to later finding interested and influential inside clients, and then having some of its recommenda-

---

*There had been a court reform movement for many years (e.g., American Judicature Society, the Foundation for Modern Courts); but the focus tended to be on such issues as judicial selection and legislative and constitutional amendments. It was not on how to run the courts.

tions implemented. The important implications that such a political analysis points up constitutes the main theme of the chapter.

SOME IMMEDIATE PRECONDITIONS

If the schools were in a state of crisis when EDC began its work there, the situation in the courts was even worse. When EDC arrived in 1969, the New York City Criminal Court had reached such a state of disrepair and accompanying public outcry for reform, with the *New York Times* and other media continuously publicizing atrocity stories of institutional breakdown, that the term "catastrophe" rather than "crisis" best describes its condition. In 1970 there were two major riots in the city's overflowing jails, forcing Mayor Lindsay into negotiations with prisoners about prison and court conditions and producing a historic confrontation between him and the senior judges of the city and state court systems regarding their conflicting views as to what was wrong and who was to blame.[3]

One of Lindsay's main arguments was that despite the city's having doubled its expenditures for the courts in the previous four years, and despite his having added twenty judges to the Criminal Court in 1969, the courts' own administrative inefficiency prevented those additional resources from being used well and had a lot to do with the breakdown. He held the state ultimately responsible, since the New York City courts were legally part of the state court system. "The courts ask us for more judges, more clerks, and more space," he noted. "But we who have to draw funds from an exhausted public treasury find it difficult to react favorably, when the request for funds comes with no plan for basic change, no indication of a commitment that supervision and discipline of judges will be priority issues, and no sign that the central administrative control authorized by statute and rule will be exercised to the utmost. Why build expensive new court facilities when the public sees existing courtrooms in session only a few hours each day?"[4]

Judge Fuld indicated in rebuttal that the city was responsible for disorders in correctional institutions that were under its jurisdiction, that the courts had already been implementing many reform programs to limit delay and ease congestion, contrary to what Lindsay had implied in his "exaggerated and excessive statements condemning others," and that "the courts are but one facet of a very complex mechanism which deals with persons accused of crime."[5] Both were right in different ways, and the intensity of their statements indicated how serious the apparent breakdown was.

At the time of the riots, the New York City criminal courts had a tremendous number of undisposed cases, including many traffic and other (city agency) summonses that they had to process. City jails were operating at close to twenty percent over capacity in the aggregate, and many prisoners, unable to post bail, awaited trial for months after they were arraigned. Severe calendar congestion and prolonged pre-trial detention had become commonplace. Indeed, City Hall and criminal justice officials anticipated the riots long before they actually happened, but somehow seemed incapable of doing anything about it. The riots, the overcrowding, the congestion and delays in the courts were all just symptomatic, moreover, of a broader institutional breakdown.

A series of developments had combined to produce the devastating conditions that EDC was to find in the courts, including: (1) *an escalation of crime;* (2) *an increase, in particular, in drug-related crimes,* New York City having become a distribution center for illegally imported narcotics; (3) *an increasingly tough police department arrest policy* and what judges referred to as a pattern of *"overindictments" by district attorneys* in response to these developments; (4) *a seemingly insurmountable glut of traffic summonses,* with all those summonses processed through the Criminal Court; (5) *a condition of pronounced underfunding of post-arrest agencies within the criminal justice system,* reflecting broader societal values;* and (6) all these pressures coming together to impose *tremendous case load increases* in an already high-volume court that wasn't even able to handle the cases it had before.

AN INSTITUTIONAL ANALYSIS

Even these conditions, however, as devastating as they are, deal with only some of the more immediate causes of the courts' breakdown. They fail to explain the courts' limited response to the problems, notwithstanding those problems' magnitude. In the atmosphere of mutual recrimination and scapegoating that prevailed, as different participants sought to explain why the breakdown wasn't their fault,

---

*For example, society's concern was with "law and order" and with hiring more police as a solution to the crime problem, rather than concentrating on the courts, correctional institutions, and rehabilitation as priorities along with better coordination among the many criminal justice agencies. In 1971, for example, (as reported by the Mayor's Criminal Justice Coordinating Council), 80 percent of the city's expenditures for criminal justice went to the police department.

criminal court officials in particular often referred to these external forces as the main source of the problem. One prominent court administrator, for example, keeps arguing that there is little wrong with the courts that more judges, space, and staff couldn't cure. He fails to recognize that the court's own internal structure and politics, as well as the broader institutional setting in which they existed, had a profound effect on the breakdown, allowing it to go as far as it did with so little corrective response.

The Criminal Court in New York City is a state agency funded by the city, creating much ambiguity regarding who is responsible for its performance. It is an agency that has grown by accretion, endlessly proliferating highly specialized courtrooms or "parts" in response to increases in the volume and diversity of its cases. It is also highly fragmented, both internally—in terms of these parts and of patterns of divided authority—and externally, from other courts and other agencies within the criminal justice system with which it must coordinate. Beyond that, it has been burdened by the judiciary's traditional independence from outside review and demands for accountability, by a tight-knit civil service, and by the absence of any internal management climate or capability. Lawyers and judges usually make poor managers, much like their counterpart practitioners-turned administrators in health, education, and welfare agencies.

Many of the limitations of the courts and of the wider criminal justice system are remarkably similar to those of the schools, and one can make almost the same general diagnosis, with some slight variations, of what ails other municipal agencies that have similarly failed to modernize. In the case of the courts, the main weaknesses include: (1) *extreme organizational and political fragmentation* that gets reflected at the most "micro" level in the proliferation of specialized "parts" or courtrooms and extends up to the various criminal justice agencies (corrections, Legal Aid, the district attorneys, the police, and the courts) at the city level and to the state-wide structure;* (2) *little coordination* or integration of these subunits, with considerable overlap and duplication; (3) *no clear lines of authority and no coherent management systems and controls*, as lawyers, judges, and civil servants (e.g., court clerks) with little management expertise have a monopoly over top administrative positions; (4) *extreme insider domination*, reflecting both civil service and political patronage, and reinforced by a tradition of judicial independence that has

---

*The term "parts" refers to a courtroom, a judge, and all the other personnel required to conduct the business of the court. See the discussion in John B. Jennings, WN-7841-NYC, *Final Evaluation of the Manhattan Calendar Project*, The New York City–Rand Institute, June 1972, pp. 1–2.

insulated the courts and the judges from outside review and accountability (the functional equivalent of demands by educators for
professional autonomy); and (5) *the limited activity of outside civic
groups pressing for reform*, unlike in the schools where many such
groups were at least politically active if not always successful. These
characteristics of the courts and of the wider criminal justice system
in which they were embedded merit further discussion in completing
a diagnosis of the setting in which EDC worked.

Intra-agency Coordination. The conditions of fragmentation
within the criminal courts and extending up through the entire
criminal justice system particularly hampered the development of
any efficient or effective management. Just within the courts themselves, an incredibly complex specialized "parts" system had developed to accommodate the increasing volume and diversity of cases.
Rather than enabling the courts to better handle their increasing case
load, these specialized parts seem to have contributed to the continuing deterioration of court management.

There are several breakdowns in case processing and general court
productivity that result from a parts system. First, the same case may
appear in half a dozen or more parts, as it fails to get resolved in
earlier ones, for any number of reasons, including the nonappearance
of any of the participants, or delaying actions or shopping around for
a lenient judge on the part of one or more parties. Second, there is
no continuity in legal representation or among judges when that
takes place, as all the new participants have to become informed
about the case in each new part. (Such chaos may often help
defendants, as cases eventually get dismissed or never come to trial.)
The resulting inefficiency and the potential harm to society are
significant costs. Third, and perhaps most basic of all, there is little
or no accountability in this entire process, since so many judges and
other participants get involved.

This fragmented system of specialized parts had three separate
tiers, corresponding to stages in the processing of cases: arraignments
(handled by one group of parts), hearings, and trials. There were
other bases of specialization, including type of crime charged
(felony, misdemeanor, etc.) and whether or not the defendant was
being detained in jail. Many of the classic dysfunctions of overspecialization that social scientists studying organizations have documented, some of which we have just discussed, got played out quite
dramatically in this structure—particularly the patterns of divided
authority and no accountability.[6]

By the time that EDC arrived in 1969, a broad consensus had
developed within the court that something had to be done about this
overspecialization. The administrative judge had proposed a form of

consolidation called all-purpose parts in 1967, and Legal Aid had as well. EDC was to further legitimate that consensus in its reports, thereby giving consolidation more of a chance of being implemented. *

Interagency Coordination

If the management problems of the courts were just confined to them alone, they would be tough enough to handle, but they go far beyond that. The courts are part of a multiagency criminal justice system that involves vast logistical and scheduling problems vis-à-vis the police, the corrections and probation departments, the district attorneys, and Legal Aid (a private corporation serving the legal needs of poor defendants). All of these agencies are involved in court proceedings, and yet it is very difficult to get them to coordinate consistently with one another. They constitute in that sense a "non-system" that is a big constraint to improved court management. If any one of these parties doesn't appear at a given point—for example, if corrections doesn't have enough vans to transport prisoners, or if probation reports are not available—then a case is delayed. And this was too often the routine rather than the exceptional situation.

Notwithstanding the tendency of some criminal court judges and administrators to externalize the blame too much, outside criminal justice agencies' practices do affect the backlog. More arrests, for example, contributed to crowded court calendars, and one of the reasons that the courts' breakdown became such a political issue in 1969 was the Police Department's great concern with police productivity and overtime pay, as police officers spent hours sitting around the courts.† Many police had made what court officials felt were highly questionable misdemeanor arrests, and Police Commissioner Murphy finally declared a "quality arrest" policy, with "no more pretzel-vendor quota," in the words of one court official. The same backlog problem existed in the Supreme Court as a result of "overindictments" by district attorneys, also to the dismay of the judges.

Stated more generally, all these agencies are involved at every point in the process of moving defendants through the courts. The problems of informing them of appearance times and scheduling and

---

*All-purpose parts had begun to get implemented in 1969 in Queens, before EDC appeared.

†While increasing numbers of arrests indicate rising police productivity, they increase the case backlog and thereby contribute to declining productivity in the courts.

of best using their limited time once they are all convened are very complex. Then, when they don't coordinate as required, the whole system breaks down even more. The Criminal Justice Coordinating Council cites some common examples of such breakdown: "The police were making illegal arrests under various loitering statutes despite the refusal of the courts or district attorneys to prosecute. Court calendars on Fridays this past summer were uncharacteristically small, despite the desperate overcrowding in the Department of Correction detention institutions. . . . Through inattention and in some cases through deliberate policy, joint planning and coordinated operations among the component agencies have expanded much too slowly."[7]

This lack of coordination results in large part from the separation of powers between the executive and judicial branches of government, with the judiciary, as an independent branch, taking the position that formal merger with executive-branch criminal justice agencies (police, corrections, probation) is constitutionally impossible. It may cooperate voluntarily with other agencies, but it refuses to dilute its constitutional status by participation in any interagency arrangements that might subordinate it to direct executive or legislative authority. The courts' separation is, in turn, protected by long-term appointments or elective terms, designed precisely to insulate judges from the kinds of transient political pressures to which legislative and executive agencies are subject. But this attitude of fierce independence and separation is characteristic of every criminal justice agency. Consequently, nobody is in authority and no one can easily take charge when things go wrong. Early in Mayor Lindsay's first term, a commission recommended a kind of superagency for criminal justice—to combine police, corrections, probation, and the courts. The judiciary vetoed the plan, but the other departments were not that enthusiastic either.

These agencies represent competing interests: the government (Police Department, district attorneys) arrests, charges, and prosecutes; Legal Aid represents defendants who are presumed innocent until proven guilty; and the courts interpret and apply the law, oversee trials, and mete out sentences. Much of this agency separation is endemic to our legal system, designed so that basic due-process concepts of separation of powers—as between the judicial and executive branches of government—will be preserved. But the lack of cooperation, even administratively, has gone far beyond what is legally required.

Furthermore, the agencies all compete for limited funding. Each sees its own functions as most important and therefore worthy of more support than it is getting. Coordination means that agencies may become more aware of each other's deficiencies or that some superordinate authority may supervise the coordination process. That may affect their power and autonomy as well as their level of funding, all of which they have a vested interest in maintaining.

The closest the city ever came, until 1977, to effecting more interagency coordination was through the Mayor's Criminal Justice Coordinating Council, a conduit for federal grants. The council represented mayoral policy in the criminal justice system by funneling and monitoring these grants, setting priorities for a city-wide approach to crime, and coordinating agency operations. It didn't fulfill any of these functions well, however, and the city still has no effective mechanism for achieving better interagency coordination.*

HISTORICAL BACKGROUND: UNSUCCESSFUL
LOCAL REFORM STRATEGIES

There were many approaches to court reform in the 1960s that predated EDC's involvement. One was to *remove cases from the courts* wherever possible. The establishment of a Parking Violations Bureau to handle the many traffic summons cases and the early diversion of narcotics addicts and alcoholics to treatment (e.g., methadone clinics) were examples. Criminal justice officials believed that these strategies would release judges and nonjudicial staff to handle more important backlogged criminal cases. They didn't have anywhere near the positive effects that their advocates had hoped, however, owing in part to the continued poor management of the courts.

A second improvement strategy was simply to *add more resources.* The Judicial Conference Administrative Board had led a state-wide drive in the 1960s to get the legislature to increase judicial manpower, and in 1968 the legislature acceded, authorizing over 100 new judgeships throughout the state, including 20 for New York City's Criminal Court. When even this step failed to stop the courts' deterioration or significantly increase their productivity, Mayor Lindsay became outraged. As the 1972 annual plan of his Criminal Justice Coordinating Council concluded: "It simply has not been established that more resources are the principal answer to court problems. The Supreme Court budget, as well as those of District Attorneys, have

*See *Organization Report*, CJCC Task Force, Economic Development Council, January 28, 1975, pp. 1-3. As of January 1, 1977, there is a deputy mayor for criminal justice for this purpose. EDC was a main catalyst for that change.

increased considerably in the last five years . . . while the delay problem has grown worse. . . . Without steps to improve efficiency, still further major commitment of scarce resources cannot be justified."8

Still another reform strategy was that of supporting *demonstration and pilot projects* to "fine tune" the courts. Two independent, nonprofit consultants, the Vera Institute of Justice and the New York City Rand Corporation, pursued this strategy. Vera, working in close collaboration with the Criminal Justice Coordinating Council and largely funded through it, developed many new programs to ease the courts' case congestion, their inefficient scheduling, and the lack of rehabilitation services. Rand, in turn, did evaluations of Vera-initiated and other projects. Both agencies produced excellent studies and programs, resulting in many innovations that dealt with specific trouble spots within the system. But for every problem that was corrected, dozens festered. An assumption behind this strategy was that a carefully designed pilot project, tested in a small part of the court system, might eventually have system-wide effects. The end result, however, was pockets of change within a sagging system and gradual disenchantment with the "fine tuning" strategy.

In searching for a "quick fix" for the courts' increasing problems, some court officials and outside management consulting firms looked to computerized management information systems as the answer. Top administrators from the Judicial Data Processing Center of the first appellate division proposed this as a way of improving scheduling and coordination; and a top administrator in the office of the administrative judge had developed a major proposal in 1969 to computerize calendar control and centralize it in the Criminal Court.* These efforts really had little impact, however, because the courts' structure and procedures were so chaotic, authority, job descriptions, and controls so vague, and the separation of the criminal justice agencies that would have to collaborate in developing such an information system so marked, that it made little sense to move in that direction without first making progress on these problems.

The most significant reforms in operation when EDC arrived were two projects designed to revamp the specialized parts structure of the courts. They were among the last insider-initiated alternatives to EDC's proposals, which were of course dependent on many of the insiders' ideas, and they helped set the stage for EDC. One, funded through the Criminal Justice Coordinating Council, involved setting up a Master All-Purpose Calendar Complex (MAP, as it was called) in

---

*He did get a small grant to begin such work, and one computer company was also brought in to work on installing an information system.

the Manhattan Criminal Court.* The other, a variant on the first, was a system of "all-purpose parts," established in the Queens Criminal Court in 1969. The first plan involved setting up a small group of parts that would be coordinated centrally and supported by a separate administrative unit. It included a central "calendar" part for pre-appearance conferences in which prosecuting and defense attorneys could make a quick decision about adjournment or an immediate trial. There were also four "backup" (or hearing and trial) parts to process the case as quickly as possible after it had moved through the pre-appearance and arraignment phases in the calendar part. The all-purpose parts, on the other hand, involved a series of paired "calendar" and backup parts. As John Jennings, a former New York City Rand and now Criminal Court researcher, explained all-purpose parts: "In the former (calendar parts), the various parties involved in each case would be assembled, quick conferences would be held, guilty pleas could be accepted and sentences imposed, or charges could be dismissed; cases requiring hearings or (one-judge) trials were transferred to the respective backup parts."9 The main purpose of these structural reforms was to decrease congestion and delay and provide speedier justice, while still giving individualized treatment to each defendant.†

Still other reforms were proposed but not implemented. One was to have the state fund the entire city court system—a proposal that has gained stronger endorsement recently, as New York City has moved into a deeper fiscal crisis. Another was to revamp the entire judicial selection process to ensure that regardless of whether judges were elected or appointed, they would be of the highest possible

---

*MAP had a budget of several million dollars and was phased out after a few years, after failing to generate much internal support or have much direct impact.

†Each of these reforms had its own complicated politics, as one might imagine. Several insiders reported, for example, that MAP was developed partly as a way of getting around Administrative Judge Dudley, who was regarded as a poor administrator and was seen as likely to be staying on when MAP was first planned. Its director, Edwyn Siberling, a Long Island judge and Reform Democrat with excellent connections to top Lindsay administration officials (including Henry Ruth, the head of the Criminal Justice Coordinating Council), had a higher salary than any court administrator and a large staff, and reported directly to the presiding judges of the appellate divisions, over the head of the Administrative Judge, David Ross, who succeeded Dudley. MAP experienced a precipitous decline in internal support and eventually all but faded into oblivion. This multimillion-dollar project ended up producing only a twenty-four-page final report and got little credit for its many innovations that Judge Ross later incorporated.

competence and integrity. Still another was to have a deputy mayor or other top local official act as "czar" for the entire criminal justice system in the city. Some or all of these proposals may eventually come to pass and might help to improve the courts' management. But they face the difficult problem of generating the required political support. It is to the political arena that we now turn in discussing the final breakdown of the courts leading up to EDC's entry, the conditions of that entry, and the nature and impact of EDC's studies.

The Final Breakdown

From 1968 on, there was growing recognition within the courts and among knowledgeable outsiders that a breakdown of crisis proportions was taking place. Throughout this period, there was a mounting flood of public criticism from the press, state and local legislators, bar associations, district attorneys, the Legal Aid Society, and civic groups. Charges and rebuttals accumulated, along with proposals for change. The reform programs discussed above had not worked. The case backlog was mounting. The number of prisoners in jail awaiting trial had increased. The courts appeared to be repeatedly adjourning cases without dispositions, and countless critics charged that the judges were not working full-time. "Henry Ruth, the head of the Mayor's Coordinating Council," reported a City Hall official, "made what has become a legendary charge in 1970 that if judges worked eight hours a day, they could really reduce the backlog." Even five hours of active bench time would have done so.* In May 1970, New York City's Criminal Court administrative judge, Edward Dudley, announced his resignation effective as of the end of the year. In August, riots broke out in the Manhattan House of Detention (the Tombs), and in October, another riot erupted in the Queens House of Detention.

Throughout all these crises, there was no decisive movement toward a solution and no concerted effort to plan emergency measures. Given the fragmented court structure described above, nobody had the authority or power to move decisively. The group with perhaps the most power, the presiding judges of the appellate divisions, seemed incapable of taking the drastic steps required.

---

*Jack Newfield, social critic and writer for the *Village Voice*, wrote a series of articles on corruption, inefficiency, and the "non-work" ethic of many judges, including one on the ten worst judges in New York, that he later put together into a book.

Political Preconditions for EDC's Entry

It had taken many years for the New York City Criminal Court to break down, and by 1970, a solution required at least three conditions: (1) Key political leaders in the city had to have a new perception of the courts, which could no longer remain a patronage dumping ground used to fulfill political commitments and then left to run themselves. The judiciary had to be held accountable to the other branches of government. (2) The presiding judges had to have a new perception of judicial responsibility. They had to abandon their traditional laissez-faire attitude about court administration and to recognize that the courts required careful institutional management. (3) A face-saving device was needed for the senior judges, who, though not solely responsible for the crisis, could be held accountable for some of the breakdown. They had to remain independent, with their judicial prestige restored.

In sum, the judicial establishment had to save itself, and its demonstrating its capacity to do that was critical to the concept of an independent judicial branch. The best way to do this was for reform to be carried out quietly by insiders, with little public exposure and little analysis of the history of the crisis or ascription of individual responsibility for it. Perhaps the single most important action taken in this regard was the appointment in late 1970 of Supreme Court Judge and former City Council President David Ross as the new administrative judge of the Criminal Court. Ross instituted many management reforms and was to support many of EDC's recommendations, contained in reports that were completed and endorsed by the presiding justices before he arrived.

EDC became one important instrument for achieving such management reforms. Its presence indicated that the judges, having invited in such a prestigious group, were strongly committed to management reform. And EDC could benefit by associating itself with an effort to restore the credibility of a seriously discredited government agency. The judges and EDC thus needed each other and have existed in a mutually beneficial partnership since 1970.

At the same time, EDC's prestige and power assured it at least informal access to many participants: the mayor, the governor, and top criminal justice officials. Specifically, this well qualified EDC to mediate in the feudal wars between the many parts of the criminal justice system and particularly in the continuing "arms length" relationship between the appellate divisions and the administrative judge. One of EDC's biggest contributions was to help clarify relations between these two parties, in order to establish much clearer and sharper authority for the courts' management.

Not the least of EDC's appeal was the fact that it offered the senior judges free consulting assistance. Since EDC's study would be donated and would not have to wend its way through the budgetary process, its results would be quickly available long before a publicly financed, commercial consulting report could have been authorized and completed. In addition, commercial consulting firms simply could not do the sustained, in-depth observation and analysis that EDC did. Finally, EDC emphasized reforms that were "doable," without the necessity of legislation and constitutional changes.

EDC offered a methodology well suited to the political realities—detailed documentation of existing court structures and procedures "as is," with no attempt to assign blame or take strong value positions. The fact that EDC asked a lot of questions about what was going on and how it could help, rather than trying to impose any preconceived solution, and that it stayed away from policy or political questions gave it further credibility.

AN OVERVIEW OF EDC'S COURTS PROJECTS

EDC's work in the courts has gone through several stages, starting with a series of studies in the New York City Criminal Court and moving on to the State Supreme Court, including both its criminal and civil units, the state administrator's office, the Family Court in New York City and throughout the state, and, finally, the Mayor's Criminal Justice Coordinating Council. Several characteristics of its work are worth noting. First, it generally proceeded in a "bottom-up" fashion, as contrasted with the top-down approach characteristic of EDC's work in the Board of Education and HRA. Its early studies involved extensive documentation of case flows and procedures in the Criminal Court and then the Supreme Court, and later work analyzed the entire state administrative structure and criminal justice system of the city. EDC started, then, by studying "symptoms" of management problems; over time, it moved on to studies of structure that got at underlying causes.

A second feature of this work was that later studies built on earlier ones in a cumulative way. EDC's studies of case flows gave it insights that helped in its organizational structure research. Also, the type of organizational analysis and recommendations that EDC made in the Criminal Court—emphasizing a strong central authority and standardized rules governing conduct—were then used in its subsequent work, which recommended an administrative merger of the Criminal Court and the State Supreme Court's Criminal Term. This was due largely to the fact that the same administrative deficiencies—fragmented authority, no enforcement of rules, no separation between judicial and nonjudicial functions or between policy and administration—existed at every level.

Finally, the sequence of these studies reflected EDC's progressively closer consulting relationships with key court officials. It started with an invitation from Judge Harold Stevens, presiding justice of the First Appellate Division, to look at the Criminal Court, and moved from there to work closely with Administrative Judge Ross and Executive Officer Goodchild of the Criminal Court, and then with Judges Breitel and Bartlett in the statewide structure and Benjamin Altman, head of the Mayor's Criminal Justice Coordinating Council. Even court officials who were critical of EDC's early work were later more positive about its contributions. "I thought some of their early studies were quite routine, and the first organizational study was much too theoretical," an appellate administrator commented. "But the more they work with us, the more valuable they are. They have become a tremendous asset; and I'm more impressed with them as time goes on."

Perhaps the most important feature of EDC's studies was their extensive documentation of court operations, an invaluable information source for court administrators. No insiders had ever done it, because the courts had so little in-house management analysis capability. As for outsiders, the courts were a very closed agency and were not about to invite in any ordinary group to make their many weaknesses more visible. EDC got in only because of its support from Presiding Judge Stevens and because of the courts' desperate condition—and because the work was tedious and took a lot of time and money.

We may now turn to an analysis of EDC's work. We will do so by considering each of its separate sets of court projects in historical sequence. The reader should keep several things in mind. First, political forces intruded at every stage, including those leading up to the decision to invite EDC in. Second, many court officials and other consultants, some of whom were competitors of EDC or felt threatened by its recommendations, had different perceptions of the merits of what it did. We have encountered this in the other agencies where EDC worked, but it seemed pronounced in the courts, partly because the changes EDC was to recommend were fairly far-reaching.

Both the play of politics and the diversity of perceptions indicate how complex this EDC courts project was. One measure of that complexity is the "lead time" that was requested for this work. Roughly twenty months elapsed from the first meeting of EDC's Public Safety Committee in 1968 to the submission of its first report to the Criminal Court, during which time many difficult problems had to be resolved. EDC gained entree easily enough through Presiding Judge Stevens, but the real problem was to reach agreement with court officials on what it would study and to secure people on loan for the work. While the latter did not pose any great problems, getting operating-level officials to agree on particular EDC studies was a very time-consuming task. The whole process was not very different from that of a private management consultant trying to secure a government contract.

EDC's "lead time" experience broke down into several discrete stages: considerable self-education; extended work to make itself known to top court and city officials; prolonged "contract" negotiations, selling the program to member companies; and, finally, setting up an organization and doing the study itself. A key figure in this early work was Joseph Grazier, former president and chairman of the Board of American Standard, who joined EDC in late 1969 to consult on courts and corrections. Grazier's influence within EDC increased steadily, and he eventually became the director of the court studies, as well as EDC's vice-chairman and a close colleague of Champion. He was EDC's advocate of in-house task forces: he conceived the idea of having one for the court projects, and helped transfer the concept to later EDC work.*

Two other key participants in the court work were Richard Coyne, a young (early-thirties) lawyer from Dewey, Ballantine, a major Wall Street firm, who had come to EDC in November 1969 and became a member of its central staff, assigned to work on criminal justice problems; and Harold Finley, a staff vice-president in Marketing and Operations at Metropolitan Life, who arrived at EDC in April 1970 as an on-loan executive and later became a permanent staff member and director of EDC's HRA task force. Coyne provided strong administrative leadership, directing all of EDC's court and criminal justice work after 1971 and bringing important legal as well as management-analysis skills to the projects; and Finley, a student of management theory and organizational design, did the first EDC study on the organization of the Criminal Court. A third participant, who came on the courts task forces in 1973 after having worked at the Board of Education headquarters and with Finley at HRA, was Anthony Morelli, a management analysis and information systems

---

*The task force concept worked much better in the courts than it did in the early stages of the HRA and Board of Education projects, mainly because of weak leadership in the latter two and their failure to develop manageable projects or do the detailed documentations that the courts group did.

specialist, who had had extensive experience both in the private sector (at Metropolitan Life) and in New York City government.

THE CRIMINAL COURT

EDC began work in the Criminal Court in December 1969. It took until the following summer for EDC to actually get underway with specific studies. During this period, EDC made extensive observations of the courts at the "bottom"—that is, at operating levels—in addition to conducting interviews at the "top"—with the mayor, interested legal groups, and court officials.

Its work started with visits to the Criminal Court in the Bronx and Manhattan, the ones to the Bronx being particularly important. The Criminal Court there was among the most congested and physically deteriorated in the city, and EDC soon developed a picture of the chaos that existed and of the demoralized state of the judges. There was a lot of mutual scapegoating, with some lower-court judges blaming senior judges in the Appellate Division for failing to face the crisis and for being overly defensive with outside critics.

The question was what EDC might do in this situation. Its first inclination, which it later followed up on, was to support a media exposé that would dramatize the physical deterioration of the Bronx Criminal Court in particular and the neglect of the courts in general, in order to draw attention to the citywide problem of congestion.

Having familiarized themselves with conditions at the "bottom," Grazier and Coyne, the two EDC officials most active at this stage, then contacted top criminal justice and city officials. They approached, among others, Mendes Hershman, general counsel for New York Life, an EDC member, and chairman of both the Mayor's Committee on the Judiciary and the New York City Bar Association Committee on Court Requirements; David Peck, retired presiding justice of the First Appellate Division and a senior partner at Sullivan and Cromwell, one of the most prestigious law firms in the city; the assistant administrative judge and court administrator of the Criminal Court; Presiding Judge Harold Stevens, who succeeded Peck; and Mayor Lindsay, along with his advisor on court and criminal justice matters.

The meetings with the mayor were particularly important, since he had so much power over the courts' operations. The mayor had at least two agendas that were potentially at odds with EDC's priorities as he saw them. One was to force the courts to make management improvements by threatening to cut their budgets if they failed to do so. His aides were talking at this time about "starving the courts into submission." EDC, by contrast, had become publicly aligned with the judiciary and its Bar Association allies by supporting their demands for more court construction. It did this partly to gain some credibility with court officials, just as it had done so in the high schools and at Board of Education headquarters.

Lindsay was also preparing at this time to greatly expand the role of the Criminal Justice Coordinating Council, one of whose functions was to try to coordinate court reform programs. A mayoral assistant expressing concern that so many groups were becoming interested in improving the courts and anxious to avoid conflict and duplication, suggested that EDC work with and through the Council.

At this point, the first round of EDC's initial explorations was completed. Its strategy was still not clear, since it had just begun gathering information. The second stage of EDC's attempts to gain access to the Criminal Court began in February 1970 and involved numerous meetings with court officials who were responding to EDC's questions regarding how it could help. It took five more months before EDC began doing studies, during which time it was defining some general objectives, developing its task force concept and methodology, getting clearance for the project from top court officials, developing working relationships throughout the court, and recruiting task force members.

Late in February, at EDC's request, the administrative staff of the First Appellate Division prepared a memorandum making clear to EDC that some projects might soon get under way. The memorandum emphasized the court's lack of "in-house management analysis capability." It emphasized in particular the need for improved clerical procedures, statistical data, and project planning and coordination.

A series of meetings on these matters between EDC representatives and court officials took place that spring. The meetings were quite open-ended, and for the first time, the key court participants—one from the Appellate Division and the other from the office of the administrative judge—were administrators. As these two top court officials gradually became more specific about their objectives, it was clear that they had different goals. One, the head of the Judicial Data Processing Center of the First Appellate Division, wanted assistance in computerization for record keeping and case scheduling. EDC resisted, arguing that computerization was premature until the courts developed organizationally and procedurally to the point where they would know what to computerize. The other, the executive officer of the Criminal Court, wanted management and record-keeping assistance to help the courts deal with their backlog and with delays in case processing. The question remained, however, as to what specific studies EDC would conduct.

Finally, in mid-June 1970, EDC and court administrators agreed on areas in which EDC could help: (1) a citywide study of the scheduling of "universal summons" cases, to redesign and improve procedures; (2) a study in two court parts, to simplify and rationalize the forms used in case processing; and (3) an organization study of the citywide administration of the Criminal Court. An agreement was also made that the three studies would begin on July 1, subject to EDC's being able to recruit qualified people on loan.

While the recruiting did not constitute a major problem, it did require some initial persuasion. Grazier of EDC did this through personal contacts with board chairmen and other top people from three large insurance companies: Metropolitan Life, New York Life, and Equitable. At first, both New York Life and Equitable resisted, saying they had no retired staff members still living in the city with the "required experience," and offering financial support instead. When Metropolitan Life agreed to provide people on loan, however, the other two followed suit. Finley of Metropolitan Life then acted as coordinator for this task force.

The skills of the insurance company people matched the courts' needs very well, and this constituted one of the most important features of the task force. EDC had recruited capable work systems analysts and management services staff with precisely the kinds of skills required to improve court operations. Part of the courts' problem was designing effective work and case flows, and the techniques of case processing in insurance were thought to be particularly applicable. Finley's organizational design interests also meshed well with the immediate need of the Criminal Court for a more stream-lined structure.

By the end of July, the courts task force comprised eleven people. One immediate problem was EDC's possibly duplicating what other consultants were doing. The Appellate Division was going ahead with the Master Calendar Project (MAP) with federal funds already allocated for it; and there were plans to evaluate it and compare it with the all-purpose part structure set up in Queens. An Appellate Division administrator questioned, in this context, the usefulness of EDC's also studying court parts. While court officials could not very well order EDC to stop a free consulting project, they were trying to limit it. "There was already heavy involvement of many consultants in Manhattan," reported one of the EDC people. "People studying the courts were tripping over each other, so we agreed to do many of our studies over in Queens."

In late July, almost a month after EDC began its studies, one of its top officials was prepared to stop the entire project, because of what he saw as a lack of court staff cooperation at lower levels, as well as the seeming duplication by EDC of another consultant's studies. He recommended that the insurance companies provide grants to this consultant, rather than have EDC do any studies itself. EDC decided instead to continue, but the incident indicated further how difficult it was to start even some relatively simple studies in this agency.

At some critical point in the summer of 1970, Lester Goodchild of the Criminal Court, with whom EDC had been working all along, helped redirect it from doing relatively trivial studies to doing a major one on the organization of the entire Criminal Court. EDC had already proposed to do such an organizational study, but it needed strong insider support for it. The study soon gave EDC momentum and a more influential consulting role than it would otherwise have had. "Their forms and summons studies were good," reported a top court administrator, "but the big breakthrough for them came when Goodchild helped Coyne redirect their work to a big organization study, and that was the thing that made them so successful."

The mechanics and politics of access had thus occupied EDC over a seven-month period, before the study itself actually began; and some issues appeared to remain unresolved even after the formal starting date. EDC overcame many early obstacles, owing to its having found an influential insider client in Goodchild, who wanted this organizational study done, and to its own persistence. It also began a series of studies that have continued to the present time and that constitute important and productive management consulting efforts in the public sector.

EDC's Organization Study

EDC's work in the Criminal Court included both low-level studies documenting court procedures and a broad, citywide study of the court's organizational structure. The documentation work, while not nearly as important as the organizational study, enabled EDC to learn about the courts, to establish its credibility by carefully delineating procedures, forms, and work flows that court officials should have known about but didn't, and to develop key contacts within the system. At the same time, EDC became increasingly aware that sustained improvements in procedures would not be possible until the court's organizational structure was clarified. Indeed, it turned out that the court didn't have any management or structure at all and had to get one as a first-order priority.

What follows is an analysis of this EDC organization study. As in EDC's other consulting work, one cannot isolate out particular effects of its work, since other forces were operating at the same time. The most important was the appointment of a dynamic administrative judge, David Ross, two months after EDC completed the report. The combination of EDC and Ross was to contribute to critical management innovations, with most involved participants concluding that Ross was by far the more significant of the two factors. Any attempt to estimate the relative importance of each is less fruitful, however, than an analysis of the political process.

In order to orient the reader to the complexities of the city and state court structure, Figure 6-1 presents a simplified picture of the main participants and their relationships. Starting at the bottom, where EDC did, are the main operating courts in the city, including the Supreme Court, which is placed on a slightly higher level than the others, because of the higher status and salaries of its staff thoughout much of the period of EDC's studies. Originally, each of these courts had its own, fairly autonomous, administrative judge. (One effect of EDC's many studies and reorganization proposals was to consolidate and expand the authority of the New York City Administrative Judge, who acquired increasing jurisdiction over all of these courts, including the Supreme Court.) The next level up is the Appellate Divisions, which had ultimate jurisdiction over the city courts on both administrative and policy matters, including the power to appoint the administrative judge. Above them were higher-level state officials—in particular, the state administrative judge, a position that only came into existence in 1974, after EDC and the Chief Judge recommended that it be established. EDC's many years of consulting for the city and state were to cumulatively help rationalize each level, starting from the bottom.

The organization questions that EDC's Criminal Court study covered related to the court's basic *structural* problems discussed earlier. There were also problems of *politics*, relating mainly to the vested interests of the Appellate Division in preserving its authority, and others of *personalities* or *managerial styles*, in particular those of Administrative Judge Dudley and his successor.

The main issue tying together all three problems was the ambiguity of authority between the Appellate Division and the Criminal Court, resulting in a vacuum of leadership that had existed for many years. The Appellate Division had its own administrators, duplicating functions of the administrative judge and his staff, and neither group had assumed leadership during the breakdown of the Criminal Court

FIGURE 6-1. New York City and State Courts. *In order to orient the reader to the complexities of the city and state court structure, Figure 6-1 presents a simplified picture of the main participants and their relationships.*

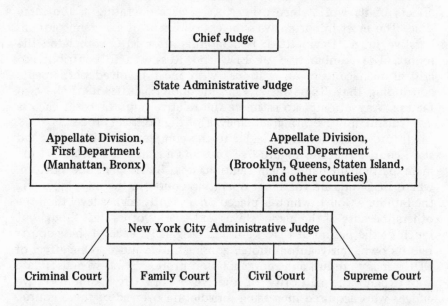

in the 1960s. The problem was in part one of the Appellate's being unwilling to delegate administrative authority to the Criminal Court on such matters as issuing sanctions against judges, attorneys, police, and other criminal justice officials who failed to appear in court at required times or to work appropriate hours. Many judges had so blatantly abdicated their responsibilities by working very short hours that administrative sanctions against them seemed essential. To some degree, however, the problem was one of Administrative Judge Dudley being unwilling to exercise what authority he had. There was blame enough to be borne both by the system and by particular top officials—but the result, in any case, was poor management and a pronounced absence of judicial accountability for performance.

Several management reforms, all of which EDC was to address in its report, seemed required for the court's recovery. They included the need for a *strong central authority;* for a sharp *separation of policy from administration;* for a *delegation of administrative authority* to the Criminal Court from the Appellate, the top policy-making body; for an equally sharp *separation within the Criminal Court of the judicial from the nonjudicial chain of command;* and for *standardized rules and sanctions* to be applied citywide. These needed reforms followed classical management and public administration principles, just as did those that EDC tried to introduce in reorganizing Board of Education headquarters.

THE APPELLATE AND CRIMINAL COURTS: NO CENTRAL AUTHORITY

Many informants indicated that a major obstacle to court reform in accordance with these principles was the Appellate divisions. They had kept tight control over judicial patronage; they continuously got into administration, refusing to delegate management authority to the administrative judge; one of their primary goals seemed to be to perpetuate the power of their unit; they stood as a barrier between the administrative judges of the city courts and top state officials, thereby preventing the latter from exercising authority; they had failed to provide leadership during the period leading up to the breakdown (1967-70); and their jurisdictional conflicts with the Criminal Court were symptomatic of many court management problems. Consider the following comments from a wide spectrum of participants:

> The Appellate Divisions controlled the assignment of judges, the rules for disposition of cases. But it was a very clubby atmosphere, and they never enforced the rules. They didn't insist that the judges work after 2 P. M.

> Power really stops at the Appellate Division. It doesn't move up to the state level.

> When Henry Ruth of the Mayor's Coordinating Council made the charge that the backlog and detention problems could be licked if the judges ever decided to work eight hours a day, they really got cracking. The problem before was the Appellate's power. They are an inside group of judges. They had felt they were above criticism, and no policing went on.

> The presiding judges in the Appellate Division are the professional power brokers of the system. They really didn't seem to want much change.

> The power of the Appellate was the main obstacle to change. They didn't want to delegate power for administrative solutions.

There was also a consensus that Administrative Judge Dudley had prevented management reforms. Court officials consistently regarded Dudley as a decent and intelligent man, but as lacking any sustained interest in or ability at management. He seems to have exercised little leadership in dealing with the court's breakdown, though one obstacle was the Appellate's reluctance to delegate much administrative authority to him.*

---

*Dudley and Presiding Justice Harold Stevens of the First Appellate Division were both black politicians, and some insiders suggested that it would have been

A key problem, then, and one on which EDC as an outside organization played such an important role, was this absence of authority at the top, reflecting a stalemated relationship between the Appellate Division and the administrative judge over who was in charge. The Appellate was legally in charge, but its functions were supposed to be policy ones, while it should have delegated authority for running the Criminal Court to its appointed administrative judge. No court official, however, could easily propose that. The proposal might be seen as self-serving; there was some career risk in pushing too hard; and no official would have enough of a political constituency to prevail, even if other conditions were favorable.

As students of organizational development have confirmed, the entry into such situations of a third party with the required prestige and legitimacy is often the catalyst that helps resolve such internal stalemates in a manner allowing for significant innovations.[10] That happened in this instance—though the third party, EDC, was effective mainly because of the actions of Administrative Judge Ross. EDC, however, was an important buffer between the Appellate and Ross, and its organizational study, by prevailing on the Appellate to delegate administrative authority where it belonged, helped establish a newly unified authority in the Criminal Court under him. It was to set the stage for Ross, and without EDC's study, Ross would have found it much harder to provide leadership.

Support and Rationale for the Study

Another critical element in the situation was the support given to EDC's organization study by Lester Goodchild, a top planner in the Criminal Court, who had become one of EDC's main insider clients. Coyne had always wanted to do such a study, and at some point in mid-1970, there was a meeting of Coyne, Finley, and Goodchild at which it was agreed on. Finley, the other EDC person involved, was a specialist in organization design, and such a study fit his interests as well. "What was missing from our other work," reported an EDC

---

difficult for Stevens to fire or transfer Dudley. Dudley had become one of the scapegoats for the breakdown.

To give the Appellate its due, Judge Stevens did take the initiative by inviting EDC in, appointing Ross as administrative judge, and allowing him to take over. The situation of the court was desperate enough for Stevens to do this. The insiders' perception of Stevens was that he, like Dudley, was not a specialist in management, nor did he seem oriented in the past toward management solutions to court problems.

official, "was how you run the court. Once Goodchild and Finley got going on this, it really moved."*

Finley directed this organization study in a systematic way.[11] First, based on his private-sector experience, he constructed a model of key administrative functions that he felt all organizations had to deal with—for example, goal setting, rules and work standards, authority, communication, clear specification of tasks, leadership, and performance measurement.† Second, he assessed the court's structure and operations in the context of this model, based on EDC's own studies, on its review of the studies of others, and on past organization charts and proposals for management reform.

Finally, Finley presented detailed charts of what the structure of the courts should be and of what positions and functions it needed to fit his model. Before the actual presentations, Finley and EDC rehearsed with informed lawyers to limit the management jargon and make the model acceptable to the judges. Even so, many judges and court staff thought it was too theoretical. "We had a meeting early in 1971," an Appellate administrator reported. "EDC suggested establishing a large number of subcommittees—capital, planning, and so on. All kinds of business terms. There was a serious jargon problem. The structure they drew up was preposterous. Straight out of a college textbook. There were about thirty judges and other court people at that meeting. On that night, those subcommittees died. Some panned it openly. The next morning Judge Ross called somebody at the Appellate Division to ask whether they were insisting on this. They told him it was ridiculous. That was it. We had no qualms about forgetting it. Some of the EDC people were very shocked and upset by this, but they stayed with us, and as I say, their organization report was fine overall; and they helped us more and more over time."
time."

*Goodchild had experienced continued frustration in his many attempts to achieve such a reorganization, and EDC was to be the effective ally that he had always needed but never before had. "In early 1967," reported a court administrator, "Goodchild recommended that the Criminal Court top administrative structure be reorganized along the lines later endorsed by EDC and implemented by Administrative Judge Ross. It was that a single administrator be appointed, with three deputies directly under him. The Appellate approved the proposal and then it went the rounds from there to the Judicial Conference to Judge Dudley, back to the Appellate, back to the Judicial Conference, and then to the mayor. But nothing happened. There seemed to be an agreement on Dudley's part that he would push it, but he apparently did nothing. Meanwhile, the walls were caving in on the court."

†For a report on the study, including its methodology, see *Organization Study of the New York City Criminal Court*, Economic Development Council Task Force, 1970, pp. 1-23.

Part of the problem was Finley's strong theoretical interest and his attention to detail, as reflected in his elaborate organizational charts, some of them big enough to fill an entire large wall. "As lawyers," reported a top EDC representative in defense of Finley's work, "they interpreted his charts too literally. For people who follow case precedent, the word is law. What he presented was only meant to be suggestive of how the courts might reorganize, and he probably spelled out in too much detail what that might involve. He wasn't telling them that they had to have this, that, or the other subcommittee, but rather that particular functions had to be performed in some fashion that were not being performed at that time, if the courts were to be at all well managed." A big part of the problem also, however, was the threat that the study posed for Appellate and Criminal Court staff, some of whose jobs might be changed or eliminated if its recommendations got implemented.

Diagnosis and Recommendations

In any case, the details of the charts are less important than EDC's diagnosis, its reform recommendations, and what happened to them. Developed in the context of Finley's management theory of universal functions, the diagnosis spelled out many of the court's weaknesses. It argued that there was an absence of coherent planning and setting of priorities, of rules and standards, of clear lines of authority, of specification of tasks and quality controls, of administrative leadership, of management support services, and of performance measures and accountability. Condensed to just a few pages of summary discussion (in sharp contrast to Finley's many charts), it was a compelling indictment of the system—though there was little in it that many court officials hadn't known for a long time.

EDC had thus crystallized key recommendations for reform that several court officials had espoused, fit them into Finley's management theory, and given them its imprimatur. EDC's report contained some of its own ideas as well; its report did, however, strongly reflect their views.

The report, submitted to the court in October 1970, contained some seventeen broad recommendations relating to administrative and judicial policy matters.* The recommendations met, not surprisingly, with a very mixed response. The main criticisms were that the report itself did not document or state the rationale for many of

---

*If one includes all the sub-recommendations under each of the seventeen headings in the report, there were close to three times that number.

its recommendations; that those recommendations relating to judicial policy issues indicated EDC's naiveté, since many of them required enabling legislation; that the report was not original, but rather picked up ideas that had been around for some time; that the elaborate structure of administrative functions and subcommittees was unrealistic and pretentious; and that the recommendations were too theoretical.

The most critical comments came from court officials who felt threatened by the changes and were skeptical of attempts on the part of business to transfer management principles and techniques from the private sector to government. "We are not an assembly line," explained one court administrator, "and many of their principles relating to management functions just don't apply." Some also came from competing consultants who felt that their work was better and more relevant than EDC's to the court's immediate problems.* The most positive responses came from participants whose own past proposals got incorporated in the report and who stood to benefit from their implementation. These included the Legal Aid Society, some Criminal Court judges and administrators, and even some people from the Appellate Division, though the latter usually had reservations about EDC and its report.†

A review and interpretation of such reactions, however, is much less important than some discussion of just what the recommendations were and what changes, if any, resulted from the report. Some bore directly on administrative reform—such as recommendations to consolidate authority and have it exercised uniformly and firmly throughout the courts, or to eliminate or transfer some functions and establish others. The rest pertained to new judicial policies that might cut the backlog and speed up the flow of cases—for example, establishing all-purpose night courts and abolishing three-judge trials. The line separating administrative from policy reforms, however, was sometimes hard to draw.

---

*I was never particularly impressed with EDC," reported one such consultant. "They mostly addressed the wrong issues—forms, documentation of clerical procedures, office layouts, trivia. The rest of their work went to the opposite extreme, head-in-the-clouds stuff. . . . The giant chart of corporate functions the courts should use as a model was silly. The analogy between business and the courts was stretched beyond all usefulness."

†"EDC gave the courts an organizational model," reported one court administrator. "It helped also with its documentation of procedures and case and paper flows. But the breakthrough was when Goodchild helped Coyne redirect their work to a big organization study, and that was the thing that made them so important."

Administrative Reform Recommendations

The EDC report included administrative reform recommendations in two broad categories. The first had to do with "vertical" relations within the Criminal Court, involving the establishment of a unified central authority, with a middle-management and staff support structure and uniform rules throughout the system to help make it work. The second focused on "lateral" work flow arrangements, mainly related to consolidating the overspecialized part structure. In general, these were not ad hoc recommendations, but rather were presented as part of a package of proposals related to Finley's and EDC's model of what constituted "sound" management principles and practice.

Vertical Authority Relations

The most basic EDC recommendation was to grant the administrative judge the authority he needed to manage the courts. Superficially, this seemed like asking for what already existed, and some insiders claimed that the recommendation was superfluous, but that wasn't the case at all. Dudley had been the administrative judge since 1967, and, whatever his own limitations as an administrator, he did not have a clear, strong mandate from the Appellate to run the court.* By contrast, Ross's mandate as Dudley's successor, at least in part because of the EDC report, was much broader and stronger.

EDC also recommended increased funds to buttress the administrative judge's authority, and it specified the kinds of powers the office would need—to appoint, reappoint, and transfer judges, and to issue sanctions against those "court personnel, city agencies, attorneys, prosecutors, etc. . . . that impede the swift application of fair justice. . . ." Though funds were never provided ("The only additional funds we got came from LEAA for the night arraignment parts," reported a court administrator), the powers were made available.

To ensure even more that the administrative judge might run the courts effectively, EDC recommended that he have an in-house management planning capability—to conduct research, redesign court structure and operations, and establish standards. Judge Ross

---

*As EDC correctly pointed out: "While this authority seems to have been implied in the approval of Administrative Judge Dudley's reorganization proposal of February 27, 1967, it needs reaffirmation and a directive that it be exercised, to make his or our proposed organization changes effective." *Organization Study of the New York City Criminal Court*, Economic Development Council Task Force, 1970, p. 12.

approved this recommendation, but such a unit would have required an annual budget of up to $400,000.* EDC tried hard to finance this unit, but it was unsuccessful. "We don't know where this was stopped," an EDC staff person told us. "We think it may have been the Coordinating Council, who didn't want the courts to have more money until they demonstrated that they could manage better." Part of the problem was the competition within the court as to who was first in line to get new money and more staff, and to this day, the kind of management analysis capability that EDC recommended and that the court needs barely exists.†

Notwithstanding his mandate, the administrative judge alone could not run the court effectively. He had to contend with the judges and, in addition, manage a large administrative support staff of over 1,000 clerks and other personnel responsible for the courts' day-to-day operations. EDC recommended in this regard that an executive officer be appointed as his second in command and that the position be vested with full authority over all nonjudicial court staff. This position was established, with the person appointed to it, Lester Goodchild, having previously been just a planner with a few assistants. His boss, Administrative Judge Dudley, instead of just supervising the judges, had also been involved in court operations in much too detailed a way, often dealing with problems that some other administrator should have been dealing with. The recommendation, then, permitted a differentiation between judicial and nonjudicial authority. It freed the administrative judge to monitor and supervise the judges, while his executive officer would be in charge of all nonjudicial staff.

One other needed change in the top management structure was to establish strong and clear lines of authority. One problem was that the position of assistant administrative judge, a holdover from the old county structure, diluted the authority both of the administrative judge and of the new executive officer. With the establishment of a strong administrative judge to monitor the judges and an equally strong executive officer in charge of all nonjudicial personnel, there was no more need for this position. "Before," reported one EDC official, "you had these three circles of competing authority—the administrative judge, his executive, and the assistant administrative

---

*This recommendation contradicted the general pattern of EDC's consulting work for city agencies, which was predicated on changes that could be made within the constraints of existing budgets.

†A New York City Rand researcher who had done good studies of court operations moved over in 1973 to take a full-time position in the Criminal Court, and he has begun to develop such a management analysis unit.

judge—and they checkmated each other. Also, the assistant administrative judge's job was very ill-defined. He had neither any particular function nor a geographic area, and all you could say about it was that he got in other people's way. It was good that it was eliminated."

This was another case of a reform proposal that got implemented only after EDC had endorsed it. Goodchild, for example, had tried to eliminate the position several years before, but encountered too much opposition. The opposition disappeared, however, at a November 1970 meeting of top court officials, much to the surprise of at least one Appellate administrator. "I had no idea there was so much support for dropping the position," he reported, "but since it seemed to be just about unanimous, I didn't put up any strong objection."*

This reform, perhaps more than any other, dramatized the nature of EDC's role. When a court official had proposed the idea, it had been rejected as self-serving. Several years later, when an outside group, EDC, made roughly the same proposal, it got through. Conditions for its acceptance were by then more favorable, the courts having deteriorated since it was first made. In addition, EDC was regarded as a prestigious business group, and it proposed the change as part of a large package of management reform proposals, many of which were favorably received.

Fixing up the top, however, was not sufficient to provide the improved management that the court needed, and another set of EDC proposals was to establish a middle-management cadre, referred to as deputy executive officers, to help Executive Officer Goodchild in managing the court. At the time of EDC's report, a very weak support structure existed. Eventually, there were deputies responsible for legal services, judicial services, administrative operations (payroll and accounting, audit, budget, and personnel), court operations (supervising the clerks and court officers), and planning and analysis (statistics, supply, space, and facilities). This was not done so as to proliferate positions, but in order to assign authority for critical administrative tasks that had not been performed systematically in the past.

Realigning particular functions was still another EDC recommendation. The Criminal Court's Mental Health Bureau was one example. Widely regarded by insiders as highly inefficient, as "not putting in a full day," as producing reports of questionable quality, and altogether as a "boondoggle," the Bureau reported directly to the administrative judge. The Appellate opposed EDC's recommendation to

---

*The fact that this administrator saw no particular value in eliminating the position indicates just how strong the force of tradition was and how little careful thought had been given to streamlining the top management structure.

have the Bureau report instead to the chief clerk and to cut its "inflated" budget, but in this instance, at least, it gave in. "The doctors were pulling end runs and going to the Appellate in opposing the reorganization," reported a court official; "they even got at least one congressman to lobby for them there. That the Appellate would allow this to continue indicated that they were not really running the courts. The problem is to get them to delegate authority on these administrative and operational matters and let the Criminal Court decide."

To further support the administrative judge, EDC recommended miscellaneous other administrative changes. Setting up standardized, citywide rules on court hours, adjournments, sentencing, dismissal, and bail was one; devising procedures for their enforcement was another. Some judges and court administrators objected to EDC's getting into these matters, on the grounds that they pertained to judicial policy rather than administration, and that they required legislation. An equally compelling argument could be made for their having a strong administrative component as well.* "EDC was quite naive about what were judicial and what were administrative functions," reported one court official, "and it got these things confused." What this person and others had overlooked, however, was that many rules on these matters had been established before EDC arrived and had never been enforced.

Lateral Relations

Turning now to "lateral" work flow arrangements, one of the most significant of EDC's recommendations was to consolidate the court's fragmented parts. Again, parts consolidation had been proposed several years before by Administrative Judge Dudley and by Legal Aid, but implementation had been limited. EDC reaffirmed that proposal as the result of an incisive management analysis by one of its top staff people, Harold Finley. As he and others pointed out, the management problems of the court increased almost geometrically with the proliferation of specialized parts. Scheduling and calendaring of cases got incredibly complicated. There was always a new place for a case to go, thereby allowing attorneys to delay its disposition in order to gain tactical advantages for their clients.

---

*Sentencing and bail were most often mentioned as judicial matters, and EDC's recommendations resulted in fact in few major changes, largely because of the need for legislation. Yet, courts have been moving nationally toward standardizing sentencing and bail practices. Rules on adjournment guidelines, on the other hand, generally regarded as a borderline case between the administrative and the judicial, did not require legislation and were enforced.

Judges no longer had the opportunity or the incentive to control their cases and take a "hard line" on adjournments. By contrast, parts consolidation allowed for continuity in case handling; it fixed responsibility on a particular judge; and it reduced the amount of time required for case disposition.

Finley pointed out the many parallels between the court's over-specialized part structure and similar work flow arrangements on industrial assembly lines. Specifically, he noted the similarity between unit assembly work flow arrangements in industry—what is often called the "product shop"—and all-purpose parts. As he indicated, the extent of "make ready" or "put away" time in any work flow system, whether in industry or the courts, is tremendously reduced by having all activities done in one place.

Conversely, the specialized parts structure in the courts is similar to "serial" work flow arrangements in industry and has many of the management problems associated with that, for example, duplication, inefficiency, and difficulties with coordination. Though several court administrators kept emphasizing that case processing in their agency was not like an industrial assembly line, because of the many participating agencies and the complex judicial policy issues involved, the parallels that EDC pointed out from its management perspective were cogent and well taken.[12]

EDC was not the first to make this recommendation, but it did endorse parts consolidation from an organizational design and work-flow efficiency point of view. Since EDC's report, this reform has proceeded in all five counties. While that might have happened anyway, EDC's endorsement probably helped ensure its diffusion.

Judicial Policy Recommendations

The other part of this EDC study dealt with judicial policy issues, on which EDC again collected various insider proposals. They included establishing all-purpose night courts in Manhattan and Brooklyn to handle their big volume of adult arrest cases; phasing out the court's Identification Bureau, which did fingerprinting; and abolishing three-judge trials. Even though these were insider ideas, EDC came in for some criticism about them. The last, an Appellate proposal, required legislation that eventually got passed. The Identification Bureau has been slowly phased out, without legislation. The night courts proposal came under particularly strong criticism as vague, as not based on an analysis of case volume, and as probably costing more than it might be worth. Ross was to reduce the court's huge case backlog, but through a different policy.

Finally, EDC recommended that the courts coordinate much more with other criminal justice agencies, which was also not an original proposal. While some small progress was to be made on this under Judge Ross, the courts had too many internal problems that took up their limited resources. Also, they didn't have enough power to order other agencies to comply with common standards, having all they could do to improve their own management.

In sum, this EDC report, though not implemented in its entirety, was a critical event in the modernization of the New York City Criminal Court. For EDC, the report gave it visibility and stature as a consultant that it might not otherwise have had and paved the way for future work. For the Criminal Court, the report crystallized a consensus of disparate reform proposals that various insiders had developed over the years and gave them a legitimacy that increased their chances of implementation. Furthermore, EDC had, through this report, helped resolve a stalemate between the Appellate and Criminal courts as to who was in charge and who should have what powers. For reform-minded insiders in positions high enough to wield influence themselves, EDC became a prestigious tool to use against those court officials who refused to accept the necessity of major management reforms.

EDC also helped bridge the gap between Edward Dudley, who resigned as administrative judge in May 1970, and Ross, who took office in January 1971. It actually set the stage for Ross's regime by reaffirming the importance of a strong administrative judge. Though Ross was not to accept all of EDC's recommendations, the strong mandate he received from the Appellate, as well as his supportive management structure centered around Executive Officer Goodchild, were given a big boost by EDC's report. He was then able to use them as a basis for the management reforms that he undertook. One top court administrator summarized it well: "There were few new ideas in this 1970 EDC report. But EDC pulled it all together and lent prestige. Its key contribution was its support for old recommendations to reorganize the top. Also, it served as a buffer and broker between the Appellate and Criminal Court structures. EDC's uniqueness is that it put it all together. It was an impetus for change. It lent prestige to many ideas other people had been pushing for years. . . . The emphasis was on things that were doable."

The New Administrative Judge

The most important single event in the New York City Criminal Court in 1970, however, was not EDC's organizational study, despite its significance, but rather the appointment of a new administrative judge who was to become, in the words of several insiders, almost a "one-man show." EDC helped set the stage for him, and he provided administrative leadership that the Criminal Court had never had before.

Dudley had resigned in May 1970, and in October, Presiding Justice Stevens appointed former City Council President and Supreme Court Judge David Ross to the position. Neither EDC nor the more influential Bar Association had been consulted on the appointment, and both had reservations about him, though EDC was to quickly change its mind.*

A consummate politician who had become increasingly bored and frustrated in his Supreme Court judgeship in the Bronx, Ross had no past experience or training that might have indicated his administrative qualifications for the position or that would have helped one predict the outstanding job that he did. He had, however, a lot of respect from "lower court" judges, having come from the Supreme Court; and he had the political skills required to deal with judges and other court officials. A driving and intensely ambitious man, his success in introducing management reforms to the Criminal Court and later as the administrative judge first of an administratively merged Criminal and Supreme Court and then of all New York City courts (family, civil, criminal) not only rescued him from boredom and oblivion, but may some day gain him wider recognition.

Ross was such a powerful figure that his arrival overshadowed EDC's contribution. Without EDC, however, he might not have received the mandate that he did or been as able to sell the Appellate on all of his administrative innovations. The problem that his leadership was to pose was whether the innovations introduced would be institutionalized and hence sustained after he left. As one city official noted: "The integration of modern-management expertise into government agencies will take a long time. EDC's contribution is obscured by the fact that the criminal courts have become a one-man show under Ross. Whoever gets the credit, and I think 90 percent of it should be given to Ross, the system could produce another Dudley at any time. The changes have not really been institutionalized."

In contrast with his predecessor, Dudley, Ross took charge immediately and innovated with a vengeance. Even before he formally assumed office, he reviewed the many new programs, studies, and

*The Bar Association hadn't even included Ross on its informal list of six candidates that it had submitted to Stevens. It represented a "good government" point of view according to which Ross's political machine ties were ill suited to his appointment. By contrast, Mayor Lindsay, despite his ethnic and class affinity with Ross's Bar Association and reform critics, was reportedly delighted with him, even though Lindsay and Ross had had political differences.

reform proposals that had been made, including those of EDC. "He had a list of some sixty reform measures," reported a court administrator, "some of which were EDC's, translated into his own language and style." Indeed, both Ross and Goodchild were to select only those EDC recommendations that most fit their management styles. The ones that they particularly picked up on related to establishing a strong top-management group and to having uniform rules governing judicial conduct throughout the five counties.

That part of the EDC report that they discarded was its overelaborated structure, particularly the many committees that Finley had recommended. They both functioned much more informally, and each set up his own cabinet or council—Ross with ten judges, Goodchild with his top administrators. EDC now recognizes in retrospect that their response made sense. "The committee structure was something we now feel was most inappropriate," reported an EDC person. "The committees we suggested were much too cumbersome for Ross. He and Goodchild both had their own councils, and both were much less formalized than what we had suggested. What we recommended represented too unadulterated an effort to apply theory to practice." One court administrator suggested that EDC's committee recommendations assumed that the courts would have a weak administrative judge succeeding Dudley and that they became irrelevant when that proved not to be the case.

Ross immediately made a number of administrative changes in the course of establishing his own regime. First, he differentiated the judicial hierarchy, for which he was responsible, from a nonjudicial one, the responsibility for which he happily delegated to Goodchild. Second, Ross appointed five supervising judges, one for each borough, to ensure close monitoring of judicial conduct. This gave him much more control over the five counties than any of his predecessors had had.

Ross also began to exercise leadership in a way that had never been done before. His style was direct and blunt, and he exercised strong sanctions against judges who were not putting in enough bench time—such as transfer to other, less desirable, boroughs or parts. He also used his power to appoint and reappoint judges, encouraging the Appellate to delegate more of that to him, as EDC had recommended. "Ross is changing the whole concept of court administration," a criminal justice agency official explained. "He is demonstrating that the court administration job is to set standards and evaluate whether or not people meet them. He is very fair but tough and really works the judges." Another agency official noted, with reference to a later Supreme Court reorganization: "Ross kicks people around. He understands that the goal is not to be loved but to administer the courts. One day I ran into him giving it to a Supreme Court judge in the hall. He said: 'Look, I was in your courtroom at 3:30 yesterday and you weren't there, and they told me the court was adjourned for the day. Now I am going to be back at 5:30 this afternoon, and I expect to see you there and working. Period.' The guy is a miracle man. It works. I don't have any direct measures of bench time, but I know our lawyers are putting in more trial time."

Still another Ross innovation was to make rational assignments of judicial manpower, matching a judge's skills to the case. As one agency official explained: "Some judges can handle a really major case, but they go to pieces in arraignments. They can't handle the pressure. You have to discriminate between the people who can handle a fast-moving case load and those best at big cases. Ross is very good at this. Dudley wasn't. He would get up in the morning worrying that X wanted this, Y wanted that. He accommodated the whole system to the judges, not the real need. And now, if they don't like it, Ross is likely to farm them out somewhere."

One technique that became a hallmark of Ross's administration was what some court officials referred to as "front-end loading." It involved concentrating some of the best judges and court resources in the arraignment parts—the earliest stage of case handling—to see if as many cases as possible could be disposed of or otherwise handled quickly. The term "blockbuster" parts was also used to describe this practice. It reflected Ross's style of selling his aggressive policies to the judges. A court administrator explained: "Ross sold his approach to the judges by this front-end loading. We will cut your calendars down by this, he was saying. We will give you time to be a judge." Court staff repeatedly indicated that they had become more productive in his administration as a result of such practices, and that their morale had also improved. "We had a meeting of many judges and court staff to talk about what changes were being made and how it was going," reported an EDC person, "and so many clerks, judges, and administrators told us how much happier they were and how much more they got done."

Ross's general style, then, was one of aggressively bulldozing cases through the courts to clear up the backlog, minimize delays in case processing, and decrease the number of defendants in detention. He was successful over the short term, but there was some question as to whether his style would in fact lead to sustained improvement, or whether it even constituted management reform in any sense. "The whole Ross policy was to make the entire criminal court system into an ongoing, semi-permanent blockbuster situation," reported one of the few critical outsiders. "This was not reform, but a kind of institutionalized crisis management."

Though these assertions were true, steps were taken after Ross arrived to make the changes he instituted more permanent. A later EDC project that helped establish a strong state administrative judge, having regular contact with the city courts and effectively bypassing the Appellate, was a direct attempt to sustain these innovations.

Some Propositions about Success

EDC's work with the courts was a case, then, of an outside management consultant group, EDC, and a new inside top administrator, David Ross, complementing each other's contributions to produce significant management innovation. EDC gave Ross and Goodchild the underpinning they needed by helping establish their authority and then supporting many of Ross's specific management proposals.

The contrast with EDC's other studies in this regard is quite sharp. In the Board of Education headquarters and Human Resources Administration cases, EDC lacked clients powerful enough to have many of its recommendations implemented. Ross had the power that top administrators in these other agencies did not have, and that, along with his political skills and strong commitment to reform, helped make the difference. A further positive factor was the relevant skills of the EDC people—Finley's management and organizational design interests (notwithstanding the negative reception by court officials of some of his work), Coyne's legal knowledge and strong management of the EDC task force, and the insurance company people's knowledge about work measurement, forms, and techniques of case processing.

From the perspective of assessing EDC's role, the timing of its arrival in late 1969 and of Ross's a year later was critical. EDC arrived at the peak of the court's breakdown, when the desperation of the presiding justice was so great that any outside agency that did not impose any particular solution would have been welcomed. The fact that this outsider was a prestigious business group, willing to do studies on the courts free of charge and having no axe to grind, only made it more attractive. EDC was especially good for the court's image: "They were a demonstration to critics that we were committed to modern techniques," a court administrator pointed out. EDC then submitted its reports just before a powerful new administrative judge was appointed.

At first glance, then, it might appear that there is little to be learned from this case, since largely fortuitous conditions were critical in determining the impact of EDC's intervention.

There are broader implications, however, to be drawn from the experience. First, the probability of success is greater when there is both strong outside pressure for reform and new inside leadership. Second, many insiders invariably have excellent ideas for reform that an outside consultant should elicit and support. Third, traditional power centers within an agency often block reform, and a consultant will have to deal with the stalemated conflicts that result. Mediating and acting as a broker between various insider groups is one of the most important contributions a consultant can make; simply coming in and developing a good report is generally a futile exercise if no attention is paid to the politics of the situation. And finally, the presence of a strong central authority is one of the most important preconditions for achieving change. In the lack of such an authority to implement management reform recommendations, the consultant's limited resources would be better spent elsewhere.

The Impact of Ross and EDC: "Turning Around the Courts"?

Starting with the 1971 Annual Report of the Criminal Court, that court is referred to as having "turned around" under its new administration, with the improvements attributed to Ross and EDC. We have reviewed the main changes in structure and procedures, but the question of court performance still remains. The evidence through 1973, the last year the Criminal Court issued reports, was quite impressive. In terms of a whole series of performance indicators, the trend is overwhelmingly positive, and recent interviews indicate that the gains have been sustained. One of the most dramatic improvements is in the court backlog: it was over 59,000 cases at the end of 1970 and had come down to 17,386 after the first nine months of 1973. The calendars are now current, with case dispositions averaging 99 percent of filings in 1973, roughly what they have averaged every year since Ross arrived.

The warrant situation also improved, declining from 53,790 cases for the first nine months of 1971 to only 34,838 for the corresponding period in 1973. This decline reflects the more current calendars, the dramatic reduction in length of adjournment, and Ross's policy of "front-end loading," discussed above.

Two other indicators of court activity—the average duration of a case and the average length of adjournment—show equally dramatic improvement. The average case took 6.29 weeks in 1971, compared with 3.53 weeks in 1973. Likewise, the average length of adjournment went from 2.75 to 1.50 weeks during that same period. These trends, along with the sharp reduction in case backlog, eased the overcrowding in the prisons.

Data on the number of defendants in detention show a marked decline as well. There were 4,207 such defendants in October 1969 and only 1,849 in 1973. Also, the average number of appearances per case declined very slightly, from 3.37 in 1971 to 3.32 in 1973.

All these are indicators of the speed and efficiency with which defendants move through the courts; but there is the question of quality of justice as well. One indicator of quality is the number of calendared cases per judge day. That number had dropped from 57.78 in 1971 to 43.26 in 1973. One may conclude, then, that the goal of speedy administration of fair justice, endorsed by both the courts and EDC, was realized to a greater extent after this modernization than before.*

These results are not easily interpreted, however, since court performance is a function of many factors, not just of internal management. The criminal justice system is a multiagency one, and the practices of such other departments as police and corrections also affect court productivity. The easing up of Police Department arrest policy, for example, contributing to fewer arrests, undoubtedly also improved the court's performance, since its work load declined. Some of the improvements attributed to Ross were undoubtedly a function of this. As a top city official noted: "In evaluating Ross's indicators of court performance, you have to understand that there are many different things that bring down the statistics—the nature of cases, the trial strategy of lawyers involved, and so on. . . . There is no way to determine the extent to which the court's productivity gains are the result of changes in part structure, in Ross's policies, in case volume, or what." Even recognizing all this complexity, however, the Criminal Court had undergone major management innovations since 1970, owing mainly to EDC and Ross, and some of its improved productivity undoubtedly reflected these improvements.

In addition to its organization study, EDC's work in the Criminal Court had included work measurement and forms studies of New York County Summons Parts in 1970 and parallel studies of the handling of arrest cases the following year in Queens. The Queens work, in addition to documenting procedures and work flows, also analyzed the specialized part system and the workings of the county clerk's office, studies EDC would use later. By late 1971, however, EDC's work in the Criminal Court had slowed down a lot, as Judge Ross and his executive officer, Goodchild, were running the court

*These kinds of performance data were never available before 1971. There is, therefore, no way of knowing how bad the situation in the courts was before then.

themselves, having taken what they wanted from EDC's studies and others. And by late 1971, they seemed to have many Criminal Court problems more nearly under control.

SUPREME COURT TASK FORCE

While the crisis in the Criminal Court was easing up, with reductions in its case backlog and the many other improvements just reviewed, conditions got considerably worse in the Supreme Court. Its backlog of felony cases increased so precipitously in 1970 and 1971 that court officials began talking about a severe crisis there, for which something drastic had to be done. There were at least two reasons for the increase. First, as the Criminal Court started processing cases faster, it passed them on in increasing numbers to the Supreme Court. All felonies in New York State thus started in the lower court, with those not disposed of there moving on to the higher court through the convening of a Grand Jury. The growing number of such felony defendants awaiting final disposition of their cases by the Supreme Court soon became the primary cause of overcrowding in the city's detention facilities; and the same kind of public clamor for improvement that had developed around the Criminal Court's break-down now emerged. A new law and court decision mandating prompt trials for felony cases and limiting plea bargaining further increased the case load.

Judge Stevens, who had committed himself to EDC's proposals for reorganization in the Criminal Court and had built support for them among his less enthusiastic colleagues in the Second Appellate Department, then asked EDC in the fall of 1971 to come in and try to help out in this situation. It formed a Supreme Court Task Force in November 1971, comprised of eight management analysts from insurance companies, and immediately began field work, documentation, and organization studies very similar to what it had done in the Criminal Court. It had thus gotten involved again in a "crash" management consulting project to deal with an immediate problem; but the proposals it was to make again had long-term implications. That is, they dealt with an immediate problem in a way that might increase the management capability of the agency to the point where the problem might be less likely to recur with such devastating impact.*

*Those court staff and outside agencies who had singled out Dudley as a scapegoat for the Criminal Court's problems claimed that his reassignment to the position of administrative judge in the Supreme Court contributed to its poor

Several features of this work were important. First, EDC built on much of the methodology, diagnoses, reform proposals, and contacts that it had used in its earlier work. Though the Supreme Court differed in many ways from the Criminal—and these differences were to pose serious problems at the implementation stage—it nevertheless had many of the same organizational characteristics and management deficiencies. Furthermore, the fact that there was so much similarity in the kinds of work handled by the Criminal Division of the Supreme Court and the Criminal Court—indeed, they dealt with many of the same cases—made EDC's earlier work particularly relevant. Both its organization study and its studies documenting procedures and forms used in various parts in the Criminal Court thus proved helpful in the Supreme Court work.

Second, many of the same organizational solutions that EDC had recommended for the Criminal Court applied to the Supreme Court as well. In particular, the latter had the same need for a strong central authority, more consolidated parts, and more supportive services.

Finally, court administrators agreed that the quality of EDC's reports was uniformly better in its Supreme Court work than in the Criminal. "Its material has become much less fuzzy, much less technical in the wrong ways, and much more practical and directly helpful," reported a top court administrator who had worked with EDC on both sets of projects. Its reports contained the same kinds of detailed observations as before on court activities and proceedings, but they had many more concrete and implementable proposals for change and spelled out more how administrative improvements might be carried out. EDC had learned a lot from its earlier work, then, particularly about the outlook of court officials and about what kinds of management structures and procedures were and were not transferable to the courts. It was not to repeat, for example, the problems it had had with all the subcommittees and organization charts that it had generated in its Criminal Court organization study. It also did not have the same "start-up" problems and delays in gaining entry. It was a known quantity to the courts, they found its methodology acceptable, and they obviously needed immediate help.

The scope of EDC's work in the Supreme Court was quite extensive, including a reorganization study and a series of more specific studies dealing with particular court problems. Though the organization study was important, court officials also found the others useful, especially those on courtroom utilization, the part

---

management and caseload problems. Broader institutional and "systemic" factors that EDC was to point to were much more important, however.

structure, reorganizing clerical services, arraignment and pre-trial conference parts, the probation office, and the county clerk's office. Most of the studies dealt with the criminal branch of the Supreme Court, but there were several on the civil branch as well. Ross used many of these studies, as he had EDC's prior Criminal Court ones, to push through management reforms that he felt were needed.

Organization Study

We will concentrate on the organization study, since it was so basic.[13] It illustrates quite dramatically the transferability of EDC's earlier Criminal Court work. It contained some twenty-two major recommendations that paralleled quite strikingly, in both substance and intent, the ones it made in the Criminal Court study. EDC's main recommendation was for an immediate city-wide administrative merger of the Criminal Division of the Supreme Court with the Criminal Court, based on the rationale that they were dealing with the same or similar cases, and that there would be substantial economies of scale if they were joined.

The diagnosis that EDC made as the basis for this proposal was similar to one it had made before—namely, that the Supreme Court and its related agencies were too fragmented to effectively handle their increasing case load. As the report indicated: "The fragmentation inherent in the present system seriously inhibits mobilization of existing resources to deal with critical high-priority problems in providing prompt, sure application of criminal justice. . . . the greatest need for this organizational change is in Manhattan, the Bronx, and Brooklyn, where heavy volumes and growing felony case backlogs are beyond the administrative capabilities of the present fragmented system."

EDC pointed up three types of fragmentation: a horizontal one, along geographical lines, among the Supreme Courts of three judicial districts covering New York City; a vertical one, between the Criminal and Supreme Court administrations; and one between the separate Criminal and Civil divisions within the Supreme Court. Its reports and recommendations were concerned mainly with the second type.

Much of this organization report, as well as all subsequent ones, detailed the many benefits of administrative unification: more balanced utilization of resources, more continuity of case handling, less duplication, better supervision and monitoring, more flexibility in the assignment of judges and nonjudicial staff, and much more adaptability on the part of the courts to changing (and often increasing) caseload demands. The administrative rationale given for the merger, buttressed by extensive documentation of the excessive costs, rigidities, and redundancies of the old system, made this report particularly compelling, even though there was to be a lot of resistance from the Second Appellate Department.

The administrative merger recommendation was presented as part of a larger package that included three sets of proposals—one dealing primarily with top and upper-middle management, a second with administrative support structures, and a third with the parts structure. The first recommended the transfer of EDC's unified top management proposal, implemented in the Criminal Court, to this new, merged structure. As the report noted: "The management structure recommended builds directly on the successful and proven administrative structure previously recommended by EDC for the Criminal Court. A major part of the proposed administrative structure is already established, funded, and working smoothly within the Criminal Court." EDC emphasized that such an administrative unification did not involve superimposing an additional layer of administration but rather adapting the existing administrative structure of the Criminal Court to the new, merged unit. "The top administrative structure of the Criminal Court should be elevated two steps to enable it to address itself to all criminal matters in the Criminal Court and Supreme Court Criminal parts."

This top-management structure included a single, strong administrative judge in charge of the merged court, an executive officer with authority over all nonjudicial functions, various deputy executive officers, and at least one supervising judge for each county. There was considerable emphasis, as in EDC's Criminal Court study, on the Appellate Division's granting broad authority to the administrative judge, particularly with regard to judicial assignments to criminal parts in the Supreme Court. To further consolidate this new authority, EDC also recommended that existing administrative judges in the supreme court devote full time instead to running the Civil Division.

The second set of proposals, buttressed by many separate studies of particular court units as well as by extensive documentation, related to consolidating administrative support services. This included various categories of court officers—security staff, court reporters, interpreters—as well as library facilities, probation services, the Law Department, and miscellaneous other bureaus. The biggest obstacle to implementing these proposals was the marked status and salary differential between the Criminal and Supreme courts, with staff in the latter considering themselves way above those in the "lower court" and not wanting the change; and EDC included a proposal to revise the existing promotional ladders, salary and grade levels, and assignments of court personnel to positions based on this.

Finally, there were many proposals relating to parts consolidation, the Supreme Court having the same problems of overspecialization that the Criminal had. EDC particularly emphasized the ways in which parts consolidation could encompass both courts. One recommendation, for example, was for additional "combined Supreme Court–Criminal Court parts, staffed by Acting Supreme Court Justices designated from the Criminal Court and handling dual calendars."

Implementation

Many of these proposals were eventually implemented under Judge Ross, who became the administrative judge of an administratively combined Supreme and Criminal Court; but he faced a lot of resistance, much more than in the Criminal Court. Most of it came from the Second Appellate, covering Brooklyn, Queens, and Staten Island, whose legal staff, judges, and other officials called the merger unconstitutional and prepared exhaustive briefs to support their contention. One of their strong objections was, as an insider related, "not to have that crime czar from the Bronx (David Ross) have authority over them in Brooklyn and Queens." Informally, the Second Division had less political power in New York City than the First and had traditionally felt alienated from the Manhattan courts, where the central administrative offices were, and from the mayor, who controlled its budget. Also, that division was preoccupied with its many outside counties as well, including Westchester, Nassau, Putnam, and Dutchess.

This EDC-proposed merger passed by a 3–2 vote, with the five votes being cast by the presiding justices of each of the state's Appellates, plus the state's chief judge. The latter was able to secure the upstate vote, but lost out on Presiding Justices Stevens and Rabin of the First and Second Appellates covering New York City. This merger, of course, further consolidated administrative authority in the courts, extending a development begun with the Criminal Court reforms. Once the vote was in, Presiding Justice Stevens fully committed his authority to the success of the effort, but opposition from the Second Appellate had been so great that the final merger took place only in the First Appellate, covering the Bronx and Manhattan. Even that merger took almost a year to be implemented. EDC's organization report was submitted in June 1972, and it wasn't until the following March that Ross was appointed administrative judge of both criminal courts.

This partial implementation was rationalized in Ross's first quarterly report, in which he indicated that because of the legal uncertainty about the merger and the "great difficulty in fashioning an administrative structure for all of the criminal courts of the city without the experience which can be gained in a more modest initial configuration," he was recommending it be tried initially in the First Appellate Department. Even there, however, he mentioned several delays—in the Bronx court, regarding parts restructuring; in the state's funding of a management information system for this newly merged structure; and in the court's separating out nonjudicial personnel of the civil and criminal divisions.

Despite these initial problems, considerable implementation did take place. The top-management structure of the Criminal Courts was in fact transferred to this newly merged structure; middle-management positions were created and filled by key people in the Supreme Court; an assistant deputy executive officer and chief clerk were designated; several specialized administrative bureaus were coordinated to service both the Criminal Court and the Criminal Branch, though there was not the complete administrative unification EDC had urged; procedures were instituted to provide judicial coverage in emergencies, including the temporary assignment of Criminal Court Judges to the Supreme Court; Ross continued to issue sanctions for lateness or nonappearance; the same council and cabinet from the Criminal Court held regular meetings for the formulation of policy; regular management reports were issued on the operations of each part; an integrated law department was created, with a single law library; part consolidation was begun in both the Bronx and Manhattan; payroll, personnel, and budget functions of the two courts were merged; the court took over control of all Criminal Term calendars from the district attorneys; and there were the beginnings of a management information system.

Court Productivity

The ultimate test of any reorganization would, of course, be the court's productivity; and as in the Criminal Court, significant improvements took place just after these management innovations and were probably in large part a result of them. In the Bronx court, for example, where the unified administration began earlier, a comparison of court productivity for the period June–October 1973 with the same period for 1972 indicated the following: dispositions increased by 38%; dispositions as a percentage of arraignments went up from 61.4% to 104%; trials increased by 13%; pending cases dropped by 8%; average duration of a case declined by 35%, from 16 months to 10.6 months; and the number of defendants in detention declined from

1,101 at the end of October 1972 to 1,029 at the end of October 1973. On January 4, 1974, the number dropped to 864.

In New York County, while no major operational changes were made until November 1973, when the part structure was reorganized, numerous administrative improvements were made, and these were accompanied by improvements in court performance, albeit less substantial ones than in the Bronx, where the changes were more extensive. Nevertheless, dispositions went up from 4,305 to 4,542; dispositions as a percentage of arraignments were 113.6 as compared with 93.1 in 1972; trials increased from 214 to 367; pending cases dropped from 3,466 to 3,252; average duration of a case dropped from 6.6 months to 5.7; and defendants in detention numbered 1,379, compared with 1,458 the year before. On January 1, 1974, that figure dropped to 1,108.

A further area of concern related to the utilization of judicial resources. EDC made detailed observations of nineteen courtrooms of the Criminal Parts of the Supreme Court in New York County during the period from February 28, 1972 through March 24. Coding each observation under one of three categories—"court open—no actions," "court in session," and "court closed"—it documented with detailed data a condition of substantial underutilization in each of the nineteen parts. The general pattern was that considerable time was lost between 9:00 and 11:00 A.M. with no action other than general "housekeeping" from 9:00 to 10:00 and a daily average usage by judges active on the bench of only 58% of the time between 10:00 and 11:00 (for all nineteen courtrooms combined). Courtroom usage by judges active on the bench increased to 71% for the hour between 11:00 A.M. and noon, but as the report pointed out: "This hour is the beginning of the peak period of the day for transacting court business, where it might be expected that each part utilization would reach somewhere in the neighborhood of 85% to 90% of capacity." Utilization then got considerably worse after 2:00 A.M. with the average less than 51% between 2:00 and 5:00.

The study indicated the causes of these conditions: poor calendaring, poor staff support, the absence of procedures for transferring work from one part to another, overspecialization of parts, and the mutual isolation of parts. The problem was worse, for example, in felony cases, where the parts were set up to handle only trials, rather than the whole range of activities. Based on EDC's observations and its analysis of the causes of the problems, it made many recommendations for improving courtroom utilization that were later adopted. At least in part as a result of this study, there was improvement in courtroom utilization over the next couple of years. Thus, the court convened an average of 32 minutes earlier in November 1973 than in the previous December; the average time of adjournment was 55 minutes later; and the average available bench time increased 35%, from four hours and ten minutes in December 1972 to five hours and thirty-seven minutes in November 1973.

The improvement was probably also a result of this study's having been made public after its submission to the administrative judge and the presiding justices of the appellates, presumably by a court or other government official.* Its release created a strong public reaction, which may well have led to more action than if the report had remained confidential.

Other EDC Studies

EDC did other studies of the Supreme Court as well, and a few were important enough to merit discussion. One, on the part structure, complemented in many ways the utilization study. It took its recommendations on parts consolidation from the organization report and provided extensive documentation—pointing up the inefficiencies of the existing system—to support them. Moreover, it spelled out, for each recommendation, the concrete actions that could be taken to ensure its effective implementation. The main emphasis was on innovations to speed up the processing of cases, including all-purpose or "individual calendar" parts,† each of which might handle cases at all stages; more flexible staffing arrangements, with provisions for transferring judges from the Criminal Court to become "acting" judges in the Supreme; longer hours; physical changes in the courtroom (for example, a "check-in" desk); having "ready" cases on reserve in each part; and regular monitoring of court part operations. Again, the concrete and implementable nature of these recommendations made them particularly helpful to court administrators. Thus, the recommendation regarding monitoring included a methodology for doing so.

EDC also studied the Civil Branch of the Supreme Court. "We were asked to look at the civil branch and felt we shouldn't do it," reported an EDC person, "but Stevens and Tolman of the Appellate prevailed on us, saying that you couldn't understand and improve the system without dealing with all of its parts. We took on the civil side and felt we did a good job, but it was the sore thumb of the Supreme Court."

*EDC released the study as it did all others it conducted in the courts, but only several months later.

†Individual Calendar parts were the Supreme Court's early equivalent of consolidated all-purpose parts in the Criminal.

EDC documented procedures used in civil parts, developed a procedures manual based on this, and did some courtroom utilization studies as well. Indeed, it used the court's own data on the functioning of civil parts in New York County as the basis for pointing up the poor utilization of courtrooms that existed there. Later, after direct observations of the same parts from January to April 1972, EDC noted a significant improvement, probably due in part to its earlier studies. As its report noted: "On a number of mornings, the percentage of courtrooms being utilized by these parts at the time of the daily observations ranged from 85% to 100% in the mornings, as opposed to an average of only 75% during the preceding 1971 period." Later, there was to be an informal administrative merging of the Civil Division of the Supreme Court with the lower Civil Court, for the same reasons as on the criminal side, and with EDC's studies again buttressing the move. "40% of the Supreme Civil cases are now decided by city civil judges," reported an EDC person, "and this has contributed to a big decrease in the backlog. There was never a formal report on the merging of the two civil courts, but Dudley was backed into a corner on it, and Thompson, the administrative judge of the Civil Court, agreed to it."

In brief, EDC repeated in the Supreme Court the same consulting work it had done earlier in the Criminal, in response to the same kind of crisis. The Supreme Court then improved over the next couple of years, even though there was much more organized resistance to implementation, both from the Appellate and from the Supreme Court itself. Much of the resistance arose, as we have discussed, as a result of status differences between the Criminal and Supreme courts. Though they dealt with the same cases and were located in the same building, Supreme Court officials had higher salaries and prestige. After EDC pushed hard to revise the existing "promotional ladder," to distribute needed skills among all criminal parts, and to eliminate status differences, much of that resistance eroded. "There were people in the same building who had not communicated for seventeen years," reported an EDC person, "not even chief clerk to chief clerk, and they are literally in the same building. Not even Goodchild and people at that high administrative level knew that much at first about the Criminal Division of the Supreme Court. That has all changed now."

The fact that the EDC's proposals did not require new legislation or much additional money undoubtedly helped ensure at least some implementation. The question remained, however, as to how enduring the changes would prove to be if Ross was replaced at some point by a less dynamic successor. That nagging question came to the forefront in the next important stage of EDC's involvement.

THE STATE COURT MANAGEMENT AND
TASK FORCE

Some time in mid-1973, EDC got an invitation from top state court officials to do management studies of the Office of Court Administration, similar to what it had done before at the city level.* "Tom Chittenden, from the Judicial Conference, contacted us and asked us in," reported an EDC person. "He said that with trends toward more centralization there had to be better state management, and that we were best qualified to help. We felt ready at that time to look at the highest levels of the court."

This represented a logical next step in EDC's court reform activity. It was particularly important in sustaining the changes that had taken place in the Criminal and Supreme courts. EDC and the courts had thus moved incrementally to first improve the lower court and the Supreme Court and then try to do likewise with the state administrative superstructure that had ultimate authority over these courts. "I felt that if we wanted to protect the gains made in the city," explained an EDC person, "if we were to keep the great achievements of Ross, we had to gain the state's support. And we would have to help overhaul the state structure, to fill in a vacuum at that level that was very weak before. We came up with a blueprint for reform that State Administrative Judge Bartlett feels was implemented, and I think it helped."

As in EDC's previous work, it did a basic organization report and several others dealing with particular functions—one on budgeting and others on records management, personnel functions, statistics and data processing functions, and laws and procedures relating to judicial discipline. The organization report, which analyzed and documented the many management problems resulting from the weak state administrator's office, was again the most important one. It proposed a strong administrative judge along with a supportive management structure around that position, and indicated how it should relate to the Appellates and to the New York City courts.† As was not the case with its proposal for the administrative merger of the Supreme and Criminal courts, EDC was here once again picking

---

*The Office of Court Administration, formerly referred to as the Judicial Conference, is the administrative organization that has authority over all courts in the state.

†There was a very brief discussion at the end of the organization of courts outside the city, but that was peripheral to the main part of the report and will not concern us here.

up on proposals of insiders and providing documentation and legitimacy for them. While it was.not a new discovery that the state administrator was a weak office, EDC did a lot of management analysis indicating how and why it was so weak, and what had to be provided to make it strong.

The main reason for the office's weakness was its diffuse line and staff responsibilities, and yet the Appellate divisions had not been willing to delegate the authority and provide the resources and services required for the office to run the state courts effectively. As of January 1974, when the Chief Judge, Charles Brietel, and the Appellate presiding justices unanimously designated a new state administrative judge, Richard Bartlett, the office still did not have the organizational capability to carry out its functions. It was responsible for administering the state's unified court system, but had no authority to do so.

EDC's report, documenting in detail the main limitations of the office, also analyzed what was wrong with the entire state structure. It listed ten organizational problems related to the office, which boiled down to the fact that it did not have enough centralized control over key management and legal functions, and what functions it did control were either illogically combined, ambiguously defined, or both. Furthermore, too much power still remained with the Appellates, through their departmental directors of administration and their various committees—which, themselves, constituted a most cumbersome and confusing structure.[14]

The report, based on EDC's interviews with key administrators, a questionnaire survey, and analysis of past organizational charts and other studies, contained detailed proposals both for reorganizing staff services within the office and for clarifying its line authority and responsibilities. The proposals for consolidating staff functions were developed after extensive discussions with the state administrative judge and his deputy, the latter having dealt extensively with EDC while he was a top administrator in the mayor's Criminal Justice Coordinating Council. The main recommendation, which was largely implemented, was for a new deputy state administrator to preside over such central staff functions as legal counsel, training for judges and top court officials, internal management consulting, budgeting and finance, and policy and standard setting.

The other part of the report, dealing with "line organization" recommendations, proposed the same kind of unified state authority under a strong administrative judge that EDC had previously recommended for the Criminal and Supreme courts. It also proposed that he have a deputy in charge of all staff functions, as Ross had in his executive officer, Goodchild.

All these proposed changes followed the same management principles that EDC had endorsed throughout its court and other agency consulting efforts. One set related to *centralization* and *consolidation* of management functions in a strong central authority, in this case the state administrative judge. Another guiding principle was to *shorten the chain of command* between this position and the city's administrative judges, further cutting down on the authority of the Appellate Division presiding justices and their administrative staffs. To further streamline state-city relations, EDC supported a similar centralization and consolidation at the city level, through the establishment of a single administrative judge for all trial courts in the city.[15] This last recommendation simply amounted to EDC's endorsing for the city courts a proposal developed by Chief Judge Breitel and State Administrative Judge Bartlett. It involved almost the complete demise of Appellate power over court administration and carried that process of radical change in the court's authority and power arrangements to its final step.*

The specific EDC studies of state administrative functions complemented this broader organization report. One that received particular support among state officials had to do with budgeting procedures. EDC proposed that the state court system change from line-item to purpose budgeting, and that change did in fact take place. "We would have gotten it anyway, in the next several months," reported a state court administrator, "but the EDC report was good. They had a first-rate guy doing it, and we adopted the proposals."

CONCLUSIONS: RESOLVING AUTHORITY AND POWER RELATIONSHIPS

Changes in court authority and power relationships took place very quickly in 1974 and 1975, all in the directions indicated in the EDC state organization study. Chief Judge Breitel was the leading figure in these changes, as Ross and Stevens had been before at the city level. The main changes involved increasing the authority of city and state administrative judges, at the expense of the Appellates. Though EDC was not the only group to recommend this—a state investigation commission, for example, having also proposed a strong state administrative judge-its studies were an integral part of the reforms.

*The "politics" of this change are still getting worked out.

Administrative judges in each of the main city courts—civil, family, and criminal—began to report directly to the state administrative judge, and that change gave the state much more control than it had ever had before. The consolidation of line responsibility and staff functions in the office of the state administrative judge, resulting from the combination of Chief Judge Breitel's leadership and EDC's studies, gave the state the authority it had always needed (but never before had) to administer the unified state court system. Meanwhile, top administrators in the Appellates were being phased out of their jobs. "McGivern, the presiding justice in the First Department," reported one observer, "voluntarily forfeited all administration, and he kept asking his top administrator, who had been there a long time and was very competent and knowledgeable about New York City courts, when he was going to move. The guy eventually ended up in a state position."

Early in 1974, Chief Judge Breitel, having followed EDC's work closely and being strongly in favor of centralization at both the city and state levels, quickly extended administrative unification by making Judge Ross and his executive cadre the nucleus of a single court administration for the entire city—including civil, family, criminal, and supreme courts. This was a sweeping reform instituted to improve the pooling of staff and other resources across all city courts. It represented the culmination of a process of both vertical and lateral integration of court management that had begun with the first reforms of the Criminal Court in 1971. State- city linkages and those across city courts then became much more direct than before, improving efficiency. "Thus we have, as of mid-1975," wrote Richard Coyne of EDC, "numerous judges from the lower courts who are sitting full-time on the Supreme Court Branch as Acting Supreme Court Justices dealing with severe felony case backlog problems. There has been a substantial transfer of civil cases from the Supreme Court to the Civil Court. Civil Court judges are helping out a hard-pressed Family Court. What makes this easier is that there has been a beginning at ending the fragmentation of the courts through administrative and management reforms in New York City."

At the same time, the changes have taken place so fast that court officials have not completely adjusted to them, and major questions of authority and jurisdiction remained unresolved as of the end of 1976. The Appellate still had a lot of informal policy-making power, and it was still unclear how much authority it was willing to delegate down to a city administrative judge and up to the state administrative judge. Yet, many significant changes have come about.

What is so amazing, given the traditionally slow pace of change in the public sector, is that the most entrenched group, the presiding justices of the Appellates, kept cooperating. The most recent reform, establishing a city-wide administrative judge with jurisdiction over all local trial courts, effectively removed them from much court management. Several insiders suggested that Breitel secured the justices' support for the changes by promising them something in return. Thus, in 1974, both Stevens and Rabin were given positions on the higher Court of Appeals, and McGivern, Stevens's successor, was told that he would have to deal with strong city and state administrative judges. He has since resigned and Stevens has returned to the position, but the changes have nevertheless remained.

EDC's Most Recent Criminal Justice Work

Since completing its work at the state level, EDC has been involved in still other court and criminal justice projects. It began work in the New York City Family Court in late 1974, largely as a result of state Administrative Judge Bartlett's concern about that court's internal management and coordination problems. The Family Court gets involved in many child welfare and youth-related agencies and has been widely regarded as one of the most insider-dominated and poorly managed of any of the city courts. Resistance to change within the New York City Family Court is so strong that it is still too early to see many results from EDC's various studies there.*

Finally, beginning in September 1974, and extending through January 1975, EDC studied the Criminal Justice Coordinating Council, the mayor's policy-making and administrative agency for criminal justice activities. Though the council had competent directors and staff people while John Lindsay was mayor, it had never performed effectively on any of its three major functions—monitoring federal grants, setting priorities and developing a comprehensive plan for reducing crime and improving criminal justice in the city, and coordinating all criminal justice activities locally. The council's new director under Mayor Beame, Judge Benjamin Altman, immediately sought outside help when he took office in early 1974. "Altman had been talking to Bartlett about the mess he had inherited, and he came to us," reported an EDC person. "We said we would try to make some sense out of it."

EDC produced the same kind of organization report on the council that it had done in previous studies. Its main recommendation was for the mayor or a deputy mayor to become chairman of the council, in order to give it the authority and power it needed to more effectively carry out those three functions. By now, establish-

*EDC also began studies of family courts in other parts of the state in the summer of 1975, at the request of Bartlett and under a federal grant.

ing strong central authorities had become a hallmark of all EDC's organization reports; and of course it made a lot of sense in this case. This proposal was to be supported later by the City Charter Revision Commission's parallel proposal for a high-level "coordinator" of all criminal justice activities in the city. Mayor Beame finally established such a position in 1976, with the first coordinator, former Corporation Counsel Nicholas Scopetta, to begin operations in January 1977. Given the separation and competition among criminal justice agencies that we have described (and that EDC described in its report), it remains to be seen how effective the new coordinator will be.

Other, less important, recommendations have been implemented since the report's submission in February 1975. They relate to improving the council's grant administration (by separating responsibilities for grant development and applications from those for monitoring and evaluating programs); having a stronger executive committee that meets more often than in the past (monthly or bimonthly rather than quarterly); and improving the council's central filing system and audit capability.

Given the city's many fiscal problems and the modest capabilities of many of the council's staff members—some of them patronage appointments by the Beame administration—it is too soon to tell how effective the council will be. EDC was one important catalyst, however, in the move to set up a strong central coordinator for all criminal justice activity in the city, and that reform may have some positive impact in the future.

Comparisons with Other EDC Management Consulting Efforts

In conclusion, EDC has done a fairly extensive amount of management consulting work for the New York City courts and related criminal justice agencies. It has had an important impact on these agencies, giving legitimacy and support to strong administrators who would have tried to do most of what it recommended anyway. If EDC had not been around, these court officials would probably have been less successful.

Several factors contributed to EDC's successes. The crises were severe enough to force reform actions. EDC consistently gravitated toward strong "inside" administrators who became its main clients and who took from its many studies those proposals that they wanted to implement, in their own way. Furthermore, the agencies, while large, were not nearly as large as the Board of Education or the Human Resources Administration, making it more likely that a coalition of strong, innovation-minded agency officials and a prestigious outside consultant might reach the critical mass necessary for significant change. On EDC's side, its leadership and task force members had many relevant skills. Coyne was a lawyer and a forceful administrator who rapidly became a competent management analyst. Finley made important early contributions in EDC's first Criminal Court work. Morelli, Coyne's associate in the later state and city studies, had had extensive experience in the public and private sectors and on other task forces. The insurance company work measurement and management systems people had already developed a methodology in the private sector that had important applicability to the courts. Finally, the continuity of EDC's task force leadership and staff was also critical.

A combination, then, of positive circumstances (for which EDC was not responsible) and its own capabilities contributed to a successful series of management consulting efforts. While it would be inaccurate to impute some preconceived plan or strategy to EDC's work in the courts, that work certainly did proceed in an incremental way that built on past successes. And there was a clear pattern to the political and organizational changes that took place at both the city and state levels. Though there were many false starts and though some of EDC's assertions about its successes oversimplified what actually went on, the general quality of its work not only improved over time, but represented some exemplary management consulting in a public-sector agency.

A central pattern to the EDC work, relating back to the earlier discussion in the first chapter, is that it proceeded in a "bottom-up" fashion. EDC had started working on the lower courts in New York, helped support reforms there, and later moved to the state level to endorse the kind of strong central authority needed to sustain those reforms. Had it begun at the top instead, it probably would not have been as effective. Securing entry in the diffuse state structure, with its many participants, might have been more problematic. Moreover, if EDC had started at the top, it might have been very difficult later for it to gain access and credibility locally, since the state never had much local credibility until very recently. While this is mostly speculation, the case does illustrate the possibilities inherent in a "bottom-up" approach. EDC task force leaders indicate that the policy of starting at the bottom and working their way up was a conscious one. It is a strategy that might well be worth following in other public-sector consulting work.

Before making an overall assessment of EDC's consulting work, however, and of its potential relevance for future urban development efforts, it is important to analyze in greater depth EDC itself. The way that EDC was organized, its degree of success in generating corporate support, the quality of the people it recruited, and how they saw its programs are all particularly important. It is to those questions that we now turn.

7. EDC And Its Member Corporations

We have now reviewed three cases of EDC involvement in city agencies. Each illustrated the strengths and weaknesses of the management transfer strategy, in terms of the conceptual scheme presented in Chapter Two. Basically, the only way for EDC to have much impact on the city through this strategy is to develop a large constituency for management reform in New York City, beginning with its own members. Though EDC now has almost 200 corporate members, few have loaned executives to the program; and even among those that have, the quality of the people they have sent has been uneven, as we will discuss in this chapter.

EDC's experience has, in fact, simply reflected the general New York City experience with regard to big-business participation in civic affairs. As noted in Chapter Three, big business in New York, unlike its counterparts in cities such as Pittsburgh, Philadelphia, Chicago, St. Louis, Boston, Detroit, Atlanta, and Dallas, has remained quite remote from civic involvement. Where business has closer relations with City Hall and with other power centers, there may be better possibilities for successfully incorporating many parts of this program than there were in New York.

This chapter deals with a number of questions related to the issue of business involvement in the EDC program. First, how much support was there and from what companies? Second, what did EDC do to try to generate, sustain, and increase such support? Third, how did the program look to the people on loan?

EDC AND ITS MEMBER COMPANIES: MOBILIZING SUPPORT

"The one thing I hope comes out of your book," remarked a top EDC official, "is the fact that many corporations in New York City are still asleep, even though this is one of the best civic programs that business has ever developed. They're not supporting it in the way they should, and I hope some of them soon change their minds. We get some good people, but our biggest problem is to sell this program. We've tried and we're still trying, but we're not doing nearly enough, and the corporations have yet to give us the kind of help we need."

A critical problem for EDC, then, has been to expand the base of its corporate support. Though EDC has had a management consulting program since 1968, most business people on loan have come from only a few corporations, even though that number is slowly increasing. As of July 1974, IBM, New York Telephone, Equitable Life, Chase Manhattan Bank, Metropolitan Life, New York Life, Consolidated Edison, Chemical Bank, General Electric, Western Electric, Irving Trust, and Union Carbide—twelve companies—had provided 63 percent of all the on-loan executives, and only 47 of EDC's 200-odd member companies had provided anyone at all. Those corporations that have provided the most people on loan are ones whose top executive officers and board chairmen are business associates and friends of George Champion.* Nine of the twelve are on EDC's own board of directors, represented in almost every case by their board chairman.

STAGES IN EDC RECRUITING

Recruiting has been one of the most difficult parts of the EDC program. At the beginning there was no precedent in New York City for an effort of this kind; and it wasn't clear at first what talents were needed. And because of big business's limited commitment to the city, EDC had to take whoever it sent. "You can't look a gift horse in the mouth," explained one EDC person in describing the situation in the early years. "We had to take what we could get, even though some of the people the companies sent were not as good as we would have liked."

---

*Many supported the program "on its merits" as well, but Champion's personal influence was critical.

EDC's recruiting has gone through three stages. For the first several years, much of it was done by George Champion himself through his own personal contacts, or by Champion's associate, who recruited for the courts task force. As one EDC official explained: "When we needed somebody, George or Joe [Grazier] would get in touch with one of his associates—Smith from Equitable, Ellinghaus from New York Tel, Wriston from Citibank, or Fitzhugh from Met Life. And then the word would travel down the chain of command until it got to an urban affairs or personnel director." This was a necessary strategy, since Champion had so many contacts among corporate board chairmen and presidents, and they were the ones who had to be convinced to support such a program.

For any program like this to sustain itself over time, however, recruiting must be institutionalized, so that it does not depend on one or a few people. Champion's contacts were almost always at the very top, and the request sometimes got garbled as it moved to lower levels or was vague to begin with.

As the task forces began to assume more autonomy, their directors did their own recruiting. They were better informed than Champion about their needs, and as they established their own corporate contacts, they didn't have to rely on him. This change helped rationalize the recruiting, since each task force director could then directly communicate his needs to EDC's member companies.

Champion kept a hand in recruiting, however, and occasionally there were questions as to who was ultimately responsible. Also, the task force directors did not clear with each other their recruiting efforts, which led to confusion on the part of EDC's member companies. "The same urban affairs guy might get requests from two or three separate EDC task force directors over a short period of time," reported an EDC official, "and it got to be annoying for some of them. They wondered if all three people were contacting them about the same EDC assignment or two or three different ones, and who was really representing EDC."

A limitation of EDC in this second stage was its lack of any central staff function to handle problems like recruiting. While the task force directors might do a better job in recruiting than Champion alone, they couldn't give it the attention it required, and duplication and confusion was the result.

Champion made recruiting a central staff function in June 1974 and brought in a person on loan full-time for this purpose. This person, a salesman from IBM, recognized many weaknesses in EDC's recruiting. Job descriptions were often not explicit; unqualified people were seldom sent back to their companies before they began the assignment; and people on loan were seldom helped with re-entry problems. Little attempt had been made to get companies to provide people on a regular basis. Furthermore, EDC did not publicize its program enough, and it generally didn't keep a company well enough informed about a loaned person's work and its potential for improving city-agency management. Finally, sometimes the companies themselves gave little recognition to the accomplishments of the people on loan.

EDC did write letters to the companies evaluating the people on loan and held various meetings and testimonial dinners, particularly in connection with the court task force. It also helped some people with re-entry problems. That wasn't enough, however, and if EDC had invested in this task a fifth of the resources that it devoted to consulting, its program might have been more successful.

With regard to job descriptions, for example, several urban affairs officers have complained that EDC has been too vague. "Their job descriptions are still not good," reported one such urban affairs person in 1975, "and if they are going to sell this program they'll have to do more homework and develop a better product."

A particularly difficult problem was the fact that as many as one-half of the people who went out on loan were marginal to their companies and had no clear sense of what kind of job, if any, might be awaiting them when they returned.* Where it became known within companies that an assignment to EDC might indicate that a person was not in good standing and if so might entail serious re-entry problems, it became difficult to obtain competent people.

The theme that emerged most strongly from personal interviews with roughly fifty people on loan as well as with urban affairs officers, task force directors, and city agency officials was that EDC had not done enough to sell its program. Some typical views were:

> EDC has to provide much more information to us on what it is doing, on the background and impacts of its task forces. It has to really show that there is a need that it can fill. The concept is great, but EDC has to decide that it really wants to sell it.
>
> Urban Affairs officer

> EDC is really not selling it well. I've been around the city for many years, and the first I heard about this program was when I came over to this job. The way they get people is for Champion to go to the chairman of the board, who does it as a personal favor, rather than on the merits of the concept and what EDC has accomplished.
>
> Urban Affairs officer

---

*Being marginal did not necessarily imply that a person was incompetent, and some people in this category were very able. They might still have job insecurity in their company, however.

> Several of us keep telling George that he has to do more to sell this program to business, but that still hasn't happened as much as it should. He agrees we should do it, but then we don't.
>
> Top EDC official

One result of EDC's limited recruiting efforts was that the quality of people on loan was uneven, and it does not seem to have improved appreciably since the recruiting position was established in 1974. "You'd have to say," reported one urban affairs officer, "that some of these people in the early years were surplus people in their corporations. The first reaction was to farm out people you didn't know what to do with. Then, at the end of the year's assignment, you still hadn't solved the problem."

To illustrate, the school headquarters task force received three people on loan from a major bank in 1973, all of whom had been told beforehand either that they were fired or that there might not be a job for them when they returned. Neither the bank nor the three people informed EDC about this, and when EDC found out, it was understandably angry and made its feelings known to top bank officials. "At one point, we finally told many of these urban affairs directors that they had been giving us their five percenters, their losers," reported an EDC recruiter.* "They were the people the companies didn't know what to do with and wanted to farm out. We went back and checked out these cases, people who had been here in the past, like the three from that bank and many others, and found out the truth about them. At first, the leadership of EDC didn't agree that this was happening. 'Is this a problem we're having?' was the question asked in some disbelief."

A candid comment from a top urban affairs officer in an EDC member company that had provided several people on loan over the years sums up the general problem that EDC faced. "You never send complete incompetents over there," he said, "but you do send misfits, people at loose ends, malcontents, people two years from retirement. You do it primarily because that is the only kind of person available. If you go to the profit centers of the company and ask for a high-potential executive who can do things for EDC and New York City, you don't get too much response. To take yourself out of the mainstream of the company for six months is political suicide. Also, operating managers are always reluctant to send people on such an outside assignment. Some of these managers will tell you point-blank that 'if I could give you a top person, it would mean that I am overstaffed and it wouldn't look good at all.' "

---

*The term "five percenter" refers to somebody who is out of favor and is on the company's list to be let go if the budget gets cut by, say, 5 percent.

The effectiveness of EDC's management consulting was obviously limited when people were recruited who had only average ability and were laden with career anxieties. "It was tough for the task force projects to keep the attention and energies of some of these people," reported one of their colleagues on loan. "You could see that for some of them the last couple of months of their EDC assignment they were so preoccupied with finding another job or a decent one back at their companies that it was hard for them to concentrate on what they were doing here."

The public-agency administrators EDC worked with were quick to recognize when it had sent such people, and sometimes shunted them aside or found "busy work" to keep them occupied. Having such people on loan hurt EDC and the corporations and raised questions for city-agency administrators about business's commitment to this program and about the program's ultimate worth.

At the same time, EDC recruited some very competent people, who did excellent consulting work in the different agencies. Every task force had many of them, and our analysis of three major EDC projects in the preceding chapters highlighted the important work they did. The warehouse, auditing, fiscal, budget, accounting, management information systems, and general management people at the school headquarters task force; the human resources and organizational development specialists in the high school projects; many of the accounting and computer specialists at HRA (a project not reviewed here); and the management systems analysts in the courts all were able to apply their private-sector skills to their respective agencies. The basic policy question for the future is whether such successes could become more the rule than the exception, both in New York City and elsewhere.

The EDC programs have involved several actions. Many were not sustained for long, but some were. Even those that weren't could usefully be implemented by other cities.

The main new recruiting techniques included having the corporations sign a contract with the person on loan, actually committing them to take the person back at a particular grade and salary level; instituting quarterly visits by the people on loan to their company; refusing to take everyone recommended and threatening to have the leadership of EDC go to the president or board chairman if urban affairs staff were not cooperative; developing kits indicating how the EDC assignment represented a "return on investment" to the company and the person on loan; writing more standardized job descriptions; pressing companies to build into their annual budget a fixed amount for loaning executives to EDC; and awarding a public service medal to everyone on loan.

The court task force had already been using extensions of some of these techniques—for example, holding banquets attended by leading judges, awarding plaques, and having people stay close to their companies by not even giving up their offices—but the others had not done so nearly as much. Since 1974, some companies have held lunches attended by top management at which they presented medals to their on-loan people and wrote an article accompanied by a photograph for the company house organ. For many people who had been on loan to EDC and felt they had not received much company recognition, this was an important symbolic gesture that, several acknowledged, meant a lot to them.

Some of the kits and speeches were also useful. The speech emphasizing the return on investment was tried in several companies and contained important arguments about the benefits of the program to the company and the loaned executive alike. Perhaps the best single idea to come out of this recruiting effort was to get the companies to build into their annual budget a fixed amount for loaned executives. Some had been doing this for several years—for example, Citibank and IBM—and a few others began to do so, after the EDC recruiter arrived.

On balance, however, two and a half years after the new position was established, EDC's recruiting had not improved. Several task force officials and on-loan people reported in 1975 and 1976 a decline in the number and quality of loaned people, for reasons that were not that clear. One task force director reported that EDC's recruiting sagged considerably in 1976, when the city's and EDC's need for such people was greater than ever. Apparently much resentment had built up among corporate urban affairs officers at the first EDC recruiter's going to their presidents and board chairmen when they were slow in providing competent on-loan people. They complained to EDC and to the company from which the recruiter had come.

EDC AS VIEWED BY ITS ON-LOAN PERSONNEL

We turn now to an analysis of how people on loan viewed the EDC experience. As we have indicated, the program's success depended very much on the number of people EDC's member companies were willing to provide on loan, their quality, and the timing of their being made available. It was important in an assessment of EDC to elicit their opinions in a systematic way,* and a questionnaire was sent out in the summer of 1974 to 145 of these people. After continued follow-up, aided by letters from several EDC task force directors, 80 replied.†

The questionnaire elicited information in the following areas: (1) *the backgrounds of these people;* (2) *their career problems, if any* (which might have some bearing on their assessment of the program); (3) *the interest that their company took in the program;* (4) *their perception of EDC's responsibility relative to their re-entry;* (5) *their overall evaluation of the EDC program;* and, finally, (6) *their evaluation of the management transfer strategy generally.*

Who Were They? Viewed in terms of such background characteristics as age, salary level, functional specialty within their firm, and education, the people EDC recruited were quite heterogeneous, as Table 7-1 indicates. They came from virtually every age group, with a preponderance of those over 40—representing many "mid-career" and "near retirement" people. (This confirms what outsiders who had come into contact with EDC had reported—that it had many older people.) Both categories were part of that large marginal group that EDC had tapped.

As one might expect, the level of formal education was quite high, 76% having had at least four years of college. As for their salaries, one indicator of their level within their corporations, there was a broad range—from a small group (8%) in the under-$10,000 category to a larger one (24%) over $30,000. The biggest concentration (53%) was in the middle- or lower-middle-management category, with salaries ranging from $15,000 to $30,000.

These people came from a variety of functional specialties within their corporations, including management information systems, data processing, and computerization (30%); personnel (19%); general management (20%); management services (10%); accounting (6%); and finance (5%). Only 10% were women, almost all of them serving in the high schools project.

*As the people on the "firing line," they had first-hand knowledge of the workings of the task forces. Also, since they went back to the private sector after their assignment with EDC, they had less of a vested interest in the program's future than did the more permanent EDC staff and were therefore more likely to give an "objective" assessment of how well it functioned.

†The biggest group of non-respondents were people who had moved to some other area of the country, or at least outside metropolitan New York. Others included people from a particular task force or company who decided it was not in their interest to reply. In some cases, they were people with severe re-entry problems who did not want to discuss them.

T A B L E 7-1 Background Characteristics of Executives on Loan

Age (N = 77)

Under 40	39%
40 - 55	48
56 and over	13
Total	100%

Education (N = 67)

High school graduate	5%
Some college	19
Completed college (or higher education)	76
Total	100%

Salary (annual) (N = 72)

Under $10,000	8%
$10,000 - 14,999	15
$15,000 - 29,999	53
$30,000 or higher	24
Total	100%

Management specialty (N = 84)

Information systems	30%
Personnel	19
General management	20
Management services	10
Accounting	6
Finance	5
Other	11
Total	100%

Finally, a majority were on the assignment for more than just a few weeks or months. Seventy-four percent served for more than 10 months, and only 6% were there for less than 6 months.

The "typical" person on loan, then, was just over forty years of age, had a salary of about $25,000 a year, was male, and was a college graduate. He was most likely a specialist in management information systems (including data processing and computers), in general management, or in personnel, and he spent about one year on an EDC assignment.

Career Situation: Marginality, Re-entry Problems

Two questions were asked to ascertain how widespread was the marginality within their firms of people on loan. One related to how they perceived their *career progress* ("How would you characterize your career in your firm at the time you came to EDC: moving ahead quite well; making modest progress; at something of a standstill?''), and the other to *how integrated they felt within their firm* (''How would you describe your relation to this firm when you went to EDC: felt very much a part of it; felt somewhat marginal to it; felt very much an outsider?''). Answers to the second question did not confirm the marginality thesis, with 75% responding that they felt very much a part of their firm. The question about career progress, however, did point to problems. Some 30% answered that they were making modest progress, 23% were at something of a standstill, and another 16% weren't sure. Only 30% stated unequivocally that they were moving ahead quite well.

Company's Interest in Their EDC Assignment

To further ascertain how marginal these people were, questions were asked about the interest on the part of both their immediate supervisor and their top management in what they were doing at EDC. Of particular concern in this context was how prevalent the "out of sight, out of mind" attitude was, at least as these people on loan perceived it. It apparently was quite widespread, with less than 40% indicating that either their own immediate supervisor or top management was very interested in what they were doing at EDC. Apparently a majority of companies did not value this on-loan assignment as a training experience, or as an activity that might help the city or provide the company with needed information about city problems. These people on loan may have been more cynical about their companies' interest in the program than was merited, but many companies indeed seemed to take little direct interest.*

EDC's Responsibility Relative to Re-entry

Several people had indicated in personal interviews that they felt let down by EDC for not supporting them when they had trouble returning to a satisfying position. In fact, EDC does send letters of

*From interviews with people on loan and with EDC recruiters. Personal interviews indicated that those companies that provided most of the people on loan—for example, Citibank, Equitable, IBM, J. C. Penney, and some of the other big banks and insurance companies—did take more of an interest. Walter Wriston of Citibank reportedly met frequently with his people working at New York City Board of Education headquarters, inquiring at length about what they were doing and what impact, if any, it was having.

evaluation back to the companies, but it does not usually intercede on behalf of people who have problems. We asked two questions related to this issue, the first about how helpful EDC had been in the person's making the transition back to his company and a second on whether EDC should assist people on loan with re-entry. Less than one-quarter (23%) reported that EDC had been helpful, while 59% answered that EDC should assist people on loan to make the transition back to their companies. In brief, a large group felt that EDC had some responsibility to help them.

Overall Evaluation of EDC

Despite their frustrations with EDC's not having helped them with re-entry as much as they would have liked, the on-loan people's evaluation of the program was predominantly positive: 55% responded that it was excellent or very good, with 42% expressing more negative views.

General View of the Management Transfer Strategy

One of the more interesting findings related to how these people felt about the management transfer strategy generally. Even though many had experienced career frustrations and were to experience more on the task forces, 73% answered that the strategy had considerable merit, a much higher proportion than had given EDC a favorable evaluation. Another 21% felt it had some merit. Their belief in the social benefits of this strategy still held, then, notwithstanding their disappointments with (and many critical comments about) EDC.

TASK FORCE DIFFERENCES

Many of these findings for the total sample are not as important from a policy point of view, however, as are the sharp differences that emerged across task forces. They first became apparent in comparing the respondents' overall evaluations of EDC. Only 38% of both the school headquarters and Human Resources Administration task forces gave EDC a favorable evaluation, compared with 91% of the high schools group and 88% of the courts one.

In attempting to account for such differences, two factors, taken together, are critical. One is the backgrounds of the task force members. The other is their experiences on the task force. Though the sample as a whole was heterogeneous, there was considerable homogeneity within each task force. The directors tended to selectively recruit people from particular functional specialties who most fit their definition of what the assignment entailed. Beyond that, each task force director probably had some preference as to the types of people he wanted. At any rate, there were definitely four different sets of people on loan.

It is possible from interview and questionnaire data to develop profiles of the kinds of people in each task force. For example, the high schools group had many more people from human resources, personnel, and related specialties than other task forces. The high schools project was initiated to help those schools better prepare their students for employment; many of the people EDC recruited for this project were primarily interested in the connection between school and work. They had been involved in manpower training for minorities in their companies, and their work in the high schools was an extension of that work.

This on-loan group also had many minority people, primarily middle-class blacks and some Puerto Ricans, several of whom lived in the city and were oriented to helping minority youth. They constituted for many students examples of people who had "made it" out of poverty. Thus, 67% of the sample from the high schools project were minority people, in contrast to none on the courts and HRA task forces and only one person on the Board of Education one. As we indicated in Chapter Five, there was a network of such minority people who saw in the EDC program a way of directing corporate resources to minority youth, while also making the schools more responsive to the manpower needs of business.

The high schools group had other differentiating characteristics as well. Thirty-seven percent, for example, were not college graduates, in contrast to 6% and 7% for the HRA and school headquarters task forces, respectively. Furthermore, their salaries tended to be much lower than those of HRA or Board of Education task force members, with 60% earning under $20,000 a year when they came to EDC, in contrast to 42% for the HRA people and only 19% for the Board of Education ones.

The courts task force people, on the other hand, came from either management services or management information systems and data processing backgrounds. They were by far the oldest of the task forces; they had quite low-level positions within their companies; and they had little prospect of future promotions. They were in a situation that in the corporate world might almost be called "stable poverty," with an average salary of under $15,000, an average age of 47, and a self-proclaimed position as either "at a standstill" (50%) or "making modest progress" (25%).* Furthermore, they had the least education, with 75% of them having not graduated from college, far greater than the other task force members, as indicated above.

Both the high schools and the courts groups, then, were lower-level corporate staff people. The schools group had been recruited for their people-oriented skills in education and training, particularly as related to minority youth; the courts people for their technical skills.

The Board of Education and HRA task forces were completely different. The former were primarily general management (29%), management information systems–data processing (29%), accounting (14%), and personnel (14%) people, while most of the HRA people were in data processing and related budget and financial fields (75%). The Board of Education task force was the highest-status group, as indicated by education (45% had more than college) and salary (35% earned over $30,000), and its members were more likely than those in other groups to characterize themselves as moving ahead or at least making modest progress in their careers. They were recruited for management skills that the school headquarters task force director saw as necessary for modernizing the Board of Education. Many with backgrounds in general management worked on the headquarters reorganization, while people in data processing–information systems, accounting, and personnel worked on functions related to those specialties.

The HRA task force was another high-status group, though not as much so as that at the Board of Education. Many were young executives and staff people on the way up, though 44% did characterize themselves as "at a standstill." This group was involved primarily in data processing and management information systems, having been recruited specifically to set up such systems. They were much younger than the group at the Board of Education and not as experienced in general management.

What we have, then, are two groups: one, in the courts and high schools task forces, who evaluated the program positively from the perspective of their own experience, and the other, in the Board of

*The response rate was lowest in this group, however, and the survey missed a few higher-salaried people.

Education headquarters and HRA groups, who did not. Some analysis of why this was so is important.

The courts and high schools groups derived more immediate satisfactions from their work than the other task forces. Coming in at lower operating levels within the agency, they saw more of their proposals implemented, more often in the courts but in the high schools as well. The high schools group got many satisfactions working directly with minority youth, and they saw specific projects started at those schools as a result of EDC's presence.

Similar short-term results were visible in the courts. Their task force members were not "people-oriented," as the high schools group was, but they could transfer their skills in case processing and work methods analysis from their insurance companies.

The task forces with the most dissatisfaction, on the other hand, were involved in complex projects that did not easily lead to immediate results. In the Board of Education, implementation was seriously delayed on EDC's proposed headquarters reorganization and then on several key projects in auditing, management information systems, budget and financial operations, personnel, and other areas. Interviews with twenty members of this task force indicated tremendous frustration with the glacial pace of change in that agency.

The same frustrations existed at HRA. EDC came into that superagency in 1971 at the request of its administrator, Jules Sugarman, to help streamline its administrative structure and to introduce a computerized information system that would help the agency keep track of its clients and of what it was doing. EDC proposed a complete reorganization to simplify the agency's structure and programs. In theory, the plan took a fragmented superagency delivering services in a duplicative and disparate way and redesigned it to eliminate those problems. In theory, and on paper, the plan made a lot of sense. Politically it proved unviable, as special units within HRA felt they would be phased out, proceeded to organize their constituencies to protest, and were successful in stopping the plan's implementation. HRA's ethnic and other client politics affecting its organization and programs were so pervasive that EDC's work there kept being stalled. Those people who worked on the HRA task force at that time experienced endless frustration.

In brief, the goals of these two task forces were so diffuse that short-term successes were difficult or impossible to attain. Both were undertaking to completely redesign the headquarters bureaucracies of massive, highly politicized agencies that were in a constant state of turbulence. As one HRA task force member reported: "You'd have to be a superman to change the administrative organization of HRA. We took an unrealistic view of what we could contribute and were nowhere near having the key factions within the agency on our side or even close to supporting what we were recommending."

We have, then, four task force groups, two of which had a feeling of accomplishment, the other two experiencing frustration. The two that felt they accomplished something were working at operating levels in the agencies, where services were delivered and they could see concrete results arising from their consulting. The others, removed from operations, were engaged instead in the more formidable task of changing an entire agency structure. It is not surprising that they had more negative responses to the experience.

HOW EDC COULD BE IMPROVED

The survey also elicited relevant ideas on how the EDC program might be improved. At several points, informants were asked to indicate EDC's main strengths and weaknesses and what improvements they would recommend.

People on loan to all the task forces made extensive comments in response to the open-ended questions on these issues. Even those who gave EDC a positive overall evaluation had many constructive suggestions as to how it could be improved. The comments could be sorted out into *those that pertained mainly to the people on loan themselves*—their re-entry problems; what EDC could do, if anything, to help them make the transition back to the private sector; and what it could do to get member firms to provide more of them; and *those that pertained to the program itself.*

Taking the most positive comments first, on the personal level some people reported that the assignment was a valuable training experience, that it led to promotions or salary increases, and that it brought them into contact with many interesting and dedicated people.

> I mention my present salary, not in a boastful fashion, but as another indication of how EDC assisted me and made me more valuable to my firm. EDC gave me my first "executive" training. This, coupled with my previous corporation training, gave me balance. Recently, a non-minority member of my company had an EDC assignment. His experience was similar to mine. It has brought him "up." This is another side of EDC. Please mention it in your book.
>
> High Schools Task Force
>
> I can say without reservation that EDC was one of the most exciting experiences of my career. I enjoyed every minute and learned a great deal

from Mr. Finley, Champion, Busse, Grazier, and Morelli, as I hope they did from me. I would do it again and make whatever the task a success.

> HRA Task Force

I received a merit increase while in the EDC. The company organ wrote a full-page article re EDC and my role.

> Board of Education Task Force

On a regular monthly basis, I was invited to lunch by a member of our organization, who checked out my work performance, asked my impressions, and asked to be placed on our EDC mailing list. Furthermore, I was given a merit (salary) increase for my performance at EDC while *at* EDC.

> High Schools Task Force

I was given a bonus for the work I did at EDC by the chairman of the board, when I returned.

> High Schools Task Force

There were even more favorable comments about the EDC program itself. Several averred that EDC's expertise was indeed transferable to city agencies and had contributed a lot to their improved effectiveness. The money and management expertise that EDC made available without charge were seen as particularly important. A few of these comments are worth presenting here.

This is a very good concept as a way of breaking down the barrier between the business community and the city; as a means of introducing "practical" business techniques to city operations; and as a means of educating businessmen into problems of city government.

> HRA Task Force

The point of view of someone who is both an outsider and from the private sector is beneficial, since it is fresh and unhampered by past client policies and procedures.

> HRA Task Force

The Board of Education task force obliged a ponderous bureaucratic organization to begin to think in terms of the need for organization effectiveness and accountability. While specific movement along these lines has, on occasion, been glacial in speed, organization change and responsiveness is occurring and specific instances of improved organization effectiveness can be cited.

> Board of Education Task Force

EDC provided the incentive and the means for my high school to turn itself around. Many of the faculty and staff became interested in research and development of innovative programs which would help make the school a relevant place for students to be.

> High Schools Task Force

> My task force performed in an area beseiged by emotions of race, politics, and alienation. Lines of communication between the high school, the community, and city officials were nonexistent; and where there were lines of communication, they were distorted by a desire to maim the adversary, rather than "understand." In this setting, the business approach of problem solving was the key that opened the door.
>
> High Schools Task Force

Others, however, were critical about the way EDC was organized and ran its projects. (The courts task force members were an exception to this, owing largely to the fact that their group was one of the most effective and was run in a professional manner.) Several themes recurred in their comments.

Poor Planning and Project Definition; Diffuseness of Goals

One criticism was that EDC was not focused enough, and that by pursuing too many projects in each agency, it diffused its limited resources. Some recognized that this was EDC's response to pressure from city agency officials to "put out fires," but it still was seen as something to avoid wherever possible. Consider the following observations:

> EDC attempts to accomplish too much with too little manpower. Most often the personnel recruited are not fully aware of the scope of the job. EDC does not spend sufficient time exploring the extent of the problems posed, the degree to which the problems can be solved, the specific skills required to solve the problem, the "do-ability" of the assignment, the optimum payoff, etc.
>
> Board of Education Task Force

> More planning of the task forces needs to be made. Basic questions such as what we are attempting to accomplish, and can we do it, should be asked.
>
> HRA Task Force

> A preliminary review by EDC should be performed prior to the establishment of the task force. It would permit defining of the objectives in light of realities encountered on site. And it would permit a better definition of the needs of the task force.
>
> HRA Task Force

Some HRA respondents stated outright: "The project was not well-defined"; "The scope of the project was underestimated"; "The program was constantly altered to include more goals and tasks than could be feasibly undertaken."

Inadequate Job Descriptions; No Work Plan

A related criticism was that EDC often lacked a sharp statement of its work plan as a guide to the people on loan. Inadequate job descriptions were constantly referred to as a problem in recruiting and in maintaining job satisfaction and productivity after the person was on the assignment.

> The project was not well defined. I had the skills EDC had requested, but had the impression they did not know what to do with me.
>
> HRA Task Force

> The task force assignment was almost never clearly defined. There was a poor match of skills with the job.
>
> HRA Task Force

> I did not feel the person doing the recruiting had any understanding of the area I was being recruited for. I spent considerable time trying to educate EDC management to the point where they could understand what had to be accomplished to my functional area.
>
> Board of Education Task Force

One improvement for the future might well be for EDC to recruit many more actual consultants as its people on loan and to head up its task forces. The task force directors were retired chief executives or were from other backgrounds, but they were not trained consultants.

Inadequate Management and Supervision

The task forces' inadequate supervision and management were also mentioned. Though EDC had put so much effort into improving the management of city agencies, it hadn't always done so with its own operations. Given the size and diversity of its task forces, EDC needed more administrative and supervisory staff.

The task force directors had too many other responsibilities to be engaged in day-to-day supervision; yet this was essential for the morale and effectiveness of the task force members. Many people on loan felt they needed more assistance in orienting themselves to the assignment than EDC provided. This was a big problem in the HRA and Board of Education task forces, though not in the courts. Consider the following comments:

> We need better middle management at EDC that can interface effectively with city officials and has knowledge of the city's operations and problems.
>
> Board of Education Task Force

EDC should give closer and better supervision.

HRA Task Force

Each task force should be under a capable, successful, manager, not a retired, second-line staff man, who is constantly telling us "how we did it at my company."

HRA Task Force

Those in charge need more management skills. Some of our people on loan were not self-starters.

High Schools Task Force

We had too many people who didn't do a lot. They'd read the *New York Times*, they'd be on the phone, calling about a possible job. And they just didn't have enough supervision. We had some good people in charge, but they sometimes didn't keep close enough tabs on what was going on, and they kept leaving after a year or so.

Board of Education Task Force

I designed with help a new organization structure for one of the HRA units. They needed so much operational help that I gave it, at least partly to get the structure implemented. Because EDC gave little support in implementation, many of the benefits were lost.

HRA Task Force

There was a definite lack of interest and commitment by the city.

HRA Task Force

EDC was having a difficult time for the recommendations to be fully accepted. This was so because EDC really didn't have the clout to force acceptance.

Board of Education Task Force

Limited Implementation

One of the most frustrating aspects of the on-loan assignment was the limited implementation of EDC management reform proposals. It was demoralizing to spend months on a project and then see few results. The people working at HRA and the Board of Education headquarters felt this keenly. In fact, Champion and the task force directors were often working behind the scenes, pressing top city officials to move ahead on EDC's management reform proposals, but with mixed results. Consider the following comments:

I designed with help a new organization structure for one of the HRA units. They needed so much operational help that I gave it, at least

structure implemented. Because EDC gave little support in implementation, many of the benefits were lost.

HRA Task Force

There was a definite lack of interest and commitment by the city.

HRA Task Force

EDC was having a difficult time for the recommendations to be fully accepted. This was so because EDC really didn't have the clout to force acceptance.

Board of Education Task Force

EDC had not consistently defined its role as having a political aspect. That would have required paying much more attention to mobilizing a constituency for management reforms than it did.

Problems on Re-entry

An even stronger frustration than the one relating to implementation concerned re-entry. Some on-loan people reported that their company took little interest in them after they went to EDC and sometimes hoped they would not return, that if they did they would be likely to face re-entry problems, and that EDC had not been particularly helpful in this regard. Some were particularly concerned that their assignment too often amounted to being "put out to pasture." They recommended that EDC more frequently inform their company and their immediate supervisor of what they were doing on the assignment, and assist them on re-entry. Consider the following comments:

> As for the company's interest in me after I took the assignment, out of sight, out of mind. One more competitor out of the way. They felt they had to fill a request from the chairman of the board, and my acceptance of the assignment got them off the hook. Having not done too well since my return, my responses in this section cannot hide a deep bitterness about my decision to take the assignment, though I try not to make the answers too subjective. There was no position open for me, and I was assigned to an insignificant position in the inventory department until "something opened."

Board of Education Task Force

> I got the impression that the commitment to EDC was made by the chairman of the board and that people were sent, not because of a belief in EDC, but rather because the personnel department was told to send them. I had been forgotten, and there was some question as to whether there was a job for me when I returned. Finally a job was defined, and I was told, "Take this or a severance package."

Board of Education Task Force

The company's interest was "tokenism" only. After three months of not too much trying, the personnel people encouraged me to look outside.

Board of Education Task Force

They wanted to give the impression that the company was interested in helping the city. Ultimately I do not think the commitment was there. There was no feedback to my company until after I left. The problem would have been finding someone to give it to who would have regarded it as meaningful. There was only a thank-you letter from Mr. Champion, which has never managed to find its way into my personnel file. The job I have is way below my capabilities, has no possibilities for advancement.

HRA Task Force

For me, out of sight, out of mind. The corporation's profit position changed. No position to return to. New management team in command, and position promised was filled before I returned.

HRA Task Force

I was assigned a "task" within the Personnel Department. The bank made absolutely no effort to place me in a new position. My "career" was stopped dead.

High Schools Task Force

There was no specified job waiting for me. I had to go on numerous interviews, which was total frustration.

High Schools Task Force

I was not expected to return to the division. It had been implied when I left that I would move to corporate headquarters, but this never came about. The job I returned to was in the training department and obviously manufactured in lieu of being in limbo. I eventually returned to my previous job after one year.

High Schools Task Force

These comments illustrate problems endemic to the entire program. Two themes stand out. First, there was the companies' almost ritualistic sense of obligation to respond to a personal request from Champion, sometimes unrelated to any perception of the benefits of the program—for the city, for business, or for the person on loan.

Second, there was a career risk in going out on such a "social service" assignment. Job skills might become obsolescent; the company might reorganize and have new managers in the departments responsible for the person on loan's re-entry; and corporate politics might lead to competitors taking over the good jobs, even if the person on loan maintained contact with the company. People often reported that letters from EDC about their good performance sometimes helped, but were usually regarded within their company as pro forma.

EDC still has a big recruiting problem. It must do more to sell the program throughout its member companies and not just to the board chairmen and presidents. In that sense, EDC not only has to convert city government to good management principles, but it must also convert big business to a markedly different set of priorities as regards executive loan programs and the city's future.

THE POLITICAL PROBLEM

Getting big business to provide more and better people and to amply reward them within the corporation is only half the battle. The other half is political. As discussed in the first two chapters, the business in government movement, which began in the Progressive Era and which EDC reflects in a modern-day 1970s version, was based on outmoded concepts of public administration—that local government could be "depoliticized" and that trained "city managers" should be appointed to top positions. Such public administrators might then make more cost-effective, "objective" decisions—decisions more in the "public interest"—than would the usual political appointees. The city management movement never worked in big cities, however, because of the power of political parties and because such apolitical administrators were too remote from key constituencies to retain needed support.

Instead, all scholars and practitioners of public administration agree that all public-agency decisions have political components.* Administrators don't make decisions solely on abstract principles of efficiency, truth, public interest, or social justice, but also on the basis of alignments of political forces and interest groups, involving extensive bargaining and tradeoffs among key participants with different points of view.†

EDC sometimes assumes that business is less "political" than government, and is better managed as a result. In fact, big corporations are also political, and the retired EDC executives had risen to high positions not just on the basis of managerial and technical

*For a good recent review of public administration theory, see Nicholas Henry, *Public Administration and Public Affairs*, Prentice-Hall, 1975.

†Simon, Cyert, March, Etzioni, and Perrow are among the social scientists writing about organizations who have emphasized this point. Cyert and March's important book, *The Behavioral Theory of the Firm*, places strong emphasis on coalition formation, bargaining, and political tradeoffs as endemic to decision making in all organizations.

competence, but also because they understood this political process well and were able to function appropriately.

EDC is thus involved in a highly political program. It is "good" politics, in the sense that it tries to make city government more efficient, more effective, and more responsive, which is one reason why it is worthy of support. The only way it can succeed is to acknowledge this fact and move to develop the required constituency—for example, from among city-wide good-government groups that share EDC's values and local and neighborhood-based groups that have a direct stake in EDC's proposed improvements. Many organizations in both categories don't even know about EDC's programs.

EDC must also increase its influence with top public officials. The history of EDC's relations with City Hall indicates just how hard it is for business in New York City to gain access to the centers of political power. Remember that EDC had an abortive first venture into management consulting for the city in 1966 and 1967, when it tried to work directly through the deputy mayor– city administrator. After about a year, EDC was "cooled out," because the deputy mayor had no power, and the new budget director, Fred Hayes, had his own management consultants. Subsequently, EDC adopted an agency-by-agency approach.

The problem with this approach is that many of the key "nerve centers" of city government, which influence agency implementation of EDC's proposals, are outside EDC's or the agencies' control. This includes particularly the city overhead agencies—the Bureau of the Budget, the Department of Personnel, and the Department of Purchasing—as well as the comptroller. A top administrator in the Board of Education explained:

> Some of EDC's studies are very good, but its target was too limited. They should use their political clout to deal with agencies of city government that control what we do here. The comptroller's office was run very poorly and gives us serious problems on payroll. The Department of Personnel and the whole city civil service system is another nightmare for those of us who want to bring in competent managers. It's an endurance contest with them when you send over names of people you know are competent, that the Board of Education has unanimously voted to hire, and that EDC likes too. They can make you bleed for months at a time, and it looks like we are the ones who are stalling when in fact it's the city. EDC has to use its power to get after that problem.

Rather than trying to chip away at agencies that don't have enough control over key management functions to effectively implement its proposals, EDC should try to reform these overhead agencies at the same time.

The decline of New York in the 1960s and 1970s and its seeming escalation over the past two years obviously raises serious questions as to the benefits of EDC's management consulting and economic development projects. Given the limited imapct of these programs, an uninformed outsider might well conclude that this was just another futile effort.

One must separate out the question of ultimate impact, however, from that of the potential for the city's future development of this kind of program. Even though EDC has not dramatically reversed the downward trend in New York City government or its economy, it may well have begun a process that in due course can significantly reverse the city's decline. It is to this more basic question that we now turn in an attempt to assess what EDC's twelve years of programs all add up to.

8. Conclusions

We have described and analyzed several efforts by a major business group in New York City to provide management assistance to local government, efforts that have national significance and that comparable business, governmental, and civic groups in other cities will look to for cues to solve their many service delivery problems. Several relevant conclusions follow from the analysis. First, this management transfer strategy has much to commend it and should be supported, both in New York and elsewhere, as one useful approach to improving the delivery of services in cities. Second, having said that, one must note the complexities of carrying out such a program—in particular, the conditions under which it is more or less likely to be successful. Since New York is not urban America, and since the constraints to implementation there are so great, it is important that other cities not reject the strategy on the basis of New York City's experience alone. And third, while the strategy should be supported, it is not *the* answer to the urban crisis but simply one of several approaches that must be orchestrated together. By itself, it has limitations that we will discuss in this chapter.

EDC CONTRIBUTIONS: BENCHMARKS FOR OTHER CITIES

At a time when cities like New York are experiencing tremendous fiscal problems as well as serious problems of local government productivity, responsiveness, and accountability, almost any attempt

246

by business to improve city-agency management must be given very serious consideration. Furthermore, every effort should be made to develop a broad-based constituency for implementation of any resulting recommendations.

As we have indicated throughout the book, the EDC program contains components that other cities may well find useful, and it has had some important successes that may serve as benchmarks as well. The most significant components include the task forces; the use of retired top executives as task force directors; the on-loan people from business, taking public-service sabbaticals, who do much of the consulting work; the support given them in a three-tiered structure (on-loan people, task force directors, EDC business leaders) by Champion and his top associates, who had influence and extensive contacts with business, civic, and governmental (city, state, federal) leaders; the strategies of the EDC task forces, in particular, their collaborative approach, their avoidance of simple solutions, and their continued emphasis on implementation, even in the face of agency inertia and resistance; and the many outside resources EDC brought to city government—foundation and government grants, business funding, free consultant services, management training, and help with such technical matters as computerized information systems, budgeting, and accounting practices.

Beyond its management consulting work, EDC often advised the city's top administrators in agencies involved in economic development, manpower training, and related fields. It also helped to mobilize its member corporations to set up active urban affairs departments and become more deeply involved in New York City problems. It has been in that sense a change agent for big business as well as for city government. Relative to the magnitude of the city's problems, EDC's impact may not appear significant, but business has become more involved in New York City as a result of its efforts.* Thus, many business leaders active in trying to improve the city's finances and governmental efficiency generally through such new commissions as Big MAC and the Emergency Financial Control Board had been introduced to city problems and informally trained by EDC.

As for EDC's specific contributions, we have reviewed many in the preceding chapters. The school headquarters task force, though encountering continued problems in securing agency action on its

---

*Mayor Robert Wagner commented recently that in his administrations (1953–1965), he could never count on business for much civic assistance and that its only interest in the city was a narrow one relating to taxes. EDC was formed to correct that deficiency.

reform proposals, conducted some important projects: the inventory control and warehouse storage work in the Bureau of Supplies; the assistance in streamlining the payroll system; the consolidation of administrative functions in construction; the assistance in developing computerized management information systems; and the work in rationalizing administrative structures and practices in community school districts. It also did many studies that may later be acted upon in the auditing bureau—on teacher accountability, on management styles of high school principals, and on construction. Even its headquarters reorganization, though not resulting in marked-management improvements, has begun a process of administrative rationalization that may well continue.

The work in the high schools, utilizing a quite different structure and mode of operation, had similarly positive results. A self-renewal process has been activated; several exemplary programs have been developed; and the beginnings of a broad-scale replication of both the process and the programs have been seen in recent years.

Turning to the courts, EDC's work there is in many respects the most impressive of all. The cumulative and increasingly valuable management assistance that EDC provided many criminal justice agencies at the city and state levels constitute models of public-sector management consulting that can be applied elsewhere. That has in fact happened through inquiries from several states and cities, and it may well increase as other places learn more about what EDC did in the criminal justice field and as they commit themselves to management improvements.

The particular roles that EDC played in these agencies, typical of what many effective consultants do, are worth recounting. Several offer particular promise.

Supporting Innovation-minded Insiders

EDC was often a catalyst, helping to move an agency toward changes that some of its administrators knew were needed but hadn't yet initiated themselves. Regarded as a prestigious outsider, EDC legitimated ideas that some innovation-minded agency staff members had had for many years. The most dramatic case in which EDC played this role was the courts, where it endorsed insiders' reform proposals, absorbing some of the criticism that those insiders would otherwise have received. This is as much a political as a technical role, and EDC and other business groups would do well to take that EDC experience as a model for future management consulting efforts.

Playing a Third-Party Mediating Role

A second role that EDC played was as a third-party mediator between agency factions that had been stalemated before in a way that had stalled reform. Some instances of this were in relations between the appellate divisions and the administrative judge in the courts, among the many contending parties (parents, students, and the administration) in troubled George Washington High School, and between the state and city manpower agencies in HRA. As a respected outsider, espousing no particular policy position and having considerable mediating skills, EDC got these contending groups to collaborate in adopting new programs and structures. Students of urban politics and management have concluded that the establishment of mechanisms for effective conflict resolution is one of the most important public policy problems the cities face today, without whose solution they may never appreciably improve the delivery of services.[1]

Bringing in New Resources

Finally, EDC brought in new resources to city agencies. It provided needed research and operations analysis that were not available through "in-house" staff and would have been expensive if purchased from outside. In the high schools, it brought in curriculum and instruction materials, federal and foundation money, and skilled executives. It represented local schools at headquarters to ensure that more resources would be made available for program development, and it introduced into the schools a research and development climate that has promise for application elsewhere.

It would be both inaccurate and of little public-policy relevance, however, to conclude from the above that the EDC program has been an unqualified success or that EDC followed consistently productive courses of action. Like any program of its kind, it faced many obstacles and had many weaknesses that may best be summarized in the context of a comparative perspective on EDC's projects.

CONDITIONS FOR SUCCESS IN PUBLIC-SECTOR CONSULTING

This study shows that several conditions must be met for management consulting in the public sector to be successful.[2] Some conditions relate to characteristics of the target agency and its situation, while others concern the strategy and style of the consulting work itself. With regard to the first set of conditions, when the agency (1) is perceived to be in a situation of crisis by its top policy makers and administrators, who (2) have both the power and the commitment to effect management reforms, (3) are supported by an inside "core group" of agency officials at several levels, and (4) work in a setting that is not too large, the prospects for management reform are much greater. All these conditions existed in the EDC court projects, but they were present to a much smaller degree at school headquarters and in the early work in HRA. The school headquarters task force director worked continuously to develop a strong and supportive client group, but despite his political skills and perseverance, he met with only mixed results. By contrast, the court projects always had the support of powerful judges and court officials (e.g., the presiding justice of the First Appellate; the administrative judge of the Criminal Court, the state administrative judge, the deputy mayor for criminal justice), and that was critical in the successes that they had.

Such top agency support must be supplemented by support from a core group of agency staff. EDC's nonthreatening strategy maximized the possibilities of such support, and it existed to varying degrees in different agencies. In the courts, for example, EDC found administrators and judges who wanted management improvements and who used its recommendations to implement their own proposals that had been stalled until then. The same thing happened in the high schools, where the participative planning, R&D, and self-renewal processes that EDC helped begin there released the energies and talents of many teachers who had all but given up hope. Working at school headquarters and HRA was more difficult in this regard, since these agencies were big and highly politicized and had many vested interests.

A related set of findings pertain to the effects of EDC's consulting style on its success. Taking the school headquarters work as a case in point, those projects worked best—that is, effected the most changes in agency structure and procedures and had the most impact—that (1) were well defined; (2) had identifiable and measurable goals; (3) were relatively short-term; (4) operated in limited parts of the agency; (5) dealt with technical managerial functions not enmeshed in political controversy; and (6) with respect to which there was a good fit between the skills of the on-loan people and the agency needs. Thus, EDC's work on such projects as supplies and payroll was much more effective than was its attempt to reorganize the entire headquarters bureaucracy or the early HRA structure. While EDC was successful in a similar effort to reorganize the

Criminal Court, it had more inside support there than in the other agencies, as already indicated. The courts were also much smaller than the Board of Education and HRA.

These findings are not very startling, but they have important implications for future management consulting efforts in local government. They suggest that EDC-type programs will probably work better in agencies of manageable size in cities smaller than New York, and when dealing with technical administrative problems. The larger the agency in which such consulting activities are conducted and the more policy-oriented and controversial the management reforms suggested, the greater the likelihood of political resistance. (Large agencies are usually more differentiated internally and have more vested interests as a result—e.g., entrenched, semiautonomous bureaus and departments. They will also have greater numbers of outside constituencies demanding more services and thereby deflecting their limited resources from management reforms.)

One immediate implication of the findings is that a consultant like EDC may limit its effectiveness if it spreads itself out over several projects whose effectiveness requires a lot of resources and political leverage. In the school headquarters task force, for example, EDC undertook many projects at the central board's and professional staff's request. This helped EDC establish a deeper relationship with the agency and got it into important consulting activities. However, it didn't allow for the concentration of EDC's limited resources in any one place. In trying to take on so much, EDC had less impact than if it had assumed fewer projects. And the headquarters reorganization, while it produced many benefits, was simply too overwhelming a task for any outside consultant. Again, important management improvement efforts were begun which EDC, later consultants, and school officials might continue, but it was difficult to show dramatic improvements in such a project and therefore demoralizing to the on-loan people who worked on it and to the corporations that made them available. The same problems existed in the early HRA projects.

The reader may recall in this regard that the school headquarters and HRA task forces reported the greatest frustration of any on-loan group. This may well have reflected the fact that the task EDC and the agency had defined for them was too overwhelming to yield immediate results.

This central finding relates to the two most difficult problems of the entire program: recruiting competent on-loan people in the numbers and at the times required, and gaining the required political leverage to have proposals implemented. The bigger the projects in which EDC got involved, the more difficult it was to show results and, consequently, to keep the support of its member corporations for on-loan people. While EDC claimed results in its public relations statements, the on-loan people were also reporting back to the corporations. When they indicated negative or at best limited results, these corporations were less willing to send more people to those task forces.

The main problem, then, was the political resistance encountered in large, complex projects like reorganizing school headquarters and HRA. Since all efforts at changing organizations have a political component—that is, they require bringing together a dominant coalition inside to arrange the necessary tradeoffs and overcome the inevitable resistance to change, EDC's selection of such large targets was in some respects self-defeating.

DILEMMAS OF THE EDC PROGRAM

The EDC program thus faced many dilemmas common to any public-sector management consulting program, including: (1) the political one of developing enough leverage for implementation while pursuing a collaborative, technical-assistance strategy; (2) that of maintaining continued business support for projects for which it was difficult to show results; and (3) the even broader question of whether management consulting, even if successful, is the most effective way of improving city government.

The political dilemma results from having to pursue seemingly contradictory strategies. If a management consultant like EDC is to gain entry, secure the information necessary to do its studies, and be effective, it has to work collaboratively with the agency. When it then moves on to implementation, however, a more aggressive strategy is often required, since top agency officials often don't have strong enough incentives to embark on proposed management reforms and don't perceive that they have the required constituency support.

Moreover, in seeking to maintain a continuing relationship with the target agency, the consultant runs the risk of being co-opted. It must often accept the agency's priorities and "rules of the game"—in, for example, not going public with critical studies; doing studies reflecting agency priorities even if this means spreading itself too thin; and not going outside to develop constituencies for change, lest the agency be undermined. Where powerful inside clients whom the consultant carefully cultivates have a genuine commitment to management reform, as in EDC's courts work, the collaborative strategy can be effective, but that may have been an exceptional case.* There are usually many more constraints on the power of top administrators inside their own agency than existed in that instance, and these limit the power of the consultant as well.

In brief, a consultant like EDC often has little bargaining power, making it very difficult to effect change no matter how "expert" its consulting work may be. Purely "technocratic" strategies of intervention are thus inadequate in the political setting of government—as, indeed, they often are in the private sector.

The second dilemma facing a management consultant like EDC is how to maintain continued corporate support in the face of limited bottom-line results. Change takes place more slowly in the public sector than in business, and it is often not even clear what the public sector's goals are. Since business, by contrast, is so results oriented, unless a consultant like EDC can show that it has had measurable impact, it will have difficulty generating continued corporate support. Corporations are not easily swayed by arguments that the public sector is more complex than business, that its performance is not that easily measured, or that productivity gains may be a long time in coming. The result is that EDC has trouble convincing its corporate members to keep supplying quality on-loan people.

Still a third dilemma relates to the fact that this strategy often focuses on problems of administrative operations, when big improvements in urban service delivery may come about only through policy and political decisions relating to, for example, collective bargaining practices, or legislation affecting agency structure and financing.†

In this regard, social scientists have distinguished three separate levels of organizational responsibility and control: the technical, the managerial, and the institutional. The technical level, which is the lowest, is concerned with the efficient operation of the organization's main activities—e.g., teaching students, processing defendants, providing social services for welfare recipients. The managerial level is concerned with linking these activities internally. Finally, the institutional one relates the organization to its environment in terms of its legitimacy, financing, securing of clients, and relations with suppliers and competitors. It is easiest to get change at the first, technical level, which is where EDC did much of its work, and

---

*It was also exceptional in that EDC made all its reports public in that case.

†Examples include the school decentralization law, prospective legislation to have the state take over more of the financing for city courts, and bloc grants to permit more local flexibility in designing and implementing federally funded programs.

increasingly more difficult at the second and third levels, which is where the most important changes may have to be made.

This distinction among organizational levels helps in understanding EDC's limited success in such projects as the early HRA and school headquarters reorganization. EDC concluded in the latter that procedures for selecting the central board and the chancellor increased their vulnerability to the kinds of political pressures that prevented their acting on management reform proposals. As a result, it has collaborated over the past year with many civic and educational leaders in designing and securing political support for a new top structure that would link the school system more closely to City Hall by having the mayor select the chancellor, abolishing the central board, and creating a new agency structure that might be more responsive to such management reform proposals. EDC had spent most of its resources on managerial-level problems, only to then see the need for placing the highest priority on institutional ones. In the meantime, some of its member corporations had become so discouraged with the slow progress of the headquarters reorganization project that they were increasingly reluctant to provide more on-loan people.

POLICY AND POLITICAL PERSPECTIVES:
ORCHESTRATING MANAGEMENT CONSULTING
WITH OTHER STRATEGIES

We have referred in passing to the benefits of orchestrating EDC's collaborative strategy with a more consumer advocacy one, and the implications of that bear further discussion. Stated very simply, there are two kinds of change strategies that outside, private-sector groups like EDC can follow, as either an *affiliated* or *unaffiliated* change agent.[3] In the first, one works collaboratively with people in the target agency, acting as a nonthreatening catalyst for change. One may do this by providing resources and technical assistance and playing a mediating, third-party role in conflicts within the agency and in its relations with outside groups. These are essentially the things that management consultants and organizational development specialists do, and EDC followed this strategy in all its projects.

The other strategy is one of working from the outside, in a consumer advocacy and adversarial role, not in collaboration but rather in conflict with people in the target agency. It is a constituency-building strategy that is in fact helpful to those agency staff people oriented toward change in that it indicates to them the political support that exists for their reform proposals. Most agency staff, however, view it as a threatening.

As Walton has pointed out, each strategy has its strengths and limitations.[4] The problem with the collaborative strategy is that one can easily get co-opted by staff in the target agency and have one's programs and resources diluted. This happens not necessarily because those staff members are incompetent, uncommitted to change, or otherwise evil, but simply because institutions, as systems, have various attributes that constitute constraints on change efforts—constraints that people working within the institutions must tolerate lest they be regarded as too visionary or impractical or perhaps even as "irresponsible." The main attributes of municipal agencies in this regard are their *strong status-quo politics*, reflected in defensive actions taken to protect jobs, programs, and divisions in the face of demands for change, and their *still defective delivery systems* that blunt even those reform efforts that are politically acceptable to the people inside. EDC had many successes that we have described, but in the important instances where it did not succeed, the power of vested interests to resist change and EDC's limited constituency for management reforms contributed to the failure.

Though advocates for the collaborative strategy argue against confrontation and adversarial roles, on the grounds that such activity will preclude needed collaboration with agency staff members in the future, much change gets initiated only as a result of such outside pressure. This is particularly so when the agency in question is large and bureaucratic, involves many jobs, contracts, and other economic interests, and is highly politicized. Collaborative relationships are sometimes hard to establish in such a situation, and where they do get established after years of effort, it may take many more years before they result in significant organizational change and improved agency performance. This is not to urge their abandonment, but simply to suggest that they must often be balanced by other approaches.

Furthermore, as long as agency staff members have much more power than outside reform groups, they will have little incentive to change. One way to alter that power relationship is to build up outside pressure and constituencies, and that requires an adversarial role.

It is incorrect to assume in this regard, as some collaboration advocates do, that pursuing the power and advocacy strategy from the outside invariably cuts people off from later negotiations and collaboration with the target agency. As Walton notes: "The substantive gains obtained by the power strategy almost always result in temporary setbacks in terms of the level of friendliness and trust between the groups; but in the somewhat longer run, the result may be better affective relations." Taking as an example the civil rights movement, Walton observes that "one reason why more positive attitudes may develop via the initial power strategy is that the commitment and self-respect which the Negroes usually demonstrate in pursuing the power strategy may engender respect on the part of the larger white community—after the initial heat of conflict has subsided."

One useful way of orchestrating these strategies is to have a division of labor among the various private-sector groups pursuing agency reforms, in which some would adopt a power strategy while others, like EDC, would be more collaborative. Thus, EDC's close affiliation with the Chamber of Commerce and Industry, through their common board of directors, may allow the Chamber to pursue a more political strategy through outside lobbying for agency reforms, while EDC continues to work within the agencies, providing technical assistance with implementation.

A case in point is the New York City Board of Education's budget priorities, which became such a big issue over the past couple of years, with the drastic fiscal cuts. Despite diminished funds, the Board of Education's 1976-77 expense budget was virtually the same as previous ones, indicating a failure to reexamine priorities through evaluations of programs and agency functions. As a result, citizen groups and new agencies formed to deal with the city's fiscal crisis put much pressure on the Board of Education to take such steps. EDC became involved in the controversy, since it had been asking the board for several years to reexamine its priorities so that the headquarters reorganization might proceed more rapidly. It took the increasing outside pressure, however, to get the board to finally respond to EDC's many requests.

In self-defense, the central board asked EDC in early 1976 to do some of the research that civic groups had demanded and had already done themselves.* EDC then developed a review and evaluation procedure and urged the board to implement it quickly. As of the end of 1976, little change had resulted from EDC's work. Whatever leverage EDC did have in that process it owed in large part to the panel and to other outside groups; without those groups there would have been even less board action. As pressures from the outside continue to increase, such an orchestration may eventually show some payoffs.

*The Educational Priorities Panel, a coalition of 21 civic organizations, had conducted research that criticized the board's priorities and subsequently went public with it, exposing many agency inefficiencies.

In exploring the broader public-policy implications of the EDC effort, it is important to place it in historical context. EDC was originally established to promote the economic development of New York City, and it tried to do that through a strategy designed to increase the number of private-sector jobs, through constant communication with corporations thinking of leaving the city and others thinking of coming, and the creation of industrial parks throughout the city. It was relatively unsuccessful, because of the fact that broader economic and technological forces outside any local control determine the locational decisions of corporations. The main trend in New York, mirroring that in every other older, industrial city in the Northeast and Midwest, has been one of an exodus of manufacturing and a shift to a service economy. New York City has suffered, as well, from a continuing exodus of corporate headquarters; and the net result of both trends has been a substantial shrinking of employment. Since 1969 alone, the city has lost almost 500,000 private-sector jobs, and the trend seems to be accelerating. The expanding sectors of the city's economy are local government and such service fields as health, with the government having become in New York (at least until the city's fiscal crisis in 1975) as well as in other cities an employer of last resort.

Some time in 1968, George Champion and other top EDC officials shifted from a job strategy to a management consulting one. They reasoned that some of the business exodus was caused by the city's increasing taxes, along with the failure of city government to provide needed services at reasonable costs. If EDC could help improve the management of key city agencies, they argued, thereby increasing efficiency and improving the delivery of services in the city, perhaps business would not move. Moreover, if it could improve those human resources agencies directly involved in providing a literate and employable labor force—for example, the schools and manpower training agencies—that would be particularly effective, since many corporations that had left had complained about their inability to find adequately trained employees in the city. EDC's work with the Board of Education and HRA reflected that strategy.

As of this writing in late 1976, after several years of EDC efforts with this management transfer strategy, enough evidence is in to indicate that it works under some but not all conditions. The problem is that the politics of local government are so pervasive, and so consume agency administrators' limited resources, that it is difficult for a management transfer strategy to attract their attention in any sustained way. Even if successful, such an approach will not by itself solve the urban crisis. Yet it is useful in many cases, and if it could ever gain broader corporate support and be "sold" politically, it would stand a much greater chance of success.

The various commissions set up to deal with the city's fiscal problems were an attempt to alter New York City politics by countering the power of the "insiders"—unions and civil servants—through introducing new players in the game—mainly, the banks and some academicians and politicians, particularly the governor. The purpose was to take out of politics many key decisions regarding wages, levels of staffing, and levels of particular services—to indicate that they were not negotiable and not subject to patronage or interest-group pressures. It seems unlikely, however, that such a strategy will solve the problem, or be politically viable, if people are put out of work as a result.

A key limitation of these commissions and of the EDC program lies in the fact that improving the efficiency of city government does not deal directly with the larger problems of unemployment, fewer private-sector jobs, and the role of local government as an employer of last resort. These efforts assume, even if only implicitly, that city government's main function is to deliver services, and that the more efficiently it does that, the better. It is also a deliverer of jobs, however, and short of dramatic reversals in the private sector, something not likely to happen, what business, the banks, and reform groups regard as "make work" and "featherbedding" practices are in fact important ways to provide employment to groups that desperately need it. Efficiency programs indicate how the same amount of work can be done by fewer city employees, and their recommendations serve to help phase out or dismiss "redundant" personnel. Many of these people only end up on the welfare roll, however, and that only further drains city government of much-needed resources.

Management consulting is legitimate and can effect needed improvements in city government, if it is pursued in a modest way and if no claims are made about the likelihood of its reversing any city's economic decline or solving the urban crisis. It does not deal with many pressing public-policy questions bearing on the future economic and social vitality of the city. Many such questions involve national decisions—e.g., monetary and fiscal policies affecting the state of the economy and the availability of private-sector jobs; federally established incentives affecting business location decisions; housing and transportation policies affecting business decentralization from inner cities to suburban counties, and the like. They must also be handled on a metropolitan-area and regional basis. No local group, acting alone, can deal effectively with these issues. National and regional economic planning, with an awareness of the impact of federal policies on metropolitan areas, seems essential.

Related to this is a broader political struggle regarding the future role of the public sector. One prevailing point of view, reflected in the push for federal decentralization and revenue sharing, is that the trend toward centralization and big government must be reversed. Government is regarded as a poor manager and a bad deliverer of services, for all the reasons mentioned in the first chapter. It is seen as burdened with an accretion of rules, regulations, bureaus, and programs that have gotten out of control and that make it difficult if not impossible to get anything done. The assumption is that productivity becomes alarmingly low when government takes over any activity. The solution, for many conservatives, is to phase down government wherever possible, with New York City being pointed to as a prime example of what happens when government gets too big and when liberal social programs are allowed to run rampant.

Another solution, the EDC strategy, is to introduce modern-management techniques to make government more efficient. Now that the latter has been tried, even if only on a limited basis relative to New York City's scale and needs, it is clear from the evidence that while it may lead to improvements and should be supported, more than it is required to have any major impact. Nobody has indicated just what the solution may be, and there is not likely to be any single one. Surely efforts to improve efficiency in local government should be encouraged, provided one does not lose sight of the wider economic development problems of the city. Since improved efficiency in city government often contributes to a shrinking of the local public-sector work force, other strategies must be devised to take up the slack. Ultimately, we come back to the basic question of how to provide employment for the city's many minority members and other poor people as well as for its middle class. This has to be done in a way that does not necessarily so perpetuate make-work practices in city government as to reduce efficiency, thereby contributing to an intensification of citizen discontent, the continuing exodus of business and the middle class, and a steadily decreasing quality of life.

Many social scientists, social policy analysts, and concerned citizens and public officials are searching for some answers or at least for preliminary strategies for dealing with the problems of the cities. EDC was an important business group in the nation's largest city that developed such a strategy and tried to make it work. Its program has important national implications, indicating as it does the strengths and limitations of that strategy and the role of political forces in affecting the likelihood of its success. The politics of the cities and of the nation at large that have in the past prevented effective action on these problems may well be amenable to change in the direction of greater support for such action, especially if conditions in cities and in metropolitan areas continue to worsen. In the meantime, it is good for local groups like EDC to undertake governmental reform programs, but only under the conditions I have specified and without expecting that such programs will solve the urban crisis.

The unique characteristics of New York City are also relevant to an evaluation of EDC and the management transfer strategy. New York's size and tremendous diversity of interest groups make its agency-related politics particularly complex and volatile. The size and power of its municipal employee unions and of its civil service (the latter a product of its middle-class reform politics) also constitute major obstacles to modernizing city government. Finally, the limited civic involvement of big business in New York relative to that in other large cities is another serious problem, as I indicated in Chapter Seven when I described EDC's great difficulties in getting more than a small handful of its 200-odd member corporations to provide competent and high-quality people on loan for its program. One generalizes from a single case at great peril, and when the case is as extreme as New York, generalizations may make no sense at all.

At one time, I seriously entertained the title *Anywhere But New York* for this book, so convinced was I of the national potential of the management transfer strategy. I still believe in its potential. Business and reform groups from other cities, counties, and states who read this book should not lose heart, then, from any negative EDC experiences in New York. Provided they face up to the political aspects of municipal reform and abandon the traditional reformer's fantasy of eliminating politics from local government, they may well have some success. And it may well be that with a strong enough coalition, EDC or some similar-type group could be more successful in New York City. Even if it were, that still would not deal with the broader problem that EDC began with and that it was unable to make much progress on—namely, jobs. Until that is effectively dealt with—and it requires a concerted national effort—management transfer and improvement programs will not significantly reverse the economic or the decline in the quality of life in our nation's cities.

Notes

CHAPTER 1

1. See Richard S. Rosenbloom and Robert Marris, *Social Innovation in the City*, Harvard University Press, 1969, for a well-formulated explication of this view. See also Rosenbloom and John R. Russell, *New Tools for Urban Management*, Division of Research, Harvard University, Graduate School of Business Administration, Boston, 1971; and Alvin W. Drake, Ralph L. Kemney, and Philip M. Morse (eds.), *Analysis of Public Systems*, The MIT Press, Cambridge, 1972.

2. See Douglas Yates, "Service Delivery and the Urban Political Order," in Willis D. Hawley and David Rogers (eds.), *Improving the Quality of Urban Management*, Sage Publications, 1974, chap. 8.

3. Morton Grodzins, "The Federal System," in *Goals for Americans*, The American Assembly, Englewood Cliffs, N.J., 1960, p. 265.

4. See the Committee for Economic Development, *Reshaping Government in Metropolitan Areas*, February 1970, and *Modernizing Local Government*, July 1966.

5. *Report of The National Advisory Commission on Civil Disorders*, U. S. Riot Commission Report, Bantam, 1968.

6. In addition to the above sources, see Fred Hayes and Rasmussen, *Innovations in States and Cities*, San Francisco Press, 1972.

7. See, for example, Lyle Fitch, *Fiscal and Productive Efficiency in Urban Government Systems* draft, December 1972, p. 233.

8. See the many publications of the National Commission on Productivity, including its report, *Improving Productivity and Productivity Measurement in Local Governments*, by Harry P. Hatry and Donald M. Fisk, The Urban Institute, Washington, D.C., June 1971.

9. Lyle Fitch, *Fiscal and Productive Efficiency in Urban Government Systems* draft, December 1972, pp. 5 ff.

10. Examples include Edward Banfield, *The Unheavenly City*, Little Brown & Co., Boston, 1968; Peter Marris and Martin Rein, *Dilemmas of Social Reform*, Atherton, New York, 1967; and such journalistic works as Mitchell Gordon, *Sick Cities*, Penguin, Baltimore, 1965; and Richard Whalen, *New York: A City Destroying Itself*, Morrow, New York, 1965.

11. *The Public Interest*, no. 34, Winter 1974, special issue on "The Great Society: Lessons for the Future."

12. Anthony Downs, "Competition and Community Schools," in Henry M. Levin (ed.), *Community Control of Schools*, Clarion, New York, 1970, pp. 219-49.

13. See E. S. Savas, "Municipal Monopolies Versus Competition in Delivering Urban Services," and Lyle C. Fitch, "Increasing the Role of the Private Sector in Providing Public Services"; chaps. 15 and 16 in Hawley and Rogers, *op. cit.*; and Peter F. Drucker, *The Age of Discontinuity*, Harper and Row, New York, 1969, part 3, for discussions of this strategy.

14. See, for example, Hayes and Rasmussen, *op. cit.*

15. For some historical analyses of this movement, see Samuel Haber, *Efficiency and Uplift: Scientific Management in the Progressive Era*, University of Chicago Press, 1964; and James Weinstein, *The Corporate Ideal in the Liberal State*, Beacon Press, Boston, 1968.

16. See Max Lerner, *America as a Civilization*, Simon and Schuster, New York, 1957, chap. 6, for a discussion of this.

17. See Callahan, *op. cit.*

18. See Theodore J. Lowi, *At the Pleasure of the Mayor*, The Free Press, Glencoe, Ill., 1964, esp. chap 8.

19. Edward C. Banfield and James Q. Wilson have an extended discussion of these two coalitions in their *City Politics*, Harvard and MIT Press, 1963. See also Raymond E. Wolfinger and John Osgood Field, "Political Ethos and the Structure of City Government," in Terry N. Clark (ed.), *Community Structure and Decision-Making*, Chandler, San Francisco, 1968, chap. 8.

CHAPTER 2

1. Lyle C. Fitch, "Increasing the Role of the Private Sector in Providing Public Services," in Hawley and Rogers, *op. cit.*, pp. 514-16.

2. First Annual Report of the National Commission of Productivity, March 1972, p. viii.

3. *Improving Productivity in Local Government*, CED, April 1974, a proposal, p. 28.

4. Herbert Simon, Smithburg, and Thompson present this view, for example, in their widely used text, *Public Administration*, Knopf, New York, 1950.

5. See Gary L. Wamsley and Mayer N. Zald, *The Political Economy of Public Organizations*, Lexington Books, Lexington, Mass., 1973.

6. For extended discussions on these matters, see Wamsley and Zald, *op. cit.*, chap. 1; Robert Golembiewski, "Approaches to OD in Government and

Business;" Richard M. Cyert, *Management of Non-Profit Organizations*, an administration paper, Carnegie Mellon University, W. P. #C1-74-2; Mel Horwitch, "Private and Public Management: Is There a Difference?" unpublished paper, Harvard Business School, Spring 1973.

7. See Lyle Fitch, "Increasing the Role of the Private Sector in Providing Public Services," in Hawley and Rogers, *op. cit.*, pp. 514–16.

8. *Horwitch, op. cit.*, p. 29.

9. For a discussion of this strategy, as well as a broad review of ways of conceptualizing and measuring public service quality, see Harry P. Hatry, "Measuring the Quality of Public Services," in Hawley and Rogers, *op. cit.*, chap. 2. Arie Y. Lewin and Robert W. Blanning's "The Urban Government Annual Report," chap. 3 in the same volume, is also useful.

10. Theodore Lowi, *The End of Liberalism*, Norton, New York, 1969.

11. Cyert, *op. cit.*, p. 11.

12. For an extended theoretical discussion of line and staff authority in business and professional organizations, see Amitai Etzioni, "Authority Structure and Organizational Effectiveness," *Administrative Science Quarterly*, January 1959, pp. 43–67.

13. Horwitch, *op. cit.*, p. 16.

14. See Alfred Chandler, *Strategy and Structure*, MIT Press, Cambridge, 1962.

15. Cyert, *op. cit.*, p. 9.

CHAPTER 3

1. Emanual Tobier, "Economic Development Strategy for the City," in Lyle C. Fitch and Annmarie Hauck Walsh (eds.), *Agenda for a City*, Sage Publications, 1970, pp. 56 and 79. See also *New York City in Transition*, U.S. Department of Labor, Bureau of Labor Statistics, Regional Report Number 34, July 1973.

2. Two journalistic commentaries that documented this decline appeared in 1965: *New York City in Crisis*, prepared by the staff of the *New York Herald Tribune* under the direction of Barry Gottehrer, Pocket Books, Inc., New York, 1965; and Richard J. Whalen, *A City Destroying Itself*, William Morrow & Co., New York, 1965.

3. For extended discussions of these points, see David Rogers and Melvin Zimet, "Business and the Local Community," in Ivar Berg (ed.), *The Business of America*, Harcourt, Brace and World, 1967, Chap. 2, esp. pp. 50–54; Edward C. Banfield and James Q. Wilson, *City Politics*, Harvard University Press and the MIT Press, 1963, chap. 18; and Edward C. Banfield, *Big City Politics*, Random House, 1965.

4. I am indebted to William Herbster, former Vice President of Urban Affairs at Citibank, for some of these ideas. See also Peter H. Clark's unpublished doctoral dissertation, "The Chicago Big Businessman as a Civic Leader,"

Department of Political Science, University of Chicago, 1959, for some further discussion. Clark's ideas are summarized in Banfield and Wilson, *op. cit.*, pp. 247–51.

5. This discussion is based on interviews with officials from all these organizations and from their brochures and annual reports.

6. From membership lists provided by EDC.

7. From interviews with EDC staff.

8. From extended interviews with EDC officials over several years and from attempts to provide advice on how they could improve their programs.

9. The discussion to follow is based on interviews with EDC officials and on reviews of its annual reports and various internal memos.

10. *The New York Times*, September 11, 1974. This does not include 300,000 to 400,000 more private-sector white-collar jobs that the city has lost since 1969.

11. *The New York Times*, August 29, 1976.

12. Economic Development Council, *Organization and Operation of the Department of Social Services*, October 1969.

13. *Business, The City, and The Future*, 8th Annual Report, Economic Development Council.

14. See Demetrios Caraley, *New York City's Deputy Mayor: City Administrator*, Citizens Budget Commission, New York, 1966.

15. *The New York Times*, October 21, 1966.

16. See Jack Newfield, "They Made a Desert and Called It New York: How the Power Brokers Profit," *The Village Voice*, April 26, 1976. See also Newfield and DuBrul, *op. cit.*

CHAPTER 4

1. For a listing of studies done prior to 1968, see the bibliography in the author's book *110 Livingston Street*, Random House, New York, 1968, pp. 534–35. Recent reports include *School Decentralization in New York City*, prepared for the State Charter Revision Commission for New York City, June 1974; and *The Role of Local Community School Districts in New York City's Expense Budget Processes*, Citizen's Budget Commission, June 1975. Both contain materials that are critical of headquarters' management.

2. *School Decentralization in New York City*, prepared for the State Charter Revision Commission for New York City, June 1974, p. 151.

3. Richard Cyert and James March, *The Behavioral Theory of the Firm*, Prentice-Hall, Englewood Cliffs, N.J., 1973.

4. See Paul R. Lawrence and Jay Lorsch, *Organization and Environment*, Division of Research, Harvard University, Graduate School of Business Administration, Boston, 1967, chap. 8, and Herbert Simon and James March, *Organizations*, Wiley, New York, 1958, chap. 2, for good explications of the theory.

5. Indeed, they are quite pronounced in the private sector. See, for example, Paul Lawrence and Jay Lorsch, *Organization and Environment*, and Richard E. Walton and John M. Dutton, "The Management of Interdepartmental Conflict: A Model and Review," *Administrative Science Quarterly*, 1969, 14, pp. 73–84.

6. For a review of some of the deputy chancellor's many reports, see his office's *The 1973–74 Allocation Formulae: An Analysis*, Policy Paper No. 1, May 1, 1974; *The 1974–75 Allocation Formulae*: Policy Paper No. 2, June 27, 1974; *Information Systems Planning*: Phase 1, October 30, 1974; and *Description of the New York Educational Information System: Pupil Personnel Information Subsystem*, Nov. 8, 1974.

7. *A Report on the Study of Board of Education Bureau of Supplies Purchasing Function*, by John Manelski, consultant, Economic Development Council, May 28, 1974, p.2.

8. For discussions of Lindsay's use of outside management consultants and of management techniques used to deal with the construction problem, see Fred Hayes's article in the Hawley and Rogers reader and David Rogers, *The Management of Big Cities*, chap. 11.

9. Now that school construction has virtually stopped, staff shortages are no longer a problem, though they were at the time of the EDC study: See *Office of School Building Reorganization Plan*, February 1973, Paul Lubliner, Economic Development Council.

10. The EDC study on this was *Division of School Buildings: Building Cycle Study*, Manning C. Morrill, May 1974.

11. *High School Study*, by George Sachs, David Framm, and Manning C. Morrill, Economic Development Council, September 1974.

12. *Report on Accountability*, by Herbert Friedman, manager, Special Projects, Economic Development Council, July 1973.

13. For extensive analyses of headquarters–district relations, see *School Decentralization in New York City*, prepared for the State Charter Revision Commission for New York City, June 1974; and *The Role of Local Community School Districts in New York City's Expense Budget Processes*, Citizens Budget Commission, Inc., June 1975. Both studies contain extensive recent interview data from several districts that corroborate the districts' view that headquarters has not consulted with them.

14. For a political analysis of how the board worked, see Melvin Zimet, *Decentralization and School Effectiveness*, Teachers College Press, 1973.

CHAPTER 5

1. See Neil Chamberlain (ed.), *Business and the Cities*, Basic Books, New York, 1970, esp. part VI.

2. See Chamberlain, *op. cit.*, pp. 347–55, on the partnerships of Michigan Bell and Chrysler with two Detroit high schools. A good summary of the

experiences of the more than thirty "high school partnerships" existing in late 1969 appears in the Institute for Educational Development's *Industry and Education, Study No. 2/Partnerships*, Partnership High Schools: The Search for New Ways to Cooperate, October 1969.

3. See Raymond Callahan, *Business and the Cult of Efficiency*, University of Chicago Press, 1962, for a good historical discussion of these issues.

4. Roman C. Pucinski and Sharlene Pearlman Hirsch (eds.), *The Courage to Change*, especially the chapter by Samuel Burt, "Collaboration at the Crossroads"; and David Rogers, "Vocational and Career Education: A Critique and Some New Directions," *Teachers College Record*, May 1973, vol. 74, no. 4, pp. 471–511.

5. These reports were the National Association of Second School Principals' study, *American Youth in the Mid-Seventies*; the report of James Coleman's Panel on Youth of the President's Science Advisory Committee, *Youth: Transition to Adulthood*, June 1973; the Kettering Foundation-supported National Commission on the Reform of Secondary Education, chaired by B. Frank Brown, *The Reform of Secondary Education*, McGraw-Hill, 1973; The National Panel on High Schools and Adolescent Education, supported by the U.S. Office of Education, *Discussion Draft*, 1974; and the Educational Facilities Laboratory report of a panel headed by Harold Gores, *The Greening of the High School*, 1973.

6. *Youth: Transition to Adulthood*, Report of the Panel on Youth of the President's Science Advisory Committee, June 1973, Summary, pp. 1–16. See the introduction to and summary of the report of the National Panel on High Schools and Adolescent Education by its chairman, Dr. John Henry Martin, for an excellent review of all these points.

7. Studies referred to in several of these commission reports note that contemporary youth mature two to three years earlier than at the turn of the century. See, for example, *Report of the National Panel on High Schools and Adolescent Education*, discussion draft, 1974, pp. 76–8. As the report suggests: "They are reaching adult size, shape and physiological functioning 2 1/2 to 3 1/2 years earlier than they did 100 years ago" (p. 77).

8. For analyses and descriptions of the student movement in New York City high schools during this period, see Miriam Wasserman, *The School Fix, NYC, USA*, Outerbridge and Dienstfrey, 1970, part III; and Donald Reeves, *Notes of a Processed Brother*, Pantheon, New York, 1971.

9. This was summarized in the IED report *Industry and Education*, Study No. 2/Partnerships, noted above.

10. EDC's 1974 proposal to the National Institute of Education, *Self-Renewal for New York City High Schools*, gives an account of this history. See also a manual put together by Donald Barnes and Raymond Connolly, *Participative School-Based Planning in Urban High Schools*, June 1973, for a further explication of this process.

11. For some good summary statements, sharply contrasting a collaborative, OD strategy with a political confrontation and conflict one, see R. E. Walton, "Two Strategies of Social Change and Their Dilemmas," in John M. Thomas

and Warren G. Bennis (eds.), *Management of Change and Conflict*, Penguin, New York, 1972, chap. 18; and Richard A. Schmuck and Matthew B. Miles (eds.), *Organization Development in Schools*, National Press Books, Palo Alto, 1971, chap. 9.

12. The EDC School Partnership Program, *An Evaluation and Recommendations for Future Actions*, April 1973.

13. *Participative Program Planning in Urban High Schools*: The Beginnings of Industry–School Partnerships in New York City, by Donald E. Barnes and Raymond Connolly, June 1973.

14. An extensive social science literature exists on the isolation of teachers. See, in particular, Robert Dreeben, *The Nature of Teaching*, Scott Foresman, Glenview, Illinois, 1970, pp. 85, 99; and Dan Lortie, "The Balance of Control and Autonomy in Elementary School Teaching," in Amitai Etzioni (ed.), *The Semi-Professions and Their Organization*, New York, The Free Press, 1969.

15. From *Evaluation of EDC/Bushwick H.S. Partnership Program*, F. W. Banes, February 27, 1972, p. 2.

16. See, for example, Donald Super, *The Psychology of Careers*, New York: Harper and Row, 1957. Super's ideas were used at Bushwick in developing career education courses.

17. Cited in Jean Pierre Jordaan and John Lin, *Analysis of the Effectiveness of the Career Exploration Program at Bushwick High School*, Teachers College, n.d.

18. See Asma Jamila Hamdani, *Exploratory Behavior and Vocational Development among Disadvantaged Inner-City Adolescents*, unpublished dissertation, Columbia University, 1974, chaps. III and V.

19. Jordaan and Lin, *op. cit.*, p. 33.

20. *The Bushwick PMI Math Project: Mid-Year Report*, Peter Rosenbaum April 1974, p. 14.

21. From his unpublished article, "The EDC School Partnership Project and the School Self-Renewal Project: A Collaborative Model Between New York City High Schools and the New York City Business Community," n.d.

22. Donald E. Barnes and Raymond Connolly, *Participative Program Planning in Urban High Schools: The Beginnings of Industry–School Partnerships in New York City*, June 1973, p. 5.

23. For a discussion of these concepts see Rensis Likert, *New Patterns of Management*, McGraw-Hill, New York, 1961.

CHAPTER 6

1. For discussion on how outside consultants often give legitimacy to insiders' proposals, protecting these insiders to some degree from the career risks involved in putting them forth, see Wendell L. French and Cecil H. Bell, Jr., *Organization Development*, Prentice-Hall, Englewood Cliffs, 1973, pp. 148 ff.

2. For a description of earlier efforts similar to those of EDC, see "Lay Assistance in Improving Judicial Administration," *The Annals*, May 1953, pp. 169–73. For a lucid summary of an effort to clear the backlog in the U.S. District Court for the Southern District of New York in the mid-1950s, see "Irving R. Kaufman, "Decongestion Through Calendar Controls," *The Annals*, March 1960. This effort emphasized judicial policy rather than administrative reforms. In the same issue of *The Annals*, note also "Court Administration: Housekeeping for the Judiciary," by Leland L. Tolman, who reflects thinking in New York just prior to statewide court reform.

3. See the *New York Times*, October 11, 1970, for the mayor's statement and the *New York Times*, October 18, for a rebuttal by Chief Judge Stanley H. Fuld, chairman to the Adminstrative Board of the Judicial Conference and then the state's top administrative judge.

4. *The New York Times*, October 11, 1970.

5. *The New York Times*, October 18, 1970.

6. Cf. George Strauss and Leonard Sayles, *Personnel*, Prentice-Hall, Englewood Cliffs, 1960, chap. 16, "The Impact of Specialization."

7. *Criminal Justice Plan for 1971*, p. 12.

8. *1972 Criminal Justice Plan*, Executive Committee, Criminal Justice Coordinating Council, The City of New York, 1972, p. 19.

9. John B. Jennings, *Evaluation of the Manhattan Criminal Court's Master Calendar Project: Phase I—June 30, 1971*, The New York City Rand Institute, January 1972, p. 4.

10. See Richard E. Walton and Robert B. McKersie, *A Behavioral Theory of Labor Negotiations*, McGraw-Hill, New York, 1965.

11. For a report on the study, including its methodology, see *Organization Study of the New York City Criminal Court*, Economic Development Council Task Force, 1970, pp. 1–23.

12. For some excellent organizational analyses of work flow arrangements in industry that highlight the dysfunctions of overspecialization and relate directly to this parts structure in the courts, see F. L. W. Richardson and C. R. Walker, *Human Relations in an Expanding Company*, Yale Labor and Management Center, New Haven, 1948; and E. L. Trist and E. K. Bamforth, "Some Social and Psychological Consequences of the Long Wall Method of Coal Getting," *Human Relations*, 4, pp. 3–38. See also James Thompson, *Organizations in Action*, McGraw-Hill, New York, 1967, pp. 41 ff.

13. *Phase One Organization Report*, EDC Supreme Court Task Force, 1972.

14. See, in particular, *Organization Report*, EDC State Court Management Task Force, May 15, 1974, revised September 6, 1974, pp. 1-27.

15. For a discussion of these recommendations, see *Organization Report*, EDC State Court Management Task Force, pp. 88–102.

CHAPTER 8

1. See Daniel Bell and Virginia Held, "The Community Revolution," *The Public Interest*, 16, Summer 1969; and Richard Walton, *Interpersonal Peacemaking*, Addison-Wesley, Reading, Mass., 1969, for a discussion of this process in organizations. See also my book *The Management of Big Cities*, Sage, Beverly Hills, 1971.

2. A synthesis of findings from studies of organizational change that parallel this discussion of the conditions for "success" is presented in Larry Greiner, "Patterns of Organizational Change," in Gene W. Dalton, Paul R. Lawrence and Greiner (eds.), *Organizational Change and Development*, Irwin, Homewood, Illinois, 1970, pp. 213–29.

3. These concepts are discussed in Harvey Hornstein (ed.), *Social Intervention*, The Free Press, New York, 1971, pp. 257-67.

4. Richard E. Walton, "Two Strategies of Social Change and Their Dilemmas," *Journal of Applied and Behavioral Science*, 1965, vol. 1, no. 2, pp. 167-79.

Index